MW00343391

The Presbyterian Experience
in the United States

The Presbyterian Experience in the United States

A Sourcebook

Edited by
William Yoo

WESTMINSTER
JOHN KNOX PRESS
LOUISVILLE • KENTUCKY

© 2017 Westminster John Knox Press
First edition
Published by Westminster John Knox Press
Louisville, Kentucky

17 18 19 20 21 22 23 24 25 26—10 9 8 7 6 5 4 3 2 1

All rights reserved. No part of this book may be reproduced or transmitted in any form or by any means, electronic or mechanical, including photocopying, recording, or by any information storage or retrieval system, without permission in writing from the publisher. For information, address Westminster John Knox Press, 100 Witherspoon Street, Louisville, Kentucky 40202-1396. Or contact us online at www.wjkbooks.com.

Scripture quotations from the New Revised Standard Version of the Bible are copyright © 1989 by the Division of Christian Education of the National Council of the Churches of Christ in the U.S.A., and used by permission. Scripture quotations from the Revised Standard Version of the Bible are copyright © 1946, 1952, 1971, and 1973 by the Division of Christian Education of the National Council of the Churches of Christ in the U.S.A. and are used by permission.

Excerpts from Harriet Myer Laird, *Self-Dedication*; or *Solemn Covenant with God*, from Harriet Myer Laird Papers, Presbyterian Historical Society, Philadelphia, PA, are used by permission. Excerpts from "In Unity— For Mission: A Message to all congregations from the Uniting General Assembly of The United Presbyterian Church in the United States of America," in *Minutes of the 100th General Assembly of the United Presbyterian Church of North America, Part I, May 27–June 4, 1958*, pp. 155–160, are reprinted by permission of the Office of the General Assembly, Presbyterian Church (U.S.A.). Excerpts from "A Message to All Churches of Jesus Christ throughout the World from the General Assembly of the National Presbyterian Church," in *Minutes of the First General Assembly of the Presbyterian Church in America*, December 7, 1973, are reprinted by permission of the Presbyterian Church in America. Excerpts from Eugene Carson Blake and Martin Niemöller, "The Open Door," in *The Challenge to the Church: The Niemöller-Blake Conversations*, ed. Marlene Maertens, 31–46 (Philadelphia: The Westminster Press, 1965) are reprinted by permission of the publisher. Excerpts from Timothy Keller, "The Centrality of the Gospel," © 2000 by Timothy Keller, and later appearing in adapted form in chapter 3 of *Center Church* by Timothy Keller (Grand Rapids, MI: Zondervan, 2012) are used here by permission of the author. Excerpts from Jorge Lara-Braud, "Hispanic-Americans and the Crisis in the Nation," in *Minutes of the 181st General Assembly of The United Presbyterian Church in the United States of America, Part I May 14–21, 1969*, pp. 662–671, are reprinted by permission of the Office of the General Assembly, Presbyterian Church (U.S.A.). Excerpts from Gayraud S. Wilmore, "Blackness as Sign and Assignment," in *Black Preaching: Select Sermons in the Presbyterian Tradition*, ed. Robert T. Newbold Jr., 166–173 (Philadelphia: The Geneva Press, 1977) are reprinted by permission of the publisher. Excerpts from Moon Young Choi, "From the Kitchen to the Pulpit: A Korean Woman Pastor's Journey," in *Celebrating Our Call: Ordination Stories of Presbyterian Women*, ed. Patricia Lloyd-Sidle, 49–59 (Louisville, KY: Geneva Press, 2006) are reprinted by permission of the publisher. Excerpts from Fahed Abu-Akel, "A Global Presbyterian Witness for a Global World Community," in *Presbyterians Being Reformed: Reflections on What the Church Needs Today*, ed. Robert H. Bullock Jr., 91–100 (Louisville, KY: Geneva Press, 2006) are reprinted by permission of the publisher.

Photos are courtesy of the Presbyterian Historical Society and are used by permission.

Book design by Sharon Adams
Cover design by Eric Walljasper
Cover photo: Flavio Bruno (Own work) [CC BY-SA 3.0
(http://creativecommons.org/licenses/by-sa/3.0)], via Wikimedia Commons

Library of Congress Cataloging-in-Publication Data
Names: Yoo, William, editor.
Title: The Presbyterian experience in the United States : a sourcebook /
  William Yoo, editor.
Description: First edition. | Louisville, Kentucky : Westminster John Knox
  Press, 2017. | Includes bibliographical references and index. |
Identifiers: LCCN 2017005500 (print) | LCCN 2017019605 (ebook) | ISBN
  9781611648133 (ebk.) | ISBN 9780664262143 (pbk. : alk. paper)
Subjects: LCSH: Presbyterian Church--United States--History--Sources.
Classification: LCC BX8935 (ebook) | LCC BX8935 .P74 2017 (print) | DDC
  285/.109--dc23
LC record available at https://lccn.loc.gov/2017005500

♾ The paper used in this publication meets the minimum requirements of the American National Standard for Information Sciences—Permanence of Paper for Printed Library Materials, ANSI Z39.48-1992.

Most Westminster John Knox Press books are available at special quantity discounts when purchased in bulk by corporations, organizations, and special-interest groups. For more information, please e-mail SpecialSales@wjkbooks.com.

Contents

List of Illustrations

Introduction

In 1872, Charles Hodge completed his *Systematic Theology* after nearly fifty years of teaching at Princeton Theological Seminary. At this point in his storied career, the venerable Presbyterian scholar had taught over three thousand students; preached in countless churches; contributed a plethora of writings on religion, politics, and denominational affairs; and served as Moderator of the General Assembly. But he had yet to collect all his articles, insights, lectures, and notes into one comprehensive account. Hodge delayed this endeavor in part because some of his seminary colleagues worried that its publication would reduce the school's enrollment. They surmised prospective students might not come to study under Hodge if they could simply read the distillation of his theological instruction in a tome. Hodge ended up writing over two thousand pages across three volumes. The volumes sold for three dollars apiece, and eager readers purchased more than two thousand copies within the first two years of its printing, which was considered a significant achievement for an academic work covering dense topics like supralapsarianism and soteriology. Proponents and critics of Hodge alike benefited from the publication of *Systematic Theology* because it gave them an opportunity to receive or refute his ideas as they proliferated beyond the walls of the professor's classroom into the world.

In compiling thirty-five documents from the colonial period to the twenty-first century, this sourcebook similarly invites readers to better understand what it has meant to be Presbyterian in the United States. According to Charles Hodge, the task of the theologian is to interpret the facts of the Bible using the inductive method of science with reliance on the inward call of the Holy Spirit. The task of the historian is to comb through a seemingly inexhaustible trove of historical sources to find the documents that most clearly and vividly represent important developments and viewpoints. Presbyterians in the United States have been criticized, fairly and unfairly, on a number of fronts, ranging from accusations of practicing insufficient religious piety to prioritizing conformity to middle-class American values at the expense of faithful witness. But one thing Presbyterians have never been charged with is writing too little about their experiences. Thus this sourcebook does not aspire to detail an exhaustive account of every moment in Presbyterian history, but rather it provides a representative account with a rich array of documents—such as sermons, theological treatises, constitutional records, private letters, and ecumenical conversations—that capture the internal dynamics, increasing diversity, and external influence of American Presbyterianism. It presents Presbyterians in their own words, telling the story of how a tradition progressed from its modest origins as an immigrant church to national institutions with international reach.

The documentary history also reveals the complexity of the Presbyterian experience in relation to American culture. Readers will observe firsthand the prophetic witness of Presbyterians who reformed social injustices and pursued racial reconciliation as well as the moral failings of others who defended slavery and attacked their fellow Presbyterian opponents with belligerent vitriol. Because the last book of this kind, *The Presbyterian Enterprise: Sources of American Presbyterian History*, was published in 1956, this volume accounts for the last sixty years of American Presbyterianism and revises the past historical record to shine light on essential yet previously overlooked developments in women's leadership, interreligious dialogue, racial-ethnic diversity, and transnational peacemaking. It is also intentional about the inclusion of women and Presbyterians of color alongside the more recognized writings of white men like Charles Augustus Briggs and Robert Lewis Dabney.

One of the best ways, if not the best way, to study history is through the immediacy of primary sources. Even the finest secondary interpretations of Presbyterian history cannot replicate the vibrant effect of reading the convictions of pioneers like Lucy Craft Laney and Charles Stelzle or studying the words of pastors like Louisa M. Woosley and Jonathan Dickinson. The structure of this book is therefore chronological and thematic. It moves across time, and each chapter covers different features and formative experiences that have created the many streams of Presbyterianism then and now. The first three chapters examine confessionalism, revivalism, and the Reformed shape of Presbyterian worship during the eighteenth century and early nineteenth century. The next three chapters treat distinctive elements of Presbyterian polity and theology in the eighteenth century and nineteenth century, contestations over slavery and the Civil War, and theological controversies over women in ministry and the doctrine of Scripture in the late nineteenth century. The final three chapters explore the following subjects from the late nineteenth century to the early twenty-first century: emerging understandings of mission and ministry; denominational reunions, divisions, and differing ecclesial emphases; and increasing racial, ethnic, and global diversities in church leadership. Because of the unfolding nature of recent developments on human sexuality—and the ready availability of numerous works from Presbyterians on the matter in print and online—they are not included within the pages of this book. I am hopeful the next documentary history will incorporate the robust and generative theological reflections that continue to arise from prayerful Presbyterian communities seeking divine wisdom and direction concerning sexuality and gender identity.

The Presbyterian Church in the U.S.A. produced a brief pamphlet for congregational Sunday school instruction in 1908 titled "Ten Reasons for Being a Presbyterian," which included many of the topics plainly covered in this book, such as a high view of the Scriptures, a republican form of church governance, and the right administration of the sacraments. But this book also provides much-needed nuance and depth to one of the ten reasons: to enact and embody Christ's call for unity through the Presbyterian Church. The documents reflect both the shared commitments and contrasting interpretations of Presbyterians on a host of beliefs and practices. In doing so, this volume takes readers on a journey through the past, to see what unites and divides Presbyterians in the United States.

1

Contestations over Confessional Subscription

JONATHAN DICKINSON

"A Sermon Preached at the Opening of the Synod at Philadelphia," 1722

Jonathan Dickinson (1688–1747) was born in Massachusetts, graduated from Yale College in 1706, and ordained in 1709. Like many influential theologians in the eighteenth century, he did much of his writing while serving as the pastor of a local congregation. After a long career as a pastor in Elizabethtown (now Elizabeth), New Jersey, he was elected the first president of the College of New Jersey (now Princeton University), and the school's first classes took place in his home in 1747. Among his early publications is this sermon, in which Dickinson, as moderator of the Synod of Philadelphia, began the meeting with a strong argument that Presbyterians must adhere to the sole authority of the Holy Scriptures in the making of church polity. Dickinson also opposed clerical subscription to the Westminster Confession of Faith on the grounds that it violated the Christian conscience.

IT's a bold invasion of Christ's Royal Power, and a rude reflection upon his Wisdom and Faithfulness, for proud Worms to make any Addition to that perfect Pattern, which he has given us: For how artfully soever this Mischief may be painted over, with the fair Colours of Apostolick Tradition, Antiquity, Order and Decency, The band of Union and Communion, The well Government or greater Good of the Church, or whatever other Pretence; it may be justly challenged with a WHO HAS REQUIRED THIS AT YOUR

HANDS. Since he who is faithful to him that appointed him, as Moses was in all his House, has given us a compleat Rule for Doctrine, Worship and Discipline, sufficient to make the Man of God perfect, throughly furnished to all good Works.

. . . THAT the Holy Scriptures are every way sufficient, to make the Man of GOD perfect in, and throughly furnish him for, the whole Work of his Ministry. — For the illustrating this Proposition, let us take a short view of the Man of GOD, in the discharge of the several Duties of his Function, and we shall find full and compleat Furniture from this Sacred Treasury, for every part thereof.

IF we consider him as a Teacher and Instructor of poor ignorant Souls, in the way to the Kingdom of God. Labouring to store their dark Understandings with the knowledge of the Doctrines and Practice of Christianity, and to unfold the Mysteries of Salvation. The Scripture is profitable for Instruction. 2 Tim. III. 16. Thence may he bring to the Sinners view, his fallen State and native Misery, with the blessed Remedy provided, and glorious Salvation exhibited. Thence may he shew the Sinner the dreadful Perils of Impenitency, and his last Necessity of accepting offered Mercy. Thence may he mark out the path of Life, and discover the many Precipices, Errors and Mistakes, to which the poor Pilgrim is exposed in his way to Heaven. In a Word, Thence may he be furnish'd with whatever is necessary for Faith or Practice, and out of these Treasures may he bring forth things new and old. There is nothing Needful, nothing Lawful to be added. But if an Angel from Heaven preach any other Doctrine, let him be accursed. Gal. I. 8.

. . . AND now I come to the main thing intended, to make some Improvement of this Proposition.

WE are hence instructed, that the Man of GOD has no Power or Authority to make any New Laws or Constitutions in the Affairs of God's House; or to make any Additions unto, or Alterations of those Laws, that Christ has left us in the Divine Oracles. This being an Affair that has caused much Struggle and Debate; and that has been (as I observed before) throughout all succeeding ages of the Church, the source of innumerable Mischiefs and Confusions. I shall take liberty to be something particular upon this head, and consider what it is to make New Laws; and as I pass along, disprove our Claim to that Authority.

THEN the devising and imposing any PART or MODE of Worship that wants a Divine Institution, is a Legislature that we have no just claim to. — There are indeed several circumstantial Appendages to the Worship of God, such as Time, Place, &c. that are not, nor is it possible they should be, particularly provided for in the Word of God. Wisdom is therefore profitable to direct, and determine these things, conformable to those general Rules, that require all things to be done to Edification, Decently and in Order.

BUT then to Institute any new PART of Worship, or to bring any thing into God[']s immediate Service, not expressly instituted by Christ, is a bold Invasion of his Royalty, who is Head over all things to his Church; Eph. I. 22; and whose Prerogative it is, to give Laws and Ordinances to his House. And no pretence of Innocency, Indifferency, or the like, will legitimate our thus setting our Thresholds by God[']s Thresholds, and our Posts by his Posts. Ezek. XLIII. 8. What more Innocent, what more Indifferent, than the cleanly Ceremony of washing Hands before Meat? Yet when Religion comes to be placed in it, and it's made a Decree of the Sanhedrin, God[']s Commandment is transgressed by this Tradition. Mat. XV. 3.

. . . THE forming and imposing any New Acts or Constitutions, in the Government or Discipline of the Church, I take to be an unwarrantable Legislature.—That I may clear this somthing particularly, I shall premise. . . .

1. THAT Christ has appointed a Government or Discipline in his Church. Christ has not left his Church to be a Garden without Enclosure, a City without Walls, or a Vineyard without a Hedge; nor has he left his Disciples to be Lambs in a large place, an ungovern'd Mobile; that (as when there was no King in Israel) every one should do what is good in his own eyes, take his swing in sinful and licentious Courses; to the scandal of Religion, profanation of sacred Ordinances, and destruction of his own Soul. — But that Offenders may be reduced, rotten Members cut off, Scandal restrain'd, and the Church edified; Christ has constituted an Ecclesiastical Regiment, and for that end appointed his own proper Officers, Laws, Ordinances, and Censures. The Necessity of which is manifest, from the Constitution of the Church, which consists of barren, and fruitful Branches; of Sound and Unsound; Tares and Wheat; Sheep and Goats; and must therefore quickly become a Babel, if without Discipline. The truth of which is also abundantly evident from many places of Scripture, particularly from Mat. XVIII. from 15 to 20 Verse, Tit. III. 10. and I. 13, 2 Cor. II. 6, I Tim. V. 20. cum multis aliis.

I don't now design a Dispute upon the controverted Modes of Church Government; but will venture to say with due deferrence and respect to those otherwise minded, that the Presbyterian Government appears to me the most conformed to the Laws of Christ, of any whatsoever; and does, for ought I know, as exactly quadrate with the Rule, as may be hoped for in this state of Imperfection.

But I go on to premise,

2. THAT there are some External Circumstances of Discipline, that are not set down precisely, or expressly provided for in the Word of God; but are

left to the prudent Conduct of Church Governours. To exemplify this, we in these Parts manage the Discipline of the Church in Sessions, Presbyteries, and Synods; and have doubtless the Divine Warrant for our so doing. In order to this, there must be Time and Place appointed for such Conventions, and some Order and Method for carrying on our Consultations decently, and without Confusion: And in this case there being only general Rules left us in the Scripture, it necessarily belongs to us to consult and agree upon such Methods, as may best subserve the great Ends of Discipline, the Glory of God, and the Churches Weal. — The Synod at Jerusalem mention'd Acts XV. does indeed give us considerable Light, even in this case; but leaves many necessary Circumstances to be provided for, by Humane Wisdom and Prudence. . . .

IT may be objected, How can Ministers be said to represent Christ, to preach in his Name, and by his Authority; and yet their Hearers not be obliged to receive their Doctrine; but at liberty to follow their several Sentiments, and (oftentimes) erring and misguided Consciences? But the Answer is easy.

THE Ministers of Christ do come to us in his Name, and by his Authority, when they preach nothing but what is contain'd in his Word, and we are under indispensible Obligation to receive the manifest Truths of God by them preached, not as the Word of Man, but as (it is in truth) the Word of God. I Thes. II. 13. But they have no Commission to teach us to observe any thing, but what Christ has commanded them. See Mat. XXVIII. 20. And when they teach any other Doctrine, they come in their own Names, and not in Christ[']s. — So then, we are to esteem them as Christ[']s Ambassadors, and with awful Reverence to attend their preaching, as if Christ was speaking to us by them, when we are convinced that they declare the Counsel of God: But are not bound to an implicite Faith, against contrary Convictions. It concerns them therefore, to justify their Interpretations of God[']s Word, by clear Scripture Evidence, to the Conviction of their Hearers; and thereby lay 'em under Obligations to Observance and Obedience. . . .

But to make this Case, if possible, a little plainer:

THOUGH some plain and comprehensive Creed or Confession of Faith (for distinguishing such as receive, from those who reject the Faith once delivered to the Saints) may be useful and necessary, since the worst of Heresies may take shelter under the express Words of Scripture. Yet we are by no means to force these credenda, upon any of differing Sentiments.

Source: Jonathan Dickinson, "A Sermon Preached at the Opening of the Synod at Philadelphia, September 19, 1722, Whererein [sic] is Considered the Character of the Man of God, and his Furniture for the Exercise both of Doctrine and Discipline, with the True Boundaries of the Churches Power" (Boston: T. Fleet, 1723), 2, 8–9, 11–15, 20–22.

JOHN THOMSON

An Overture Presented to the Reverend Synod of Dissenting Ministers, 1729

John Thomson (ca. 1690–1753) emigrated from Ireland to colonial North America in 1715. After his ordination in Delaware in 1717, he emerged as an influential minister as the fledgling Presbyterian Church wrestled over matters of theology and polity. He was elected moderator of the New Castle Presbytery three times and moderator of the Synod of Philadelphia twice from 1718 to 1730. In 1724, the New Castle Presbytery required all of its ministerial candidates for ordination to confessional subscription with the following words: "I do own the Westminster Confession as the Confession of my faith." Thomson advocated for the implementation of confessional subscription for all Presbyterian clergy in colonial North America. The following overture to the synod, initially introduced by the New Castle Presbytery in 1727 and then published by Thomson with a new preface in 1729, articulates how subscription would guide Presbyterians in their pursuit to create an ordered, organized, and unified Church in their new North American context.

Let us then consider our present Condition as we are a Church. As it is observed in the Overture, we are an intire Church of our selves, so as not to be a Part of any particular Church in the World, with which we are joyned as a Part. Now every Collection of People which are united together unto a Politick Body, whether Ecclesiastical or Civil, must have some Bond of Union, by which the several Parts are joyned together, to make or constitute them one intire Whole; as Kingdoms and Commonwealths are joyned, linked together by the same Government, Laws and Privileges, &c. Churches by the same Faith, Worship and Government: Now, until we fulfil the Intent of the following Overture, I am at a Loss where to find any sufficient External Bond of Union, by which we are united, and by Virtue of which we may be properly denominated one Church, as particular Churches are so denominated, either in Scripture or in the common Way of speaking; seeing that we, as a Church, have never yet so much as agreed, either about our Principles of Faith, Worship, or Form of Government.

If it be said first, That we all own the Westminster Confession . . .

2dly, If it be said, That we all take the Scripture for our Rule, and so are

United thereby. I answer, we are thereby no more united together as one particular Church, than to all other Christian Churches in the World; for they all own the Scriptures for their Rule . . . I answer, it's true the Scripture or written Word of God, is the only Rule and infallible Foundation of our Faith and Practice; but whether is it the bare Letter, or the Letter together with its true and proper Sense and Meaning, intended by the Holy Ghost, which is this Rule? Surely the latter. Now how is it possible for us to know concerning one another, or others to know concerning us, in what Sense we take or understand the Scriptures, or believe them as a Church, unless we joyn together to declare in what Sense we understand them; which I cannot see how it can be possibly done, but by agreeing upon a common Confession of our Faith, in some Form or other. . . .

Another Objection, made against subscribing the Confession, strikes in general against all subscribing of any Thing of that Kind; the Force thereof (that I may give it all the Advantage that I can) may be conceived to run thus; For a Synod to oblige their Members to subscribe the confession, is an imposing upon Men[']s Consciences, Things that are of a humane and not of divine Authority; which is Tyranny and Persecution, for which we justly blame the Church of Rome; Why then should we, or how can we be justified, while we are guilty of an Evil of the same Nature? How can a Person warrantably subscribe any Thing as containing the Articles of their Faith, but the Word of God, without being guilty of idolizing or too much exalting of Men[']s Works or Words? However specious this Objection may seem to be at the first Glance, to such as have not duly considered it; yet I dare say it will plainly appear to be not only salacious and sophistical, but in part nonsensical and trifling, if the following Answers be duly considered.

Answ. For a Church to oblige their Members to receive, embrace, acknowledge, subscribe, or practice any thing that is not founded upon the Word of God, is indeed Tyranny and Persecution; but to impose what Christ in and by his Word hath already imposed, is their indispensible Duty; and therefore if the Confession, &c. be according to the Word of God, (as I will venture to say it is, until the Contrary be made appear) it is our Duty to impose or require the Acknowledg[m]ent of it, or what is contained therein in other Words.

If it be urged, That the Confession is a humane Composure, and therefore, tho' sound, yet not of divine Authority, and therefore ought not to be imposed.

I answer, the Matter is of divine Authority, being contained in the Word of God, and the Words, tho' composed by fallible Men, being agreeable to the divine Matter, tho' falling short of that Perfection that the Scripture justly claims, must of Necessity have the divine Approbation; and so far as they are agreeable to the infallible Word, are themselves infallible, as to the Truth contained in them, tho' as hath been acknowledged, they fall short of scriptural Perfection, as to manner of Expression; for whatsoever is agreeable to an infallible Rule, in so far is itself infallible.

And further, if Persons would but consider the Nature of a Confession, truly and properly so called, they might see that the very intrinsick Nature of the Thing requires that it should be expressed in our own, tho' imperfect Words, (viz. Words that are our own by Acknowledgment and Assumption, tho' we did not compose them, as a Person who can neither write nor indite makes the Words, composed by his Clerk or Scribe, his own, by setting his Name or Mark to them, tho' he composed none of them) [t]his will appear evident, if we consider First, that when we exhibit, acknowledge, or subscribe a Confession of our Faith; we thereby acknowledge such a Confession to be our Act and Deed, viz. our Confession of our Faith, or our own Declaration of our Sentiments, and Belief in Matters of Religion; and therefore, both Words and Sense must be our own, at least by Assumption; whereas the Scripture, as such, is God's Act and Deed, viz. his Declaration of his Mind to us, and thereby prescribing a Rule for our Faith and Practice; and therefore the Scripture as such, cannot possibly be the Confession of our Faith, in a true and proper Sense. Our Confession is a Manifestation of our Thoughts; but the Scripture is the Declaration of God's Thoughts; our Faith and Knowledge is but dark and imperfect, and therefore our Confession may be so too; but the Scripture is every way perfect, being a divine infallible Declaration of his Thoughts who is Perfection itself. The Scripture is the divine Rule, but our Faith and Confession too is the Thing ruled; from all which it may appear, that it's but a trifling Sophistication, to alledge that Christians should own or subscribe the Scriptures, and nothing else as their Confession of Faith, which they neither are or can be in a proper Sense. . . .

And how nonsensical (as I may say) is it for any to make this Evasion, that they are willing to subscribe the Scriptures; the Spirit of God (so to speak with reverence) hath already sufficiently subscribed them by the many Marks and Characters of the Author's Image instamp'd upon them; and therefore for us to talk of subscribing them in any otherwise than thereby to testify that we believe them to be divine, is I think (to say no worse) to cast a great Affront upon the Scriptures and their Author too: For to subscribe an Instrument is to own it by writing as our Act and Deed, in which Sense we are to understand the subscribing Confessions; and in this Sense it would be oft blasphemous Presumption to pretend to subscribe the Scriptures; and for such to say, that they only intend or mean that they are willing to subscribe the Scriptures as a Witness, viz. by writing to bear Witness that they acknowledge the Scriptures to be the Word of God; in so saying they only trifle. For First, if they acknowledge such or such a Confession to be sound and orthodox, they can have no shadow of a Scruple to subscribe it in that Sense, that is, by subscribing to declare, that they believe such a Confession to be found according to the Word of God. But however, the Act of subscribing a Confession doth necessarily presuppose, that the Subscriber believes the Contents of such a Confession to be true; yet the true and proper Meaning, and Design of the Act itself, is thereby to assume or (if I may so express it) adopt such a Confession to be our own Act and Deed, (i.e.) our Confession of our Faith, as if at the Beginning of the Confession, or at the Beginning of every Article we had written, the Word Credo, I believe, and our Name at the End of all is to signify who or what Person this (1) is, who says he believes so and so. Now, altho' every Christian will readily acknowledge, that he believes the Scriptures to be true, to be the Word of God, &c. yet who ever dreamt of subscribing the Scriptures as their Act and Deed, or a Declaration of their Acts of Faith or Believing, altho' indeed, as is before noted, they contain the Object of our Faith, viz. the Truths believed, and that not as believed by us, but as revealed by God; whereas our Confessions, tho' they contain the same Truth, yet they express them not immediately as revealed by God to us, but as understood, received and believed by us.

Source: John Thomson, *An Overture Presented to the Reverend Synod of Dissenting Ministers, Sitting in Philadelphia, in the Month of September, 1728, and is Now Under the Consideration of the Several Members of the Said Synod, in Order to Come to a Determination Concerning It at Next Meeting, Together with a Preface, or an Epistle Containing Some Further Reasons to Strengthen the Overture, and an Answer to Some Objections Against It* (Philadelphia, 1729), 7–8, 13–16, 18–20.

SYNOD OF PHILADELPHIA

Adopting Act, 1729

As the Synod of Philadelphia convened in 1729, members representing diverse positions on confessional subscription—there were strict subscriptionists, anti-subscriptionists, and moderates calling for compromise—gathered to pray, deliberate, and decide together. Opting against schism, these church leaders, including both Jonathan Dickinson and John Thomson, produced an action, known as the Adopting Act, which advanced the benefits of subscription for the propagation of right doctrine and administration of good governance in the Presbyterian Church yet maintained freedom of conscience as a crucial principle of the Christian faith. The act also introduced a method whereby a ministerial candidate with reservations about certain articles from the Westminster Confession of Faith could share this "scruple" with the governing body. If the presbytery or synod determined the scruple pertained "only about articles not essential and necessary in doctrine, worship, or government," the candidate could be ordained. The Presbyterian Church (U.S.A.) today continues to use language from this act in its constitutional question asking deacons and elders to "receive and adopt the essential tenets of the Reformed faith as expressed in the confessions of our church as authentic and reliable expositions of what Scripture leads us to believe and do."

Although the Synod do not claim or pretend to any authority of imposing our faith upon other men's consciences, but do profess our just dissatisfaction with, and abhorrence of such impositions, and do utterly disclaim all legislative power and authority in the Church, being willing to receive one another as Christ has received us to the glory of God, and admit to fellowship in sacred ordinances, all such as we have grounds to believe Christ will at last admit to the kingdom of heaven, yet we are undoubtedly obliged to take care that the faith once delivered to the saints be kept pure and uncorrupt among us, and so handed down to our posterity; and do therefore agree that all the ministers of this Synod, or that shall hereafter be admitted into this Synod, shall declare their agreement in, and approbation of, the Confession of Faith, with the Larger and Shorter Catechisms of the Assembly of Divines at Westminster, as being in all the essential and necessary articles, good forms of sound words and systems of Christian doctrine, and do also adopt the said Confession and Catechisms as the confession of our faith. And we do also agree, that all the Presbyteries within our bounds shall always take care not to admit any candidate of the ministry into the exercise of the sacred function but what declares his agreement in opinion with all the essential and necessary articles of said Confession, either by subscribing the said Confession of Faith and Catechisms, or by a verbal declaration of their assent thereto, as such minister or candidate shall think best. And in case any minister of this Synod, or any candidate for the ministry, shall have any scruple with respect to any article or articles of said Confession or Catechisms, he shall at the time of his making said declaration declare his sentiments to the Presbytery or Synod, who shall, notwithstanding, admit him to the exercise of the ministry within our bounds, and to ministerial communion, if the Synod or Presbytery shall judge his scruple or mistake to be only about articles not essential and necessary in doctrine, worship, or government. But if the Synod or Presbytery shall judge such ministers or candidates erroneous in essential and necessary articles of faith, the Synod or Presbytery shall declare them uncapable of communion with them. And the Synod do solemnly agree, that none of us will traduce or use any opprobrious terms of those that differ from us in these extra-essential and not necessary points of doctrine, but treat them with the same friendship, kindness, and brotherly love, as if they had not differed from us in such sentiments.

Source: Records of the Presbyterian Church in the United States of America: Embracing the Minutes of the General Presbytery and General Synod 1706–1788 Together with an Index and the Minutes of the General Convention for Religious Liberty, 1766–1775 (Philadelphia: Presbyterian Board of Publication and Sabbath-School Work, 1904), 94.

2

Revivals, Dissensions, and the First Great Awakening

GILBERT TENNENT

"The Danger of an Unconverted Ministry," 1740

Gilbert Tennent (1703–1764) converted to Christianity at fourteen years of age during his emigration from Ireland to colonial North America. He studied theology under the tutelage of his father, William Tennent, who founded the "Log College" seminary in Pennsylvania, and ordained in 1726. In his ministry, Tennent emphasized experimental piety and the necessity of spiritual rebirth through conversion. He became one of the leading Presbyterian revivalists during the "Great Awakening" in colonial North America. In 1734, the Synod of Philadelphia passed Tennent's proposal that instructed all presbyteries to include in their examinations of ministerial candidates questions regarding personal religious experiences of "sanctifying grace." But three years later, the Philadelphia Presbytery rebuked Tennent for crossing presbytery boundaries to preach at a church in New Jersey. Tennent protested and defended itinerant preaching as an effective means to lead people into repentance and salvation. In 1738, the Synod of Philadelphia disagreed with Tennent and passed a resolution against itinerancy because it threatened the established order of church polity. In his sermon as an itinerant preacher at the Presbyterian Church in Nottingham, Pennsylvania, Tennent railed against those colleagues who opposed his methods of itinerancy and revivalism, comparing some of them with the "Pharisee-Teachers" that Jesus had condemned in the New Testament.

My Brethren, we should mourn over those, that are destitute of faithful Ministers and sympathize with them. Our Bowels should be moved with the most

15

compassionate Tenderness, over those dear fainting Souls, that are as Sheep having no Shepherd; and that after the Example of our blessed LORD!

Dear Sirs! we should also most earnestly pray for them, that the compassionate Saviour may preserve them, by his mighty Power, thro' Faith unto Salvation; support their sinking Spirits, under the melancholy Uneasiness of a dead Ministry; sanctify and sweeten to them the dry Morsels they get under such blind Men, when they have none better to repair to.

And more especially, my Brethren, we should pray to the LORD of the Harvest, to send forth faithful Labourers into His harvest; seeing that the Harvest truly is plenteous, but the Labourers are few. . . . And indeed, my Brethren, we should join our Endeavours to our Prayers. The most likely Method to stock the Church with a faithful Ministry, in the present Situation of Things, the publick Academies being so much corrupted and abused generally, is, To encourage private Schools, or Seminaries of Learning, which are under the Care of skilful and experienced Christians; in which those only should be admitted, who upon strict Examination, have in the Judgment of a reasonable Charity, the plain Evidences of experimental Religion. Pious and experienced Youths, who have a good natural Capacity, and great Desires after the Ministerial Work, from good Motives, might be sought for, and found up and down the Country, and put to Private Schools of the Prophets, especially in such Places where the Publick ones are not. . . .

THE IMPROVEMENT of this Subject remains. And,

1. If it is so, then the Case of those who have no other, or no better than Pharisee-Teachers, is to be pitied: Then what a Scrole and Scene of Mourning and Lamentation, and Wo, is opened! because of the Swarms of Locusts, the Crowds of Pharisees, that have as covetously as cruelly, crept into the Ministry, in this adulterous Generation! who as nearly resemble the Character given of the old Pharisees, in the Doctrinal Part of this Discourse, as one Crow's Egg does another. It is true some of the modern Pharisees have learned to prate a little more orthodoxy about the New Birth, than their Predecessor Nicodemus, who are, in the mean Time, as great Strangers to the feeling Experience of it, as he. They are blind who see not this to be the Case of the Body of the Clergy, of this Generation. And O! that our Heads were Waters, and our Eyes a Fountain of Tears, that we could Day and Night lament, with the utmost Bitterness, the doleful Case of the poor Church of God upon this account.

2. From what has been said, we may learn, That such who are contented under a dead Ministry do not have in them the Temper of that Saviour they profess. It's an awful Sign, that they are as blind as Moles, and as dead as Stones, without any spiritual Taste and Relish. And alas! isn't this the Case of Multitudes? If they can get one, that has the Name of a Minister, with a Band,

and a Black Coat or Gown to carry on a Sabbath-days among them, although never so coldly, and insuccessfully; if he is free from gross Crimes in Practice, and takes good Care to keep at a due Distance from their Consciences, and is never troubled about his Insuccessfulness; O! think the poor Fools, that is a fine Man, indeed; our Minister is a prudent charitable Man, he is not always harping upon Terror, and sounding Damnation in our Ears, like some rash-headed Preachers, who by their uncharitable Methods, are ready to put poor People out of their Wits, or to run them into Despair. . . .

3. We may learn, the Mercy and Duty of those who enjoy a faithful Ministry. Let such glorify GOD for so distinguishing a Privilege, and labour to walk worthy of it, to all Well-pleasing; left for their Abuse thereof, they are exposed to a greater Damnation.

4. If the Ministry of natural Men be as it has been represented; Then it is both lawful and expedient to go from them to hear Godly Persons; yea, it's so far from being sinful to do this that one who lives under a pious Minister of lesser Gifts, after having honestly endeavor'd to get Benefit by his Ministry, and yet gets little or none, but doth find real Benefit and more Benefit elsewhere; I say, he may lawfully go, and that frequently, where he gets most Good to his precious Soul, after regular Application to the Pastor where he lives, for his Consent, and proposing the Reasons thereof; when this is done in the Spirit of Love and Meekness, without Contempt of any, as also without rash Anger or vain Curiosity. . . .

If God's People have a Right to the Gifts of all God's Ministers, pray, why mayn't they use them, as they have Opportunity? And, if they should go a few Miles farther than ordinary, to enjoy those, which they profit most by; who do they wrong? Now, our LORD does inform his people, I Cor. 3. 22. That whether Paul, or Apollos, or Cephas, all was theirs.

But the Example of our Dear Redeemer, will give farther Light in this Argument. Tho' many of the Hearers, not only of the Pharisees, but of John the Baptist, came to hear our Saviour, and that not only upon Week-days, but upon Sabbath-days, and that in great Numbers, and from very distant Places; yet he reproved them not: And did not our Lord love the Apostle John more than the rest, and took him with him, before others, with Peter and James, to Mount Tabor and Gethsemany? Matth. 17. and c. 26.

To bind Men to a particular Minister, against their Judgment and Inclinations, when they are more edified elsewhere, is carnal with a Witness; a cruel Oppression of tender Consciences, a Compelling of Men to Sin: For he that doubts, is damn'd if he eat; and whatsoever is not of Faith, is Sin.

Besides, it is an unscriptural Infringment on Christian Liberty. . . . It's a Yoke like that of Egypt, which cruel Pharaoh formed for the Necks of the oppressed Israelites, which he obliged them to make up their stated Task of

Brick, but allowed them no Straw. (So we must grow in Grace and Knowledge; but, in the mean time, according to the Notion of some, we are confined from using the likeliest Means, to attain that End.)

If the great Ends of Hearing may be attained as well, and better, by Hearing another Minister than our own; then I see not, why we should be under a fatal Necessity of hearing him, I mean our Parish-Minister, perpetually, or generally. Now, what are, or ought to be, the Ends of Hearing, but the Getting of Grace, and Growing in it? Rom. 10. 14. I Pet. 2. 2. As Babes desire the Sincere Milk of the Word, that ye may grow thereby. (Poor Babes like not dry Breasts, and living Men like not dead Pools.) Well then, and may not these Ends be obtained out of our Parish-line? Faith is said to come by Hearing, Rom. 10. But the Apostle doesn't add, Your Parish-Minister. Isn't the same Word preached out of our Parish? [A]nd is there any Restriction in the Promises of blessing the Word to those only, who keep within their Parish-line ordinarily? If there be, I have not yet met with it; yea, I can affirm, that so far as Knowledge can be had in such Cases, I have known Persons to get saving Good to their Souls, by Hearing over their Parish-line; and this makes me earnest in Defence of it.

Source: Gilbert Tennent, "The Danger of an Unconverted Ministry, Considered in a Sermon on Mark VI. 34, Preached at Nottingham, in Pennsylvania, March 8, Anno 1739, 40" (Philadelphia: Benjamin Franklin, 1740), 15–22.

JOHN CALDWELL

"An Impartial Trial of the Spirit Operating in this Part of the World," 1741

John Caldwell emigrated from Ireland to colonial North America and served as a minister in Massachusetts. He emerged as a strong and strident critic of the Great Awakening movements across colonial North America and Europe. In this sermon, which he delivered on a visit to a Presbyterian church in Londonderry, New Hampshire, Caldwell implored the congregation to evaluate the pernicious and divisive effects of the revivals according to the Bible with the rational minds God had endowed to all Christians. Caldwell found the emotional outbursts, bodily convulsions, and spiritual arrogance of the revivalist preachers and new converts did not cohere with the faithful attestations of God's redemptive work across the pages of the Holy Scriptures and events in Christian history. Caldwell's sermon was published in both colonial North America and Europe. Caldwell's ministry came to an ignominious end as he fled to England upon the disclosures that he had committed acts of fraud and thievery in Ireland prior to his arrival in colonial North America. The contrasting positions of Caldwell and Gilbert Tennent nonetheless represent both the substantive content and the rancorous tenor of the discord between "Old Side" Presbyterian opponents and "New Side" Presbyterian supporters of the revival movements, which led to the first schism in the Presbyterian Church at the Synod of Philadelphia in 1741.

I bring the present Spirit so much boasted of in this Part of the World, to the above Rule, and unprejudicedly try the same thereby; and as it appears agreeable to, or different from the same, approve and receive, or condemn and reject it . . . I shall, with the greatest Caution, and a sincere Regard to Truth and Holiness, to the Glory of God and the Good of human Souls, proceed to consider the Nature, Effects, and Evidences of the present supposed Conversion in this Part of the World, that we may all be better able to judge of the Nature of the Spirit from whence it flows.

To any Person, that with an unprejudiced Mind hath viewed the same for these six Months past, or more, I presume its Nature will appear to be this, or very near, viz. A sudden and terrible Fear of divine Wrath, or the Miseries of Hell, occasioning in some a Sensation of Cold, in most a very extraordinary Warmth all over the Body; causing People to cry as if distracted; to shed Tears in great Plenty; throwing many into Convulsions, and a few for some Time into Despair. This continues with the Generality but for a very short Season, tho' some few feel is a little longer. In a few Days, or less, the Cloud blows, for ordinary, over; the Terror is at an End, and a more than common Chearfulness succeeds; all their Difficulties and Doubts are removed, and immediately a Certainty that all their Sins are pardoned, and that they shall be saved, takes place; and that all their after Sins, how many or heinous soever they be, will be overlooked, upon their confidently relying on the Merits of our Redeemer.

Its Effects, in general, are, a bold talking of Experiences, as soon as the Terror is over; by which, if we judge as we would in other Cases, we are to understand their Righteousness; tho' in the mean Time that they are filling our Ears with such Discourse, they would have us believe them the most humble and self-denied of Mankind; a Contempt of all others, especially such as seem to question any Thing of what they say of their Experiences; boldly calling such carnal, and sentencing them to eternal Misery, who demand more Evidence than they think proper to give, to convince them their Spirit is from God; refusing to reason upon their Principles, telling the World none are capable to judge of their Doctrines or Experiences, but spiritual Men; i.e. such as are of their Opinions. Its Effects upon many of their Teachers are very uncommon, divesting them of all Charity to such as oppose, tho' ever so conscientiously, this present Scheme; moving them to shut the Gates of Heaven against the whole human Race, but themselves and a few of their Friends, whose Sins God will not be offended at, as he will not approve the righteous and Christian Behaviour of others; To despise or lightly esteem the great Duties of Morality, so clearly taught, so powerfully enforced, and declared by our Saviour, to be necessary Conditions of Salvation.

Some of them it moves to leave their own particular Congregations destitute of the Ordinances of Christ, and travel to and fro upon the Earth, spiriting People against their Pastors, who are not of their Stamp, by representing them as carnal and dead Men, who have no more Right to preach than the Devil; to declare that many Errors in Judgment, Delusions of the Devil, and direct Opposition to God's Word, are no Proof of Mens being guided by a wrong Spirit; to reproach People for not being affected with what they say, i.e. because they do not shed Tears, fall down into Convulsions, scream, and prevent others from being benefited; to declare such as oppose them are guilty of Blasphemy against the Holy Ghost; to neglect the Information of the Judgment, and apply to the Passions, especially Fear; by almost constantly insisting upon Subjects of Terror, Hell, and Damnation, with Pathos and moving Gestures; to declare such Things as God declares he will condemn Men for, may yet be found in God's own Children.

Its Effects upon People, are Censoriousness and Uncharitableness to such as differ from them in that Point; speaking evil of their Neighbours, despising a holy and religious Life in all but themselves; fancying they are obliged to perswade as many as they can, to despise and leave the Ministry of their Pastors, if not agreeable to them; pretending to God's peculiar Prerogative, searching the Heart; taking deluded Imaginations for heavenly Visions; fancying their Noise and Uncharitableness, Religion; preferring the Discourses of an ignorant Person among them, to the most judicious and learned of such as differ from them; becoming Teachers of others, praying in Public, and some laying aside all Labour for the Support of themselves and Dependents. . . .

Nor is their Conversion rational, (and therefore not from the ordinary Motions of the divine Spirit) as even the first Appearance of it plainly proves. More like a bodily Distemper, than a religious Conviction, causing People to look and act distractedly, to shed Tears, to disturb God's Worship by their Noise, and fall into paralytick, hysterick, or epileptick-like Convulsions and Spasms: That this is not acting like reasonable Creatures in Religion is self-evident; Are they then supposeable to come from the divine Spirt? Are not his Operations rational? Can any Thing else work in an irresistable Manner, but Argument and Reason upon a reasonable Subject? 'Tis certain the Spirit of God of old manifested itself in no such Way. Were the Apostles in any such extraordinary Disorders, or agitated by Convulsions at their first Conversion, or when they received the Holy Ghost? Or any of the Primitive Christians, tho' generally Idolaters before Conversion, among whom, if any where, such extraordinary Commotions might be expected? If they were, 'tis strange they never communicated any such Things to us, to be a Rule for After-ages to judge by. 'Tis true, that several Persons were pricked to the Heart: i.e. had Remorse of Conscience upon Peter's preaching that Jesus was the true Messias, and shewing how barbarously he had been murdered; but there appears no such extraordinary Commotions among them as in our Days, nor Confusion; the Jaylor and the Apostle Paul do also enquire, what they shall do to be saved, or become acceptable to God; but they did not create a publick Disturbance, nor fall into Convulsions, neither then nor afterwards, nor go away boasting of Experiences, and damning all that differ'd from them about the Modus of Conversion. They did not fancy, as appears to us, that if they could but confidently believe that Christ died for their Sins, no more was necessary, their Sins were no Sins; nor would God be disobliged with them for Sin: No; they enquired what were the Duties they owed to God and Man, and having obtained a rational and convincing Account, go away resolved to comply with the same, and hoping for Salvation thereupon…

Is a Minister's leaving the particular Society of Christians, to which he was ordained as a fixt Pastor, destitute of Sermons, from the Divine Spirit? How different is it from the Apostolick Spirit, which enjoins Ministers to take heed to themselves, and the Flock over which the Holy Ghost has made them Overseers? Is this to take Heed to, or Care of their Flocks, to leave them destitute of the Ordinances of Christ?

Source: John Caldwell, "An Impartial Trial of the Spirit Operating in this Part of the World; by Comparing the Nature, Effects, and Evidences of the Present Supposed Conversion, with the Word of God, a Sermon, Preached at New London-Derry, October 14th, 1741, on I John iv. I" (Boston: William Parks, 1747), 9–13, 16.

SAMUEL BLAIR

A Short and Faithful Narrative of a Remarkable Revival of Religion in the Congregation of New-Londonderry and Other Parts of Pennsylvania, 1744

Samuel Blair (1712–1751) emigrated from Ireland to colonial North America as a child, studied at the "Log College" seminary, and ordained in 1734. He was the pastor of a congregation in New Londonderry, Pennsylvania when the church encountered the stirrings of the Great Awakening in 1740. Four years later, Blair published a narrative of how the revivals transpired at his church of mostly Scots-Irish parishioners. Because of Blair's lucid descriptions of his own impressions and methods as

well as his detailed accounts of lay experiences, historians view his narrative as a
particularly informative window into the life of a local congregation during the Great
Awakening. Unlike the sermons from Gilbert Tennent and John Caldwell, Blair's
writing reflects a pastor holding a moderate stance on the burgeoning revival move-
ments that welcomed emotional responses to God's grace within the guiding principles
of orderly Christian worship.

Thus Religion lay as it were a dying, and ready to expire its last Breath of Life
in this Part of the visible Church: And it was in the Spring Anno Domini 1740,
when the God of Salvation was pleased to visit us with the blessed Effusions
of his Holy Spirit in an eminent Manner. The first very open and Publick
Appearance of this gracious Visitations in these Parts, was in the Congregation which God has committed to my Charge. . . .

I had some View and Sense of the deplorable Condition of the Land in
general; and accordingly the Scope of my Preaching thro' that first Winter
after I came here, was mainly calculated for Persons in a natural unregener-
ate Estate. I endeavour'd, as the Lord enabled me, to open up and prove
from his Word, the Truths which I judged most necessary for such as were
in that State to know and believe in order to their Conviction and Conversion. I endeavour'd to deal searchingly and solemnly with them; and thro' the
concurring Blessing of God, I had knowledge of four or five brought under
deep Convictions that Winter. In the beginning of March I took a Journey
into East-Jersey, and was abroad for two or three Sabbaths. A neighbouring
Minister, who seemed to be earnest for the Awakening and Conversion of
secure Sinners, and whom I had obtained to preach a Sabbath to my People in
my Absence, preached to them, I think, on the first Sabbath after I left Home.
His Subject was the dangerous and awful Case of such as continue unregener-
ate and unfruitful under the Means of Grace. The Text was Luk. 13. 7. Then
said he to the Dresser of his Vineyard, behold, these three Years I come seek-
ing Fruit on this Fig Tree, and find none, cut it down, why cumbereth it the
Ground? Under that Sermon there was a visible Appearance of much Soul-
Concern among the Hearers, so that some burst out with an audible Noise
into bitter crying (a Thing not known in those Parts before.) After I had come
Home there came a young Man to my House under deep Trouble about the
State of his Soul, whom I had look'd upon as a pretty light merry sort of a
Youth: He told me that he was not any Thing concerned about himself in
the Time of hearing the above mentioned Sermon, nor afterwards, till the
next Day that he went to his Labour, which was grubbing, in order to clear
some New-Ground; the first Grub he set about was a pretty large one with a
high Top, and when he had cut the Roots, as it fell down those Words came
instantly to his Remembrance, and as a Spear to his Heart, cut it down why

cumbereth it the Ground? So thought he, must I be cut down by the Justice of God, for the Burning of Hell, unless I get into another State than I am now in. He thus came into very great and abiding Distress, which, to all Appearance has had a happy Issue: His Conversation being to this Day as becomes the Gospel of Christ.

The News of this very publick Appearance of deep Soul-concern among my People met me an Hundred Miles from Home: I was very joyful to hear of it, in Hopes that God was about to carry on an extensive Work of converting Grace amongst them. And the first Sermon I preached after my Return to them, was from Mat. 6. 33. . . . After opening up and explaining the Parts of the Text, when in the Improvement, I came to press the Injunction in the Text upon the Unconverted and Ungodly, and offer'd this as one Reason among others, why they should now henceforth first of all seek the Kingdom and Righteousness of God. . . . This Confederation seem'd to come and cut like a Sword upon several in the Congregation, so that while I was speaking upon it they could no longer contain, but burst out in the most bitter Mourning. I desir'd them, as much as possible, to restrain themselves from making a Noise that would hinder themselves or others from hearing what was spoken: And often afterwards I had the Occasion to repeat the same Council. I still advised People to endeavour to moderate and bound their Passions, but not so as to resist or stifle their Convictions. The Number of the Awakened encreased very fast, frequently under Sermons there were some newly convicted, and brought into deep Distress of Soul about their perishing Estate. Our Sabbath Assemblies soon became vastly large; many People from almost all Parts around inclining very much to come where there was such Appearance of the divine Power and Presence. I think there was scarcely a Sermon or Lecture preached here thro' that whole Summer, but there were manifest Evidence of Impressions on the Hearers; and many Times the Impressions were very great and general: Several would be overcome and fainting; others deeply sobbing, hardly able to contain, others crying in a most dolorous Manner, many others more silently Weeping, and a solemn Concern appearing in the Countenance of many others. And sometimes the Soul Exercises of some (tho' comparatively but very few) would so far affect their Bodies, as to Occasion some strange unusual Bodily Motions. . . . There was an earnest Desire in People after Opportunities for publick Worship and hearing the Word. I appointed in the Spring to preach every Friday thro' the Summer when I was at Home, and those Meetings were well attended; and at several of them the Power of the Lord was remarkably with us. The main scope of my Preaching thro' that Summer was, laying open the deplorable State of Man by Nature since the Fall, our ruin'd expos'd Case by the Breach of the first Covenant, and the awful Condition of such as were not in CHRIST, giving the Marks and Characters, of such as were in that Condition: And moreover, laying open the Way of Recovery in the New Covenant thro' a Mediator, with the Nature and Necessity of Faith in CHRIST the Mediator &c. I labour'd much on the last mentioned Heads; that People might have right Apprehensions of the Gospel-Method of Life and Salvation. . . . And, that neither were they to obtain or seek Peace in Extraordinary Ways, by Visions, Dreams, or immediate Inspirations; but by an understanding View and believing Persuasion of the Way of Life, as reveal'd in the Gospel, thro' the Suretyship, Obedience and Sufferings of JESUS CHRIST, with a View of the Suitableness and Sufficiency of that mediatory Righteousness of CHRIST for the Justification and Life of Law-condemned Sinners; and thereupon freely accepting him for their Saviour, heartily consenting to, and being well pleased with that Way of Salvation; and venturing their all upon his Mediation, from the Warrant and Encouragement afforded of God thereunto in his Word, by his free Offer, authoritative Command, and sure Promise to those that so believe.

Source: Samuel Blair, *A Short and Faithful Narrative of a Remarakable [sic] Revival of Religion in the Congregation of New-Londonderry and other Parts of Pennsylvania, as the Same was Sent in a Letter to the Rev. Mr. Prince of Boston* (Philadelphia: William Bradford, 1744), 10–16, 18–20.

3

The Reformed Shape
of Presbyterian Worship

DAVID MCGREGORE

"The True Believer's All Secured," 1747

David McGregore (1710–1777) emigrated from Ireland to colonial North America as a child. Soon after his family arrived, his father accepted a call to become the pastor of a Presbyterian congregation in colonial New England. In the absence of a theological school, David McGregore, like some other aspiring ministers in his context, received his education mainly through an apprenticeship, in which a local pastor tutored one or more students who desired a career in ministry. He was ordained in 1737 and served as the pastor of a Presbyterian congregation in Londonderry, New Hampshire. An ardent supporter of the Great Awakening movements, McGregore preached a sermon in Boston in 1741 that directly rebutted John Caldwell's criticism of the revivals. Six years later, he delivered this sermon in Boston on the administration of the Lord's Supper. His instructions emphasize the theological significance of a covenanted community of believers gathering at the "Lord's Table" to receive spiritual nourishment and include a stern warning to unbelievers.

2 TIM I. 12. LATTER PART.

—I am persuaded that He is able to keep that which I have committed unto him against that Day.

. . . Beloved, Here is a considerable Number of Communicants who have this Day been at the Lord's Table, among which it is to be hoped there are some Believers: some who have had Faith in Exercise, and who have been enabled to make a renewed Dedication of themselves and all their Concerns to a covenanted God in Christ. And to such as have been so happy as to do so, it may be a proper and seasonable Exercise to take a back Look upon what they have been doing. Such a Reflection will yield them sweet Complacency of Soul; while they perceive that they have committed their All into a safe Hand: one who cares for them and all their Concerns with the most tender Care, who is not only able but every Way well qualified to keep what they have committed to him, as in my Text. . . .

The Words thus introduced and explained do easily afford us this doctrinal Truth.

DOCT. That a person who knows what it is to trust in God, does confidently commit all his Concerns into his Keeping.

The Doctrine is not only a Scripture Truth, as may appear from innumerable Texts; but it is a Truth plain from this Text, as may be easily seen. In the Prosecution of it I would propose this following Method;

First, Enquire what is that which a Believer by Faith commits to a covenanted God in Christ.

Secondly, What Assurance the Person has, that the Truth shall be kept safe, and that he shall have a good Account of it in the End.

And then make Application.

I. I begin with the first of these in Order; i.e. to enquire what it is that a Believer by Faith commits to Christ, or which is the same, to a covenanted God in Christ. To this I answer in general, that he commits to this Keeper all his Affairs, publick and private, personal and relative, spiritual and secular, for Time and Eternity: In a Word, all that he is, or has, or is any Way concerned with. But to be somewhat more particular: I observe that the Believer commits all his personal Concerns to Christ[.] Now these may be divided into spiritual and temporal.

[1.] He commits to this Keeper his spiritual, personal Concerns. When the Person first closed with Christ, he saw him in every Respect so qualified, that he could freely commit his precious Soul with all its Concerns into his Hand: Nay, had he had ten Thousand Souls, he would not have thought the Trust too great to commit to such a Keeper. Now he considers that he who is the Author, behoofs also to be the Finisher of his Faith; that 'tis he who begins a good Work, that can carry it on to the Day of the Lord Jesus; that it is the great Husbandman who first sowed the precious Seed of Grace in the Heart, who best knows what Culture, what watering, what Nourishment, what pruning, in a Word, what Care of every Kind it needs in order to bring it to Perfection: And hence he commits the Keeping of his Soul to him, that he would work all his Works in him and for him; that he would gloriously accomplish what he has graciously begun; that he would never leave nor forsake him, 'till he perfects that which concerns him. . . .

[2.] As the Believer commits all his personal spiritual Concerns to Christ, in like Manner he commits all his personal temporal Affairs to the same Keeper. The Person has a practical Sense of divine Providence. He sees that it is in God he lives and moves and has his Being; that 'tis Christ who upholds all Things by the Word of his Power, and by whom all Things consist, Heb. I. 3. Col I. 17. that this Providence, which has a general Care about the whole Creation, causing the Lillies to grow, and answering the Cry of the young Ravens, has a more especial and tender Care about Believers; that these are to him as the Signet on the right Hand, or the Apple of his eye; that on the Behalf of these his Eyes run to and fro through the whole Earth, 2 Chron. 16. 9; and that he has graciously laid himself under a Covenant Obligation: These Things the Person has such a Sense of, that he chearfully commits all his temporal Concerns to Christ. He looks by Faith into the New Covenant, and there he finds Promises of every needed temporal good Thing. . . .

But farther, the Person stands in the Relation of a Member to the visible Church, and he is careful to commit the whole Body of which he is a Member to a Covenanted God in Christ. As a Man is apt to have a particular Regard for his native Country, the Believer has for the Church. And indeed no wonder; all his Well Springs are in her: Here it was that the new Man first drew Breath. Psal. 87.5,—7. This and that Man was born in her. Here the Believer has often gathered and eaten the heavenly Manna: Here he has been made the happy Recipient of those nourishing Showers of divine Influence which have made his Soul like a watered Garden to grow and increase with all the Increase of God[.] It was in these Mountains of Myrrh and Hills of Frankincense, that he has met with a Saviour, and had many a sweet Intercourse with the Father & his Son Jesus Christ. On these and such Accounts he has a high Value for the Church: as indeed it is most reasonable he should. As he regards Christ as his Father, both with Respect to Generation & Education; so he respects the Church as his Mother, in each of these Respects. . . .

To Unbelievers. Alas, how deplorable is your Condition! You cannot but be sensible that you have Eternity before you; that you have precious Souls which must quickly take their Flight into the World of Spirits, there to take up their everlasting Abode, either in perfect Happiness, or extream Misery: These are great and weighty Truths which do most nearly concern you; and yet have you not a Conscience which tells you that you have never acted like Persons who believe these Truths? You are outside Christians, and that is all: You have never seen, the Danger of an unconverted State, & what a fearful Thing it is to fall into the Hand of the living God[.] You have never had a right Discovery of the Guiltiness of your Persons, or the Depravity of your Natures[.] You have had no saving Illumination of your dark Minds in the Knowledge of Christ: All that you know of his being so well qualified in every Respect to keep a Trust, is only by Hear-say; so that you could never yet be perswaded to commit your Souls into his Hand, to trust him with all your Concerns. Have you not a Bosom-Witness that joins with me in saying that this is your Case, as I have represented it? And that you are taking little or no Pains to have it otherwise: So that your All is in the most wretched Uncertainty, and liable every Moment to be utterly lost without Remedy. Alas! what a sad Infatuation are you under! How foolish is your Conduct! Yea how inconsistent are you with your selves! You would not act in your worldly Affairs as you do in your Spiritual. If your temporal Estate be in Danger, you will not rest 'till you have it secured in the best Manner that is practicable: If your Title to any Part is precarious, you'l use Diligence to have it ascertained. If you have a Sum of Money to lend, you'l not part with it but upon good Security. If you have a Ship & valuable Cargo putting to Sea, you'l not neglect to have them ensured; especially if it be a Time of uncommon Danger: And yet you can supinely sit still in Soul Affairs, and satisfy your selves with may be's, meer Uncertainties! You say, you hope God will have Mercy on you at last; but can give no solid Reason of your Hope. Is not this to be wise about Trifles, and in the mean Time to trifle in the most important Concern? Sirs! Consider how little it will profit you, tho' you gained the whole World, if you lose your own Souls. Look to the Lord; that he would enable you to give these Things their due Weight.

Source: David McGregore, "The True Believer's All Secured: A Sermon Preached at the Presbyterian Meeting-House in Boston, March the 11th and 12th, Being Sabbath-Evening and Monday after the Administration of the Lord's Supper" (Boston: S. Kneeland and T. Green, 1747), 5–6, 8–9, 12, 18, 34–35.

JONATHAN PARSONS

"Infant Baptism from Heaven," 1765

Jonathan Parsons (1705–1776) was born in Massachusetts, graduated from Yale College in 1729, and ordained as a Congregationalist minister in 1731. Prior to his ordination, he studied theology under Jonathan Edwards. In 1745, another of his mentors, George Whitefield, encouraged Parsons to plant a new church in Newburyport, Massachusetts. Parsons agreed and became the pastor of a Presbyterian congregation soon thereafter. In addition to his extensive knowledge of classics, history, and theology, he was also interested in medical practices. The erudite minister published

sermons on a myriad of theological subjects, such as justification and ecclesiology, dur-
ing his career. This sermon on infant baptism is based on the conversion of the jailer
and the baptisms of his entire family in Acts 16. Parsons underscores the importance
of water baptism as a visible sign and seal of God's grace to a covenanted people. His
biblical and theological connections between the meanings of circumcision in the Old
Testament and baptism in the New Testament demonstrate how Reformed under-
standings of covenant theology shaped the sacrament of baptism in Presbyterian polity,
worship, and witness.

ACTS XVI, 33.

"And was baptised, he and all his, straightway."

THE diffusive goodness of the infinitely glorious God, is eminently displayed, in giving us more noble powers and faculties than the beasts of the earth, and in making us capable of more excellent enjoyments and employments, than merely sensitive creatures. But, when the world of mankind was laid under a deluge of sin and death, by the universal corruption of human nature, and there was none to help, the goodness of God was more eminently displayed in the wonderful work of redemption by his son Jesus Christ, who was the gift of the Father, and made his soul an offering for sin, that he might see his seed, and the pleasure of the Lord might prosper in his hands.

AND as God was pleased to treat with innocent man in a covenant way, a covenant of works; so he has been pleased to make a new and better covenant, which is in all things well ordered and sure, and to single out some of Adam's ruined race and bring them into the bonds of it. Thus particularly, he dealt with Abraham, and entailed it unto his seed after him, for an everlasting covenant, which gave them a claim to many great and peculiar priviledges. And these priviledges the Jews for many ages enjoyed, untill, by their unbelief, they forfeited "the adoption, and the glory, and the covenants, and the giving of the law, and the service of God, and the promises." Rom ix. 4. But what qualifies the divine severity, in the rejection of the Jews from being the covenant people of God, upon their rejecting Jesus Christ as the true Messiah, is, that "thro' their fall salvation is come unto the Gentiles," and so they are become the mystical body of Jesus Christ, or the covenant people of God.

UNTO this covenant God has appointed a token, sign or seal of induction, for a confirmation of the promises on his part, and an obligation to that duty which is their part of the covenant. Circumcision was the seal of induction unto Abraham and to his seed, under the ancient dispensation of the covenant; but since the blood of Jesus Christ has been actually shed for the remission and purgation of sin, that bloody ordinance is done away, and baptism is, by divine appointment, the badge of all the disciples of Christ; and the introduction into the visible church. Therefore all these that received the doctrine, and submitted to the institution of John Baptist, he baptised with water, as the manner of the Jews was to admit prosylites, in token of their cleansing themselves by repentance and reformation. This pointed to the baptism which our Saviour Jesus Christ afterwards ordained to be the seal of induction into the visible church, under the Christian dispensation, and was the dawn of the gospel day. And hence Christ, having received power from the father, gave a commission to his apostles, and to all his ordinary ministers, to admit his disciples into the church, by the sacred rite of baptism with water, "in the name of the Father, and of the Son, and of the Holy Ghost," as the signal of dedication to God, to be his, and for him forever. Therefore, when any of the Gentiles or others embraced the Christian religion, and made an open profession of it, they were admitted into the communion of the Christian church, by the ordinance of water baptism: and not only they, but all theirs. Thus in particular it was, with regard to the instance before us: no sooner did the jailor submit to the laws of Christianity, but he was admitted to its priviledges, being baptized, he and all his straightway. . . .

ARG. I. "IF the infants of visible believers do also belong to the visible church themselves, then they are to be baptized: but the infants of visible believers are also members of the visible church themselves[,] therefore the infants of visible believers are to be baptized."

THAT all might fully understand my meaning, I desire it might be observed, that by infants belonging to, or being members of the visible church, I do not intend that they have the badge or seal of their membership put upon them when they are first born, but in a qualified sense they are members: as a son born in the army is the king's soldier, or a child born in the king's dominions is the king[']s subject, tho' the former is not actually inlisted, nor the latter formally declared to be so. So the children of visible believers are members of the visible church as soon as they are born into the world, before they have the badge of church membership put upon them, or have the seal of the covenant put upon them. If a person did in no sense at all belong to the visible church, how could he with any propriety, have the token membership put upon him? Is it not in consequence of a person's being a visible member, that he has the token put upon him, which is the common right of all visible members, and by which token or mark they are distinguished from others? [A]nd is not baptism the token of visible membership, by which Christ would have his visible church distinguished from the rest of the world? I presume none of our neighbours who deny infant baptism, will pretend that there is any other way of admission into the visible church, either from precept or example, since Jesus Christ appointed this holy ordinance. But if they should pretend some other way, they may see themselves mistaken, by considering, that all the admission we read of, since baptism was a divine institution, were by this token or seal of the covenant. As evidence of this, I would refer them to the three thousand, Acts ii, to Simon Magus and the eunuch, chap. viii., to Paul, chap. ix., to Stephanus and his hous[e]hold, I Cor. i. 6., to Lydia, the Jailor, and their hous[e]holds, Acts xvi. All these were brought into the church by the seal of baptism; and I believe none can tell of any other way. —Nor have we any warrant from the word of God to delay the administration of this ordinance to such as are members, untill they are indoctrinated in the Christian faith, and are capable of understanding the nature of the ordinance. All the scripture examples of admission are levelled against delays. No sooner did those already mentioned belong to the visible church, but they were baptised. Nor can any man living prove, that all these were adult persons: no; so far from it, that there is no reason to think they were so, but much reason to believe the contrary. But whether they were, or were not, we are assured that it is the will of God, that disciples of Christ should be baptised without delay, as we shall consider by and by.

IN the mean time, what is mainly before me upon this argument, is to prove, "that infants of visible believers or church members, are also themselves members of the visible church, and therefore ought to have the seal of induction put upon them." And this, I apprehend, will appear to every unprejudiced mind, by a careful attendance to a few things, such as these following, viz.

I. "GOD never made a covenant with man, but what included his seed." We have two covenants represented to us in the holy scripture, viz. a covenant of works and a covenant of grace, and in both these God has covenanted with man and his seed.

THUS God entered into a covenant of works with Adam and his seed. Adam was the root of all mankind, and his posterity were the branches. God entered into a covenant of life with him, binding him and his posterity unto himself, with this condition, "he that doth these things shall live of them." And all his seed being in him as their covenant head, fell with him in the first transgression. His act was imputed to them; his guilt was imputed to them, so that as soon as his posterity are born into the world, they are condemned. The whole nature of man then subsisted in Adam, and his enormous crimes tainted his blood. "By one man sin entered into the world, and death by sin, so death passed upon all men, for that all have sinned." Rom. v. 12. As the blessings offered in this covenant to Adam and his seed, would have been secured to them had he continued in his integrity, so the curse falls upon all his posterity by his disobedience; no sooner are they human creatures, but they are morally defiled and guilty creatures. . . .

UPON the apostacy, God entered into a covenant of grace to deliver men out of an estate of sin and misery, and to bring them into an estate of salvation by a Redeemer. This covenant of grace was primarily and principally with the Lord Jesus Christ as the second Adam. And therefore he is called the surety of the covenant of grace, to adjust and make up the difference between God and his people. But, although the covenant of grace is primarily made with Christ, as the represent[a]tive of his seed, yet, in him, it is made with believers or with his seed. Hence they are said "to enter into covenant;" Psal. I. 5., to "keep covenant;" Psal. xxv. 10., to "break the covenant;" Levit. xxvi. 15, and many such like expressions, shewing that the covenant of grace is made with believers.—And parents that are believers, have their children taken into covenant with them. Whenever God has taken parents into his family and kingdom, he has taken in their children with them, and has reckoned them a part of his family. Therefore all the people of Israel, young and old, male and female, are called "the children of the Lord your God;" Deut. xiv. 1, adopted children, owned by God as his people; a people near to him, set apart for him. Hence, God directed Moses to say unto Pharaoh, "Israel is my Son, even my first born;" Exod. iv. 22, precious in my sight, and dear to me, tho' there were many in Israel that were enemies to God and children of the devil; but were taken into covenant in the right of their parents, and, in that sense, "beloved for their fathers sake."

I AM sensible that Antinomians will object and say, "that it is not possible for a person to be under the covenant of grace and the covenant of works at the same time; to be precious in the sight of God, and yet haters of God; to be children of the devil, and children of God at once. How then can the preceeding account be reconciled?"

IN answer to this objection; I grant, that as to the state of persons, all are either renewed or unrenewed; in a state of nature or in a state of grace: they belong either to the first or the second Adam. . . . For the terms of the covenants are directly opposite to each other. And therefore, if a person is admitted into the covenant of grace, by effectual calling, he is certainly cut off from the covenant of works; for, "if it is by grace" that a person is saved, "then it is no more of works: otherways grace is no more grace. But if it be of works, then it is no more grace: otherways work is no more work." —But this hinders not but a person may be in a graceless state, and yet enjoy many and great external priviledges of the church, which belong to those whom God has separated to himself, to make known his name among them. Tho' outward priviledges avail nothing to special grace, any further than means of God's appointing, yet they are priviledges, and do advance people above others, which some are favoured with, as stewards, to improve and transmit to others. Paul reckoned the priviledges of the Jewish church very great, even those that were external. Rom. ix. 4. To be dignified and distinguished by visible church priviledges, to have the symbols of the divine presence, the word and sacraments, to enjoy the means of grace, and be separated from others as the covenant people of God, is a very great favour. Now, all these privileges did belong to the body of the Jews, of all ages, as the covenant people of God; even to them that never received any saving benefit by them, as well as others. It is one thing to inherit the saving grace of the covenant, and another to enjoy the outward privileges of it. All the seed of visible believers, have a right to many of the external priviledges of the covenant, and it is the duty of parents to claim these priviledges for them.

Source: Jonathan Parsons, "Infant Baptism from Heaven: Two Discourses Delivered at Haverhill West Parish, Lord's Day, April 28th, 1765" (Boston: W. M'Alpine and J. Fleming, 1765), 5–7, 13–18.

JOHN BLACK

"The Duty of Christians, in Singing the Praise of God, Explained" 1790

John Black (ca. 1750–1802) was born in Pennsylvania, raised in North Carolina, graduated from the College of New Jersey (now Princeton University) in 1771, and served as the pastor of Upper Marsh Creek Church, a Presbyterian congregation in Gettysburg, Pennsylvania, from 1775 to 1794. During Black's ministry, church attendance grew, and a large stone building was built to replace the previous log building that had become too small to accommodate all of the worshipers. Esteem for Black waned in his last several years at the church on account of his increasing social involvement in temperance reforms. After he drafted a resolution calling for stricter regulation of liquor sales in his town, only three persons in his church agreed to sign it. In this sermon, delivered at the height of Black's popularity, he treats the roles of music and singing in Christian worship. The sermon title echoes the first Directory for Worship in American Presbyterianism from 1788, with its instruction that "the duty of Christians" is to praise God by singing psalms and hymns. Black, like most Presbyterians, moved away from John Calvin's more restrictive position that only the Psalms, the Ten Commandments, and the Canticle of Simeon constituted permissible texts for corporate singing.

ON PSALMODY.

Col. 3, 16.

Let the word of Christ dwell in you richly in all wisdom, teaching and admonishing one another in psalms, and hymns, and spiritual songs, singing with grace in your hearts to the Lord.

IT is, I presume, the indispensible duty of all rational creatures, to praise God in that manner to which the powers of their name, respectively, enable them. And, I presume also, that among all the ranks of rational creatures of which we have any knowledge, and who have either retained their innocence, or have returned to God after offending him, it will be found, that praise makes a principle part of their Devotion . . . that praising God is an act of worship which should be performed both in public and in private: for as in the one we are commanded to teach and admonish one another, so in the other to speak to ourselves in psalms, and hymns, &c.

BUT it may be enquired—Do all these expressions, psalms, hymns, and spiritual songs, signify one and the same thing: and particularly, do they mean the Book of Psalms contained in the [O]ld Testament, exclusive of all others?

THE solution of this is of considerable importance:—And to it I answer, that these terms neither mean one and the same thing originally, nor have we any reason to conclude that they refer to any one system or collection of compositions whatever, which was extant in the Apostles days for praising God, and exclusive of all others.

THE word, psalm, originally means a composition . . . performed upon an instrument of music, and was not necessary to be accompanied with either words or voice. It is derived from a root which signifies, to strike gently, or move with a certain agitation; because the strings of musical instruments require to be struck or moved with the fingers, or other instrument for that purpose. David was finely skilled in instrumental music, as well as in poetry: and it is undeniable that throughout the Jewish Dispensation, especially in his time, instruments of music were used in the worship of God. On this account it was, that the compositions of David, and of others, which were used by the Jewish Church, were called psalms, because whilst the Choir and others sung the words, the musicians always performed the tune upon some instrument. Hence it is, that we find them directing their compositions to the musician, to be performed on such, or such an instrument. And hence also it is, that they so frequently call upon the church to praise God with timbrel, psaltery, harp, organ, &c.

A hymn is a poetical composition, or verses, made to celebrate some person, or action, or to bewail some mournful event; without any regard to music. It is designed to be read or recited; and although it may be accompanied with an instrument, or the voice, yet these are not necessary to its original design.

THE meaning of the term, song, is universally known—it is always designed for the voice—to be sung with an air suited to the measure of the verse. But the Apostle directs that the songs of [C]hristians shou'd be of a particular kind, as to their subject matter, viz. spiritual; that is to say, songs on spiritual subjects—subjects calculated to give religious instruction, and to raise, or quicken devotion in the soul.

I WELL know there are many who suppose, that the Apostle, by all those various terms, meant nothing more, nor less than the Book of Psalms contained in the Old Testament. But this is mere opinion; nor have I ever seen, or heard any thing in support of it, but opinion, or bare assertion. —There are no authentic records, sacred, or profane, which prove that the psalms of David bore these various titles, or were denominated by them. On the contrary we know that whenever Christ and his Apostles quote that part of scripture, they do it under the title, psalms, —never hymns, or spiritual songs. Thus the Saviour quotes that book in the following passages, "As David himself saith in the book of psalms" Luke 20. 42. "All things must be fulfilled which were written concerning me in the law of Moses, and in the prophets, and in the psalms" Luke 24. 44. Thus also Peter, "For it is written in the book of psalms" Acts 1. 20. And thus too Paul, "As it is written in the second psalm" Acts 13. 33. —On the other hand, when the term hymn is used in the New Testament, there is no circumstance to make it so much as probable that the sacred writer had any reference to the book of psalms, or to any composition in it. The only places where the word is used, are my text—the fifth chapter and nineteenth verse of the Epistle to the Ephesians—and Mark[']s and Mat[t]hew[']s Gospels, where they record, that Christ sung an hymn with his disciples, after the institution and celebration of his supper Matt 26. 30. Now, in all these places, there is no one consideration from the scope of the context, or otherwise, to make it certain, or even so much as likely, that the Old Testament psalms were meant by it. Some, indeed, have alledged that what Christ sung, after the celebration of his supper, was the Jewish Hallel, beginning with the 113th and ending with the 118th psalm. But this is still opinion—an opinion, too, very slenderly founded: for the only reason assigned is, that the Jews always sung this portion of the psalms when they celebrated their passover feast. And surely it is very extraordinary reasoning, to conclude, that because the Jews sung this on that occasion, therefore the Saviour sung the same, when he had set that ordinance entirely aside, and had instituted a quite different one in its room. —It is just such reasoning, as if one were to say, the premises are different, therefore, the conclusion must be the same. Divine wisdom has not seen it fit to record particularly, what the Saviour sung on that occasion: but as he had then instituted a new ordinance, of which there is no hint in the Old Testament, I leave it with every one to judge for himself, whether it be not most probable that he himself composed the hymn he sung; especially, as none of the psalms directly apply to that ordinance; and especially, too, as the Evangelists, who record the transaction, call it, uniformly, an hymn.

UPON the whole,—as these terms originally signify different things— and as there is no evidence that the book of psalms, used by the Jews, ever obtained, or was known by these various titles; but that, on the contrary, indeed, the title, psalms, was appropriate to it: it will be obvious to conclude, that the Apostle did not, by all these terms, mean that book, exclusive of all others; nor, indeed, any one system, or collection of compositions then extant. The plain easy, natural, sophisticated sense of the words is, every kind of sacred poetry, whatever denomination it might come under, whether psalm, or hymn, or spiritual song; and not only those which were then composed and in use in the Christian Church, but also those which, from the fullness of the word of Christ dwelling in believers, they might be enabled, from time to time, to compose for their mutual edification, and the glory of God. . . .

With regard to the manner of performing this duty, I shall not trouble you with the controversy, whether instruments of music should be used in Christian worship or not. Perhaps this is but a matter of doubtful disputation; and the propriety, or impropriety of it, may depend much upon the sentiments of the worshipping assembly. We certainly know it was practiced under former dispensations, with the Divine approbation; and the New Testament does not forbid, neither does it command it. But this is certain, that we should praise God with the voice, in an air or tune adapted to the measure of the verse. The melody of the heart—the joyful frame of the spirit—or any inward exercises whatever, will not come up to the ordinance, nor answer its end, without the sound of the voice. Nothing can be more evident than this, both from the Old and New Testament. Many are the places where David exhorts to sing to God; yea, to sing loud Psalm 47. 6, 66. 1, 2, 81. 1—Christ and his Disciples sung Matthew 26. 20—all that followed him as he approached Jerusalem, just before his sufferings, sung his praise as they descended the Mount of Olives Luke 19. 37—and the Apostle in my text, and in Ephesians 5. 19, commands to sing.

BUT although the sound of the voice is necessary to the performance of this duty, yet the exercise of grace in the heart, which the Apostle, elsewhere, terms the melody of the heart, is as necessary. For unless those devout affections and gracious dispositions that are correspondent to the subject, be awakened and in exercise, we shall only be drawing near to God with our mouths, and honouring him with our lips, whilst our hearts are far from him.

WE must also sing with understanding and judgement. This, indeed, is necessary in every part of religious worship, —The rational offspring of the All-intelligent Father, must serve him in a way proper to the capacity he has given them: and we may just as well pray to him in an unknown tongue, as sing his praise in words or phrases which we do not understand. A piece of sounding brass, or tinkling cymbal is not more worthless, in the Divine estimation, than we shall be, if we offer him a blind, unmeaning service, which, from the nature of things, must also be unprofitable to ourselves. And therefore the Apostle declares, that although he would sing with the spirit, yet it should be with the understanding also. . . .

Moreover, the Apostle, in my text, mentions another end with regard to ourselves and others, viz. instruction, "teaching and admonishing one another, says he, in psalms, and hymns, and spiritual songs." To this purpose also, the ordinance is naturally suited. Moral and religious truths, and indeed, any matter whatever, thrown into plain and agreeable verse, generally makes a more lasting impression on the memory, than prose compositions; and when they are frequently repeated, or sung, the effect will be proportionally more lasting and strong.

Source: John Black, "The Duty of Christians, in Singing the Praise of God, Explained, a Sermon" (Carlisle, PA: Kline & Reynolds, 1790), 5–11, 13–14, 18.

HARRIET MYER LAIRD

"Self-Dedication; or Solemn Covenant with God," 1822

Harriet Myer Laird (1803–1834) was born in Pennsylvania and became an educator for young women from 1827 to 1833. She taught at a boarding school in Aurora, New York, and founded two schools in north and central Pennsylvania. She was also interested in the burgeoning world mission movements, which began in the United States with the creation of the inter-denominational American Board of Commissioners for Foreign Missions in 1810, and set out to Liberia with her spouse, Matthew Laird, in 1833. The missionary couple died from disease shortly after arriving to West Africa. This private letter, which Harriet Myer Laird composed as a personal act of worship in her late teens, illustrates her steadfast commitment to Jesus Christ, her fervent desire to serve God's kingdom, and her rich understanding of Reformed theology.

To thee therefore do I now come invited by the name of thy Son and trusting in his righteousness and grace. Laying myself at thy feet with shame and confusion of face, and smiting upon my breast, I say, with the humble Publican God be merciful to me a sinner! I acknowledge, O Lord that I have been a great transgressor. My sins have reached unto heaven, and my iniquities are lifted up unto the skies. The irregular propensities of my corrupted and degenerated nature have in ten thousand aggravated instances, wrought to bring forth fruit unto death. And if thou shouldst be struck to mark mine offences, I must be silent under a load of guilt and immediately sink into destruction. But thou hast graciously called me to return unto thee, though I have been a wandering sheep, a prodigal son[,] a backsliding child. Behold, therefore, O Lord I come unto thee. I come convinced not only of my sin but of my folly. I come from my very heart ashamed of myself and with an acknowledgment in the sincerity and humility of my soul, that I have played the fool and have erred exceedingly. I am confounded myself at the remembrance of these things; but be thou merciful to my unrighteousness, and do not remember against my sins and my transgressions. Permit me, O Lord, to bring back unto those powers and faculties which I have ungratefully and sacrilegiously alienated from thy service; and receive I beseech thee, thy poor revolted creature, who is now convinced of thy right to her and desires nothing in the whole world so much as to be thine!

Blessed God, it is with the utmost solemnity that I make this surrender of myself unto thee. Hear O Heavens and give ear O earth; I avouch the Lord this day to be my God and I avouch and declare myself this day to be one of his covenant children and people. Hear, O thou of heaven, and record in the book of thy remembrance; that henceforth I am thine[,] wholly thine. . . . In this course, O blessed God, would I steadily persevere to the very end of my life; earnestly praying that every future day of it may supply the deficiencies, and correct irregularities of the former; and that I may by divine grace be enabled not only to hold on that happy way, but daily to grow more active in it!

Nor do I not only consecrate all that I am and hope to thy service but I also most humbly resign and submit to thine holy and sovereign will myself and all that I can call mine. I leave, O Lord to thy management and direction all I profess and all I wish; and set every enjoyment, and every interest before thee, to be disposed of as thou pleases. Continue or remove what thou has given me; bestow or refuse what I imagine I want, as thou Lord shall see good! And though I dare not say I will never repine, yet I hope I may venture to say I will labour not only to submit, but to acquiesce; not only to bear what thou doest in thy most affective dispensations, but to consent to it and to praise thee for it; contentedly resolving in all that thou appointedest for me my will into thine and looking on myself as nothing, and on thee, O God as the great eternal All, whose word ought to determine every thing, and whose government ought to be the joy of the whole rational creation. . . .

Dispose my affairs, O God, in a manner which may be most subservient to thy Glory, and my own truest happiness; and when I have done and borne thy will upon earth, call me from hence at what time and in what manner thou pleasest; only grant that in my dying moments and in the near prospect of eternity, I may remember these my engagements to thee and may employ my latest breath to thy service! And do thou, Lord when thou seest the agonies of destroying nature upon me remember this covenant too, even though I should then be incapable of recollecting it! Look down O my heavenly Father with a piercing eye upon thy languishing, thy dying child; place thine everlasting arms under me for my support; put strength and confidence in my departing spirit; and receive into the embraces of thine everlasting love! Welcome it to the abodes of them that sleep in Jesus, to wait with them that glorious day, when the last of thy promises to thy covenant people shall be fulfilled in their triumphant resurrection and that abundant entrance, which shall be administered to them into that everlasting kingdom, of which thou hast assured them by thy covenant, and in the hope of which I now lay hold on it desiring to live and die as with mine hand on that hope.

And when I am thus numbered among the dead, and all the interests of mortality are over with me forever, if this solemn memorial should chance to fall into the hand of any surviving friends, may it be the means of making serious impressions on their minds! May they read it not only as my language, but as their own; and learn to fear the Lord my God and with me to put their breast under the shadow of his wings for time and for eternity! And may they also learn to adore with me that grace, which inclines our hearts to enter into the covenant, and condescends to admit us into it when so inclined; ascribing with me, and with all the nations of the redeemed, to the Father, the Son, and the Holy Ghost, that glory, honour and praise, which is so justly due to each divine person for the part he [bears] in this illustrious work!

Source: Harriet Myer Laird, "Self-Dedication; or Solemn Covenant with God," from Harriet Myer Laird Papers, Presbyterian Historical Society, Philadelphia, PA.

4

Distinctive Elements of Presbyterianism

Polity, Proclamation, and Predestination

SAMUEL BUELL

A Sermon Preached at the Ordination
of Samson Occom, 1759

Samuel Buell (1716–1798) was born in Connecticut, graduated from Yale College in 1741, and ordained in 1743. He supported the Great Awakening movements and began his ministerial career as an itinerant evangelist in colonial New England. In 1746, he was installed as the pastor of a Presbyterian congregation in East Hampton, New York. One of his early tutors, Jonathan Edwards, preached the sermon at his installation. Buell was recognized as a gifted preacher and effective administrator in both his congregation and his presbytery. He was influential in the ordination of Samson Occom, the first Native American Presbyterian minister in North America. After he helped to persuade reluctant presbytery members, who questioned Occom's qualifications on account of his cultural and racial differences, Buell preached the sermon at Occom's ordination service. The sermon excerpt presents threefold instruction: (1) to presbyteries in their responsibilities to rigorously examine candidates for ministry; (2) to Occom in his vocation as a missionary to Native American communities; (3) to other aspiring teaching elders in their preparations for ministry. In addition to Buell's religious work, he established the first public library and the first private school in East Hampton, which admitted female and male students.

Reverend and Dear Sirs,

YOU will allow me to speak out our Opinion freely. In them whom we introduce into the Ministry, we look for and expect to find, a Competency of natural Endowments, acquir'd Improvements, Orthodoxy, or Soundness in the Faith, visible Holiness of Life, as 'tis commonly call'd, and that they give us some Account of their Acquaintance with experimental Religion, such as shall appear to us sufficient for the Exercise of a rational Judgment of Christian Charity, that they savingly know the Lord. We pretend not to immediate Revelation from Heaven, and Infallibility of Knowledge in this Case, no; but we seek such Evidence, as the Nature of the Case will admit, and as Faithfulness does require. We are to form a Judgment of the spiritual State of our Fellow-Men, in the Case before us, by what they profess with the Mouth, and the Influence such a Profession has upon the Life. Men without an Intention to deceive, may impose upon themselves, and upon us; yet this is no Argument against an Examination as to these Things; yea, tis an Argument that we should be the more strict upon the Point of Examination. If we consider Faith as appearing in the Profession of it, we find the Apostle accounting the Influences of the holy Spirit, necessary to enable a Man to make such a Profession of the Faith, as was to be admitted by Christians: "No Man can say that Jesus is Lord, but by the Holy Ghost." A Man may so explain himself about his Faith, and give such an Account of his experimental Religion, and his Faith may have such Influence upon his Conduct in Life, as to leave no reasonable Ground to suspect but that he savingly knows the Lord. For a Man to appear free from those Sins, commonly called openly scandalous, and to have a Life so harmless as to afford a Kind of meer negative Charity, is not enough in the present Case: We therefore seek a Profession of Faith, expressive of the Essentials of real Piety, or that the Candidate give a rational, scriptural, and satisfying Account of a sanctifying Work of God's Spirit upon his own Heart; and that his Belief, and Experience of the Power of Divine Truth, influences him to live the Truth, so that his Light shines before Men: These Things are included in the Nature of Evidence, in the present Case, and therefore Ministers have full Authority, and just Right to demand them, and are bound in Faithfulness so to do; and of Consequence the Candidate is obliged to exhibit such Evidence, if 'tis in his Power honestly so to do. . . .

'Tis more than Time to turn my Address, Secondly, to him who is now to be consecrated to the immediate Service of Christ, and the Souls of Men.

My dear Brother,

. . . WE are glad, and rejoice, that this Day the Lord Jesus Christ calls you to bear his Name, plead his Cause, deliver his Message, spread his Fame, and display his Glory among the Gentiles. We charitably hope and believe, it hath pleased GOD to reveal his Son in you; and we trust, not only that you may finally be brought to eternal Glory, but also that you may preach him to the Heathen. We adore the GOD of Nature and Grace, who has confer'd upon you the Gifts and Graces of his Spirit, and a hopeful Measure of Furniture for the Work to which he calls you. We look upon it a Token for Good, that the Love of Christ, constrains you to compassionate your Kindsmen after the Flesh, who dwell in Darkness, and the Shadows of Death, so that you are a Volunteer in a Mission among them. You need eminent Degrees of Wisdom, Patience, Self Denial, Courage and Zeal, in the Prosecution of the Work assigned you. Perils, Hardships, Fatigues, Labours and Sufferings, no Doubt, attend your important Embassy. But, my dear Brother, let none of these Things affright you; remember, always remember, who hath call'd you to this Work; and that your Sufficiency is of, and from Him, who is your GOD, and hath said, I am that I am. His infinite Wisdom will be your Guide,—his almighty Power your Shield,—and Himself your exceeding great Reward. Take hold of that precious Promise by Faith; plead it, live upon it for Protection, Light, Support, Strength, Success and Comfort. . . .

In the Third Place, as I observe at present, a Number of Candidates for the Gospel Ministry, I take the Liberty of making an Address to them.

My young Friends,

I always feel great Tenderness toward hopeful Youth, who have serious Thoughts toward engaging in the Gospel Ministry; especially toward you, who have most of you, for a Time, sojourned under my Roof, principally pursuing Theological Studies. Suffer me therefore to address you by Way of Exhortation, to see to it that you know the Lord JESUS savingly. Presume not to rest in the charitable Opinion of others, as your Evidence, that you savingly know the Lord: You may have the Sanction of the charitable Hope and Judgment of Presbyteries, or Associations, and yet be eternally rejected by the Lord. The eternal Judge, "whose Eyes are as a Flame of Fire," and whose Prerogative alone it is to search the Heart; will one Day say to many, to Multitudes, that have prophesied, that have preached in his Name, I approve you not, depart from me. —If they who have preach'd in his Name, may perish in his Wrath, how greatly it concerns them that preach, to have satisfactory Evidence, by the Actings of Grace, that they truly know the Lord! To some, it may possibly seem a very bold Assertion, but I declare it in plain Terms, that no Man can ever prove to himself, that he was call'd of GOD, to engage in the holy Ministry, who has never been effectually call'd by divine Grace, so as to know the Lord savingly. And unless you thus know the Lord, with what Heart, with what Confidence, can you enter upon the sacred Ministry? If you should run the Risk, the awful Risk, void of such Knowledge, what Comfort can you take therein? Or what of Success can you expect thereupon? Without Controversy, it will one Day be a Soul puzzling, Soul confounding Question to many, "Man, who made you a Minister?" Who gave the Commission to treat for Christ?

. . . If you had all Knowledge, and understood all Mysteries, and could use all the Force of Persuasion, and Charms of Eloquence; were you furnish'd with all the flowing Oratory of Cicero, and all the Thunder of Demosthenes; and could you employ them in every Sermon you preach; yet, without the gracious Presence of the Lord with you, you would in Reality be but as the sounding Brass and tinkling Cymbal, that makes an empty Noise and useless Musick. I pray GOD, that the Day in which we live, may not be a Day in which the true Spirit of preaching becomes lost, for want of due Regard to the Influences of the holy Spirit. While the Study and Use of fine Language and Oratory are so much in Vogue among Preachers, and so pleasing to many Hearers, as at this Day, and tend so much to recommend the Preacher, and to promote his Reputation, the Temptation, to the young Preacher especially, is prodigiously powerful to substitute these Things in the Room of the Divine Presence and Assistance, and to rest in them. But alas, for us that preach! alas for them that hear, when it shall become thus! In the Eye of a judicious spiritual Hearer, can it look like preaching the everlasting Gospel, and having to do with the eternal GOD, and immortal Souls, for Time and endless Worlds, to make the Pulpit a meer Stage, and just to flourish out a pretty pert Harrangue, top'd up with one or two general jejune Inferences? How much soever this may please the vitiated Taste and Humours of some, the two distant Poles are not more remote from each other, than such Manner of Pulpit Work from a genuine Aptitude and Tendency to pierce the Heart, to awaken the Conscience, and to do good to the Souls of Men.

Source: Samuel Buell, "The Excellence and Importance of the Saving Knowledge of the Lord Jesus Christ in the Gospel-Preacher, Plainly and Seriously Represented and Enforced: And Christ Preached to the Gentiles in Obedience to the Call of God, a Sermon, Preached at East-Hampton, August 29, 1759; At the Ordination of Mr. Samson Occum, a Missionary among the Indians" (New York: James Parker and Company, 1761), 25–26, 29–30, 32–35.

SAMUEL OCCOM

"A Sermon at the Execution of Moses Paul, an Indian," 1772

Samson Occom (1723–1792) was born on Mohegan land in Connecticut and converted to Christianity during the Great Awakening revivals in 1740. Occom preached fluently in Mohegan and English and was literate in Greek, Hebrew, Latin, and French. After much deliberation, the Long Island Presbytery ordained the talented Mohegan preacher in 1759. Occom established Native American Christian communities, published a prolific number of sermons and hymns, and proclaimed the gospel across North America and Europe to people of all races. But racial discrimination

against Occom persisted. In 1769, he returned to the Long Island Presbytery to coun-
ter and be exonerated from spurious public drunkenness charges. This sermon was
Occom's best-known work and published in at least nineteen editions in the eighteenth
century, including in an edition by Jonathan Edwards in 1788. Moses Paul, a Wam-
panoag convicted in a highly publicized trial for the murder of a white man in 1771,
asked Occom to preach his execution sermon. Occom agreed and delivered the sermon,
which represents a clear example of eighteenth-century Presbyterian gospel proclama-
tion, on September 2, 1772.

But in further speaking upon our text, by divine assistance, I shall consider these two general propositions:

I. That sin is the cause of all the miseries that befall the children of men, both as to their bodies and souls, for time and eternity. . . .

And O eternity, eternity, eternity! Who can measure it? Who can count the years thereof? Arithmetic must fail, the thoughts of men and angels are drowned in it; how shall we describe eternity? To what shall we compare it? Were it possible to employ a fly to carry off this globe by the small particles thereof, and to carry them to such a distance that it should return once in ten thousand years for another particle, and so continue until it has carried off all this globe, and framed them together in some unknown space, until it has made just such a world as this is; after all, eternity would remain the same unexhausted duration. This must be the unavoidable portion of all impenitent sinners, let them be who they will, great or small, honorable or ignoble, rich or poor, bond or free. Negroes, Indians, English, or of what nations soever, all that die in their sins, must go to hell together, for the wages of sin is death.

The next thing that I was to consider is this:

II. That eternal life and happiness is the free gift of God, through Jesus Christ our Lord.

Under this proposition I shall now endeavour to shew, what this life and happiness is.

The life that is mentioned in our text, begins with a spiritual life: it is the life of the soul, a restoration of soul from sin to holiness, from darkness to light, a translation from the kingdom and dominion of Satan, to the kingdom of God's grace. In other words, it is being restored to the image of God and delivered from the image of Satan. And this life consists in union of the soul to God, and communion with God; a real participation of the divine nature, or in the apostle's words, it is Christ formed within us. . . . And the happiness of this life consists in communion with God, or in the spiritual enjoyment of God. As much as a soul enjoys of God in this life, just so much of life and happiness he enjoys or possesses; yea, just so much of heaven he enjoys. A true [C]hristian, desires no other heaven but the enjoyment of God; a full and perfect enjoyment of God, is a full and perfect heaven and happiness to a gracious soul. . . .

I have now gone through what I proposed from my text. And I shall now make some application of the whole.

First to the criminal in particular; and then to the auditory in general.

My poor unhappy brother MOSES;

As it was your own desire that I should preach to you this last discourse, so I shall speak plainly to you. —You are the bone of my bone, and flesh of my flesh. You are an Indian, a despised creature, but you have despised yourself; yea you have despised God more; you have trodden under foot his authority; you have despised his commands and precepts; and now as God says, "be sure your sins will find you out;" so now, poor Moses, your sins have found you out, and they have overtaken you this day; the day of your death is now come; the king of terrors is at hand; you have but a very few moments to breathe in this world. . . .

Though you have been a great sinner, a heaven daring sinner; yet hark! O hear the joyful sound from heaven, even from the King of kings, and Lord of lords; that the gift of God is eternal life, through Jesus Christ our Lord. It is a free gift, and bestowed on the greatest sinners, and upon their true repentance towards God and faith in the Lord Jesus Christ, they shall be welcome to the life, which we have spoken of; it is granted upon free terms. He that hath no money may come; he that hath no righteousness, no goodness, may come; the call is to poor undone sinners; the call is not to the righteous, but sinners, inviting them to repentance. . . . Thus you see, poor Moses, that there is none in heaven, or on the earth, that can help you, but Christ; he alone has power to save, and to give life. —God the eternal Father appointed him, chose him, authorized, and fully commissioned him to save sinners. He came down from heaven, into this lower world, and became as one of us, and stood in our room. He was the second Adam. And as God demanded perfect obedience of the first Adam; the second fulfilled it; and as the first sinned, and incurred the wrath and anger of God, the second endured it; he suffered in our room. As he became sin for us, he was a man of sorrows, and acquainted with grief; all our stripes were laid upon him . . . there his heart's blood was shed for our cleansing: there he fully satisfied the divine justice of God, for penitent, believing sinners, though they have been the chief of sinners. . . .

SIRS, We may plainly see, from what we have heard, and from the miserable object before us, into what a doleful condition sin has brought mankind, even into a state of death and misery. We are by nature as certainly under the sentence of death from God, as this miserable man is, by the just determination of man; and we are all dying creatures, this is the dreadful fruit of sin. O! let us then fly from all appearance of sin; let us fight against it with all our might; let us repent and turn to God, and believe on the Lord Jesus Christ, that we may live forever; let us all prepare for death, for we know not how soon, nor how suddenly we may be called out of the world.

Source: Published by Jonathan Edwards, and titled "A Sermon at the Execution of Moses Paul, an Indian; Who Had Been Guilty of Murder, Preached at New Haven in America, by Samson Occom, a Native Indian, and Missionary to the Indians, Who was in England in 1776 and 1777, Collecting for the Indian Charity Schools, to Which is Added a Short Account of the Late Spread of the Gospel, Among the Indians, also Observations on the Language of the Muhhekaneew Indians; Communicated to the Connecticut Society of Arts and Sciences, by Jonathan Edwards, D.D." (New Haven, 1778), 7, 13–14, 16–20.

SAMUEL MILLER

An Essay on the Warrant, Nature, and Duties of the Office of the Ruling Elder, in the Presbyterian Church, 1831

Samuel Miller (1769–1850) was born in Delaware and graduated from the University of Pennsylvania in 1789. Miller's father was the pastor of a Presbyterian congregation in Dover, Delaware. Miller declined the church's invitation to follow in his father's footsteps and instead was ordained and installed at a congregation in New York City in 1793. After approximately twenty years in pastoral ministry, Miller joined the faculty of Princeton Theological Seminary in 1813 and taught there as professor of ecclesiastical history and church government until his death. He authored approximately two hundred documents, ranging from sermons and brief pamphlets to lengthier books and treatises. One of his contributions to Presbyterian polity was his strong advocacy for ruling elders as possessing commensurate authority to teaching elders in church governance. In his treatment of ruling elders, he provided biblical warrants from the Old and New Testaments for the function and validity of the office. Miller distinguished between the roles of ruling elders and teaching elders, but he argued that God commissioned ruling elders to do equally vital and important work alongside teaching elders in Christian ministry.

RULING ELDERS ABSOLUTELY NECESSARY IN THE CHURCH.

BY this is meant, that the laws which Christ has appointed for the government and edification of his people, cannot possibly be executed without such a class of officers in fact, whatever name they may bear. But that which is the necessary result of a divine institution, is of equal authority with the institution itself. All powers of instruments really indispensable to the faithful and plenary execution of laws which an infinitely wise Governor has enacted, must be considered as implied in those laws, even should they not be formally specified.

Now, all serious impartial readers of the Bible believe, that, besides the preaching of the gospel, and the administration of the sacraments, there is very much to be done for promoting the order, purity, and edification of the church, by the maintenance of a scriptural discipline. They believe that the best interest of every ecclesiastical community requires, that there be a constant and faithful inspection of all the members and families of the church; that the negligent be admonished; that wanderers be reclaimed[;] that scandals be removed; that irregularities be corrected; that differences be reconciled; and every proper measure adopted to bind the whole body together by the ties of Christian purity and charity. They consider it as vitally important that there be added to the labours of the pulpit, those of teaching "from house to house," visiting the sick, conversing with serious inquirers, catechising children, learning as far as possible the character and state of every member, even the poorest and most obscure of the flock, and endeavouring, by all scriptural means, to promote the knowledge, holiness, comfort, and spiritual welfare of every individual. They believe, in fine, that none ought to be admitted to the communion of the church, without a careful examination in reference to their knowledge, orthodoxy, good moral character, and hopeful piety; that none ought to be permitted to remain in the bosom of the church, without maintaining, in some tolerable degree, a character proper for professing Christians; that none ought to be suspended from the enjoyment of church privileges but after a fair trial; and that none should be finally excommunicated from the covenanted family of Christ, without the most patient inquiry, and every suitable effort to bring them to repentance and reformation. . . .

The truth is, the exercise of a faithful watch and care over the purity of each other in doctrine, worship, and life, is one of the principal purposes for which the Christian church was established, and on account of which it is highly prized by every enlightened believer. And, I have no doubt, it may be safely affirmed, that a large part of all that is holy in the church at the present day, either in faith or practice, may be ascribed, under God, as much to sound ecclesiastical discipline as to the faithful preaching of the gospel. . . .

Now the question is, by whom shall all these multiplied, weighty, and indispensable services be performed? Besides the arduous work of public instruction and exhortation, who shall attend to all the numberless and ever-recurring details of inspection, warning, and visitation, which are so needful in every Christian community? Will any say it is the duty of the pastor of each church to perform them all? The very suggestion is absurd. It is physically impossible for him to do it. He cannot be every where, and know every thing. He cannot perform what is expected from him, and at the same time so watch over his whole flock as to fulfil every duty which the interest of the church demands. He must "give himself to reading;" he must prepare for the services of the pulpit; he must discharge his various public labours; he must employ much time in private, in instructing and counselling those who apply to him for instruction and advice; and he must act his part in the concerns of the whole church with which he is connected. Now, is it practicable for any man, however diligent and active, to do all this, and at the same time to perform the whole work of inspection and government over a congregation of the ordinary size? We might as well expect and demand any impossibility; and impossibilities the great and merciful Head of the church requires of no man. . . .

To obviate these difficulties, some have said, let deacons, whom all agree to be scriptural officers, be employed to assist the pastor in conducting the government and discipline of the church. . . . All that it is deemed necessary or proper to say in this place is, that an entirely different sphere of duty is assigned to deacons in the New Testament. No hint is given of their being employed in the government of the church. For this proposal, therefore, there is not the shadow of a divine warrant. Besides, if we assign to deacons the real office, in other words the appropriate functions of ruling elders, what is this but granting the thing, and only disputing about the title? If it be granted that there ought to be a plurality of officers in every church, whose appropriate duty it is to assist the pastor in inspecting and ruling the flock of Christ, it is the essence of what is contended for. Their proper title is not worth a contest, except so far as it may be proper to imitate the language of Scripture...

THE NATURE AND DUTIES OF THE OFFICE.

HAVING considered so much at large, the warrant for the office of ruling elder, chiefly because there is no part of the subject more contested; we now proceed to other points connected with the general inquiry. And the first of these which presents itself, is the Nature and Duties of the office in question.

The essential character of the officer of whom we speak is that of an ecclesiastical ruler. He that ruleth let him do it with diligence, is the summary of his appropriate functions as laid down in Scripture. The teaching elder is indeed also a ruler. In addition to this, however, he is called to preach the gospel and administer sacraments. But the particular department assigned to the ruling elder is to co-operate with the pastor in spiritual inspection and government. The Scriptures, as we have seen, speak not only of "pastors and teachers," but also of "governments;"—of "elders that rule well, but do not labour in the word and doctrine."

There is an obvious analogy between the office of ruler in the church, and in the civil community. A Justice of the Peace in the latter has a wide and important range of duties. Besides the function which he discharges when called to take his part on the bench of the judicial court in which he presides, he may be, and often is, employed every day, though less publicly, in correcting abuses, compelling the fraudulent to do justice, restraining, arresting, and punishing criminals, and, in general, carrying into execution the laws formed to promote public tranquility and order, which he has sworn to administer faithfully.

Strikingly analogous to this are the duties of the ecclesiastical ruler. He has no power, indeed, to employ the secular arm in restraining or punishing offenders against the laws of Christ. The kingdom under which he acts, and the authority which he administers, are not of this world. He has, of course, no right to fine, imprison, or externally to molest the most profligate offenders against the church's purity or peace, unless they be guilty of what is technically called, "breaking the peace," that is, violating the civil rights of others, and thus rendering themselves liable to the penalty of the civil law. And even when this occurs, the ecclesiastical ruler, as such, has no right to proceed against the offender. He has no other than moral power. He must apply to the civil magistrate for redress, who can only punish for breaking the civil law. Still there is an obvious analogy between his office and that of the civil magistrate. Both are alike an ordinance of God—both are necessary to social order and comfort—and both are regulated by principles which commend themselves to the good sense and the conscience of those who wish well to social happiness.

The ruling elder, no less than the teaching elder, or pastor, is to be considered as acting under the authority of Christ, in all that he rightfully does. If the office of which we speak was appointed in the apostolic church by infinite wisdom; if it be an ordinance of Jesus Christ, just as much as that of the minister of the gospel, then the former, equally with the latter, is Christ's officer. He has a right to speak and act in his name; and though elected by the members of the church, and representing them in the exercise of ecclesiastical rule, yet he is not to be considered as deriving his authority to rule from them, any more than he who "labours in the word and doctrine" derives his authority to preach and administer other ordinances from the people, who make choice of him as their teacher and guide. There is reason to believe that some, even in the Presbyterian church, take a different view of this subject. They regard the teaching elder as an officer of Christ, and listen to his official instructions as to those of a man appointed by Him, and coming in his name. But with respect to the ruling elder, they are wont to regard him as one who holds an office instituted by human prudence alone, and, therefore, as standing on very different ground in the discharge of his official duties from that which is occupied by the "ambassador of Christ." This is undoubtedly an erroneous view of the subject, and a view which, so far as it prevails, is adapted to exert the most mischievous influence. The truth is, if the office of which we speak be of apostolic authority, we are just as much bound to sustain, honour, and obey the individual who fills it and discharges its duties according to the Scriptures, as we are to submit to any other officer or institution of our Divine Redeemer.

Source: Samuel Miller, *The Warrant, Nature, and Duties of the Office of the Ruling Elder, in the Presbyterian Church: A New Edition with an Introductory Essay, by the Rev. William Lindsay, Glasgow* (Edinburgh: Robert Ogle, 1842), 142–45, 156, 160–62. Miller's work was initially published as *An Essay on the Warrant, Nature, and Duties of the Office of the Ruling Elder, in the Presbyterian Church* (New York: Jonathan Leavitt, 1831).

JAMES HENLEY THORNWELL

A Tract on the Doctrines of Election and Reprobation, 1840

James Henley Thornwell (1812–1862) was born in South Carolina and graduated from South Carolina College (now University of South Carolina) in 1831. After his ordination in 1835, Thornwell labored in both the church and the academy until his death. He served as a pastor of congregations in South Carolina and taught at South Carolina College and Columbia Theological Seminary. At thirty-four years of age, he was elected Moderator of the Presbyterian Church in the United States of America (Old School) General Assembly in 1847. He was also the editor of numerous journals, such as the Southern Presbyterian Review. In 1861, Thornwell's leadership was instrumental in the formation of the Presbyterian Church in the Confederate States of America. The combination of Thornwell's intellectual gifts and pastoral sensibilities, which made him of the most influential Presbyterians in the antebellum period of the United States, is on display in this tract on the Reformed doctrines of election and reprobation. After presenting a robust explication of predestination and a sharp rebuttal of Arminian theology as contrary to scriptural teachings, Thornwell concludes his argument by emphasizing how election is a doctrine that provides spiritual sustenance to the human soul and prompts the human heart to adore God.

Widely as men may differ in their views of predestination, it is generally conceded by all who profess any reverence for the word of God, that there is an election of some sort, to eternal life, inculcated in the scriptures. But there is much violent and bitter opposition to that account of it, which places a crown of absolute sovereignty on the head of Jehovah, and prostrates man in entire dependence upon His will. In deducing the scriptural argument, I shall endeavor to arrange the texts under the several heads, or rather upon the separate points made out in the explanation or statement of the doctrine from the Confession of Faith.

1. First, then, election is personal; that is, it is a choice of individuals from the corrupt mass of our fallen race, to everlasting life. I am far from intending to insinuate that, in every instance in which words expressive of election, are used in the Scriptures, a personal election to eternal life must of course be understood. On the contrary, it is freely admitted that the Scriptures speak of the choice of nations to peculiar privileges, of the choice of individuals to particular offices, and of the choice of Christ to the mediatorial work. All this is fully conceded, but yet there are passages which cannot, without unwarrantable violence, be interpreted in any other way, than as teaching the doctrine of personal election to eternal life. "According as He hath chosen us in Him before the foundation of the world, that we should be holy and without blame before Him in love." Eph. i. 4. Here election is expressly said to be personal—"hath chosen us," that is, Paul himself, and the Christians at Ephesus. The epistle is directed to "the saints which are at Ephesus, and the faithful in Christ Jesus." i. 1. Here then is not an election of nations or communities to external privileges, but an election of individuals to everlasting life. In verses 5, 6, 7, 11, we have a more particular view of the blessing which they received, in consequence of their election, and which cannot, by any ingenuity of criticism, be plausibly distorted into national advantages. "Having predestinated us unto the adoption of children by Jesus Christ, to Himself," &c.: and again, "In whom we have redemption through His blood, the forgiveness of sins, according to the riches of His grace." Those, therefore, to whom Paul was writing, were "saints, faithful in Christ Jesus, adopted to be sons, redeemed and forgiven," and all these privileges he traced to the election of which he was speaking. Are there any so blind as not to see that these are saving blessings, and that those who were addressed as possessing them, were individuals, and not communities or nations? But it has been said that Paul could not know that the whole church at Ephesus were elect. To this it may be readily replied, that Paul does not say so. He sufficiently designates the individuals of whom he was speaking, by the characteristics noticed above. McKnight, always anxious to fritter away the peculiar features of the gospel, tells us in his note on the fourth verse, that the election here spoken of, is "that election, which, before the foundation of the world, God made, of holy persons of all nations, to be His children and people, and to enjoy the blessing promised to such." Upon this singular note, it is enough for my present purpose to remark—1. That it sufficiently admits the fact, that the election here spoken of is personal. But, 2: that it was not, however, an election of "holy persons," but an election to be holy—"that we might be holy and without blame before him in love." 3. That these Ephesians, previously

to their accepting of the gospel, were "dead in trespasses and sins, walked according to the prince of the power of the air, the spirit that now worketh in the children of disobedience," &c.: ii. 1-3. They could not possibly, therefore, have been elected as "holy persons," seeing that they were utterly destitute of all pretensions to holiness. . . .

The scriptural meaning of salvation is, deliverance from the curse, power, and love of sin. The word in general implies deliverance from evil; but it is always in the Bible positive as well as negative, and imports the bestowment of a corresponding good. The blind, when healed by our Saviour, are said to be saved; that is, they are delivered from the evil of blindness, and receive the corresponding blessing of sight. So sinners are said to be saved by Christ; because, through "the faith of Him" they are delivered from the evils of their natural state, and receive the blessings of a gracious state. —Could it be possible that a man should obtain the forgiveness of sin, and afterwards fail of the blessedness of heaven, there is no assignable sense in which it could be said that he was saved. If there be any difference in the spiritual import of the words, salvation and life, it would seem to be this: that the former has a more pointed reference to the evils from which we are delivered by grace, and the latter to the benefits of which we become partakers. It is true that these words are not always used in their fullest latitude, but are sometimes confined to one, and sometimes to another feature of the general meaning. This however, is a strong proof of the inseparable connection between grace and glory. In accordance with these remarks, it may be observed: —1st. That salvation implies pardon and gratuitous acceptance. Luke i. 77. "To give knowledge of salvation unto his people by the remission of their sins." The original is, "in the remission of their sins:" that is, when our sins are pardoned, we become partakers of salvation. Luke xix. 9: "This day is salvation come to this house." Whatever else the word may mean here, pardon of sin must be one of the blessings which Jesus conferred on Zaccheus.

The curse of the law is what the Scriptures mean by the "wrath to come," and no one can doubt that deliverance from this forms an important element of salvation. But we are delivered from the curse and covenant claims of the law, in our gratuitous justification and pardon.

2. Salvation implies regeneration and progressive sanctification, or the production and development of the new nature: Titus iii. 5: "Not by works of righteousness which we have done, but according to His mercy He saved us, by the washing of regeneration and the renewing of the Holy Ghost." Here, the washing or cleansing of regeneration, which is explained to be the renewing of the Holy Ghost, is in so many words, stated to be an element of salvation. Jesus received his name by the express and solemn appointment of God, because he should "save his people from their sins." The spiritual life which

the Holy Spirit communicates in regeneration, and fosters and strengthens in sanctification, is of the same nature, though different in degree and the circumstances of its exercise, with the life of glory at God's right hand. The one is represented as an earnest of the other; and an earnest must be of the same kind with that of which it is an earnest. If then eternal blessedness is a part of our salvation, the new nature here necessarily must be. All, therefore, who are elected to salvation, are elected to sanctification, in the full scriptural extent of that word. Hence the Apostle says that we are chosen, "that we might be holy and without blame before him in love." Eph. i. 4. Hence the Thessalonians are said to be "chosen to salvation through sanctification of the Spirit and belief of the truth:" and hence it is said—"We are his workmanship, created in Christ Jesus unto good works, which God hath before ordained that we should walk therein." Eph. ii. 10...

Having thus discussed the separate points in the doctrine of election, it may be well to make a few remarks on the inseparable doctrine of reprobation. The very fact that all men were not elected, shows that some were passed by. This passing them by, or refusing to elect them, and leaving them under a righteous sentence of condemnation, constitutes reprobation. If election is personal, eternal and absolute, reprobation must possess these qualities also. There is this difference between them, however: election finds the objects of mercy unfit for eternal life, and puts forth a positive agency in preparing them for glory. —Reprobation finds the objects of wrath, already fitted for destruction, and only withholds that influence which alone can transform them. It is not intended to be denied here that cases of judicial blindness occur, in which the sinner's heart is hardened. The example of Pharaoh is a case in point. But judicial blindness is a punishment inflicted, in which God acts as a righteous judge, dealing with men for their obstinacy. Whereas reprobation is strictly an act of sovereignty, in which God refuses to save, and leaves the sinner to the free course of law. Our standards afford no sort of shelter to the Hopkinsian error, that the decree of reprobation consists in God's determining to fit a certain number of mankind for eternal damnation; and that the Divine agency is as positively employed in men's bad volitions and actions, as in their good. These doctrines we know have been frequently charged upon us with no little violence and acrimony, but we have always adhered to the position of the Bible, that God is not the author of evil; and we believe that there is no inconsistency in supposing that God may determine an action as a natural event, and yet be unstained with its sin and pollution. That the Scriptures do teach the doctrine of reprobation, as depending on the sovereignty and good pleasure of God, is manifest from the following passages: Mat. xi. 25. "At that time Jesus answered and said, I thank thee, O Father, Lord of Heaven and Earth, because thou hast hid these things from the wise and prudent, and hast revealed them unto babes." Here our blessed Saviour addresses the Father by a word highly expressive of sovereignty, and refers the illumination of some and the blindness of others, to his Father's will alone. "Even so, Father, for so it seemed good in thy sight." Rom. ix. 18: "Therefore hath He mercy on whom He will have mercy, and whom He will He hardeneth." If it be said that this refers to the judicial blindness with which Pharaoh was struck, let it be remembered that no punishment of any sort would or could be inflicted on the wicked, if they were not left under the sentence of condemnation, origi-nally pronounced upon the race. The fact of their reprobation, leaves them in that state to which punishment was justly due; and the argument of Paul is, that some are left in that state and others not, by the sovereign pleasure of God. Verse 21: "Hath not the potter power over the clay of the same lump, to make one vessel unto honor and another to dishonor?" Jude 4: "For there are certain men crept in unawares, who were before of old ordained to this condemnation; ungodly men turning the grace of our God into lascivious-ness, and denying the only Lord God and our Lord Jesus Christ." In fact, every passage of Scripture which teaches that any will be finally lost, teaches at the same time, by necessary implication, if the doctrine of election be true, that they were eternally reprobated, or left out of the number of the elect. The two doctrines stand or fall together.

Independently of the direct and immediate testimony which the Scriptures bear in support of eternal and unconditional election and reprobation, there is an indirect teaching of them, by inculcating doctrines in which they are necessarily involved—such as the fore-knowledge, providence, and indepen-dence of God, and the total depravity of man. There is no way in which these truths can be reconciled with the Arminian or Semi-Pelagian scheme. Fore-knowledge of a future event means, if it mean any thing, that the event is regarded as absolutely certain in the Divine mind, and that it cannot possi-bly happen otherwise than as God foresees it will happen. How the absolute certainty of events is consistent with contingency, which necessarily implies uncertainty, I leave it to the advocates of this strange hypothesis to determine. The scripture account of foreknowledge is simple and consistent. God fore-knows all things because He decrees them, and hence the terms are frequently interchanged. Peter says that Christ was delivered to death "by the determi-nate counsel and foreknowledge of God:" that is, by the purpose and appoint-ment of God. The doctrine of Providence by which God is represented as acting upon a plan, of which He knew the end from the beginning, cannot be conceived at all, if we deny the existence of a fixed and definite purpose in the Divine mind. In fact, to deny an eternal purpose, is a virtual dethronement of God in His own dominions; and the voice of reason remonstrates as loudly as the voice of revelation, against the ruinous results to which such a denial must lead. The will of God becomes fearfully dependent upon the will of man, and the counsel of God must be formed and modelled upon the wisdom of the creature. The truth is, Arminianism declares an open war upon the essential attributes of God, and if carried out into all its necessary consequences, it would lead at once to blank and cheerless Atheism.

The account which the Bible gives us of human corruption and depravity, is utterly inconsistent with the scheme which makes election, in any measure, depend upon the faith or perseverance of man. Sinners, in their natural state, are said to be "dead in trespasses and sins." "Every imagination of man's heart is only evil, and that continually." The necessary consequence of depravity is an utter inability to think a good thought, or to perform a good action. The understanding is darkened, the affections alienated, the will bent on evil—in short, the man is dead, spiritually dead, and therefore cannot believe or do any holy action, until quickened and renewed by the supernatural grace of God. Hence our Saviour says: "No man can come to me, except the Father which hath sent me draw him." If this then be the true state of the case, all who believe are drawn by the Father, being utterly unable to do it of themselves. Why does God draw one and not another? For it is manifest that all are not believers. Every Christian will promptly ascribe his calling and conversion to the mere grace of God, and this is election. The man who rejects election, is bound to reject the scriptural account of human depravity, if he would maintain consistency of opinion. He may resort to the superficial theory of common grace, but that will not relieve him of his difficulty. The Scriptures attribute every good disposition to God, and so the disposition not to resist common grace, must after all, be referred to special grace. No Christian would ever have dreamed of Arminianism, if he had been guided only by his own experience; hence, when the love of system is laid aside, we find all pious Arminians sober and honest hearted Calvinists, as their earnest prayers for grace and assistance unequivocally declare. . . .

I know that there are caricatures of Calvinism which represent God as having made man for the specific purpose of damnation, and as putting forth a positive agency in fitting him for hell. The reprobate are represented as poor, helpless, dependent creatures in the hands of a blood-thirsty tyrant, who in the first instance, makes them sinners contrary to their own will, absolutely forcing them into transgression, and then, in spite of all their efforts, driving them to hell, that he might delight himself with their torments; and in such caricatures the reprobate are often represented as most amiable and lovely creatures, calculated by their excellencies to soften a heart of stone; but yet the cruel God of the Calvinists frowns upon them and sends them down to hell. These gross and slanderous caricatures might pass unnoticed by, if they were not palmed off upon the ignorant and unthinking as the genuine doctrines of Presbyterianism. And the worst part of the whole is, that when Presbyterians disavow them, instead of being believed or regarded as fair judges of their own principles, they are only charged with disgraceful cowardice, or taunted with being ashamed of their doctrines. If it is to such caricatures that the charge of injustice is so confidently brought up, I have no motive to attempt an answer. It is enough for me that the charge cannot be sustained against the genuine doctrines of the Church. . . .

I have now completed my original design. It is unnecessary to say, that consequences of momentous importance, involving the fundamental principles of the Gospel, hang upon the reception or rejection of this doctrine. To the humble Christian, who has been taught it by the Spirit of God; who has been emptied of self in every form and shape, and brought in deep prostration of soul to bow at the foot-stool of sovereign mercy, it is inexpressibly precious; and he knows something of the spirit in which that song, so often in his mouth, was dictated: "Not unto us, Oh Lord, not unto us, but unto thy name, be all the glory." In this precious doctrine he finds constant food for humility, gratitude, and love; and when tempted to flag in his Christian course, nothing affords a stronger stimulant to duty, than a deep sense of God's eternal, unmerited grace—"Lo, I have loved thee with an everlasting love." This doctrine is emphatically children's bread. They are often supported by the nourishment it contains, and strengthened for the race set before them, when they can give no connected, metaphysical account of their experiences or feelings. It is eminently devotional in its tendencies; and it is to be regretted that we are so often compelled to chastise the feelings which it naturally excites, in order to enter the lists of cold-blood argument, with those who would rob us of this jewel which our Master has given us. We are often compelled to reason, when the heart would prompt us to adore. It is a scriptural duty to contend, and contend earnestly, for the faith once delivered to the saints.

Source: James Henley Thornwell, *A Tract on the Doctrines of Election and Reprobation* (Columbia, SC: Samuel Weir, 1840), 7–8, 11–12, 24–26, 33–34, 56.

5

The Problem of Slavery, the Division of the Church, and the Civil War

THEODORE S. WRIGHT

A Speech to the New York State Anti-Slavery Society, 1837

Theodore S. Wright (1797–1847) was born a free black and educated at the African Free School in New York City under the direction of Samuel Eli Cornish, one of the first African American Presbyterian ministers. Wright was the first African American student at Princeton Theological Seminary and graduated in 1828. He succeeded Cornish as pastor of First Colored Presbyterian Church in New York (also known as Shiloh Presbyterian Church) and became a leader in the abolitionist movement. He helped to found the American Anti-Slavery Society in 1833 and coauthored with Cornish a book in 1840 that opposed colonization movements like the American Colonization Society (founded by white Presbyterian minister Robert Finley) that sought to relocate free black persons to Africa. Wright also remained involved at Princeton Seminary as an alumnus. In 1836, a white southern student from the college protested Wright's presence on the Princeton campus and physically assaulted him. In his speech before the New York State Anti-Slavery Society, Wright addresses the sins of slavery and racial prejudice in the United States and offers reforms based on "the principles of the Gospel."

Resolved, that the prejudice peculiar to our country, which subjects our colored brethren to a degrading distinction in our worship, assemblies, and schools, which withholds from them that kind and courteous treatment to which as well as other citizens, they have a right, at public houses, on board steamboats, in stages, and in places of public concourse, is the spirit of slavery, is nefarious and wicked and should be practically reprobated and discountenanced. . . .

The prejudice which exists against the colored man, the free man, is like the atmosphere, every where felt by him. It is true that in these United States, and in this State, there are men, like myself, colored with the skin like my own, who are not subjected to the lash, who are not liable to have their wives and their infants torn from them; from whose hand the Bible is not taken. It is true that we may walk abroad; we may enjoy our domestic comforts, our families; retire to the closet; visit the sanctuary, and may be permitted to urge on our children and our neighbors in well doing. But sir, still we are slaves—every where we feel the chain galling us. It is by that prejudice which the resolution condemns; the spirit of slavery; the law which has been enacted here, by a corrupt public sentiment, through the influence of slavery which treats moral agents, different from the rule of God, which treats them irrespective of their morals or intellectual cultivation. This spirit is withering all our hopes, and oft times causes the colored parent as he looks upon his child, to wish he had never been born. Often is the heart of the colored mother, as she presses her child to her bosom, filled with sorrow to think that, by reason of this prejudice, it is cut off from all hopes of usefulness in this land. Sir, this prejudice is wicked.

If the nation and church understood this matter, I would not speak a word about that killing influence, that destroys the colored man's reputation. This influence cuts us off from every thing; it follows us up from childhood to manhood; it excludes us from all stations of profit, usefulness and honor; takes away from us all motive for pressing forward in enterprises, useful and important to the world and to ourselves.

EFFECTS OF THIS PREJUDICE

In the first place, it cuts us off from the advantages of the mechanic arts almost entirely. A colored man can hardly learn a trade, and if he does it is difficult for him to find any one who will employ him to work at that trade, in any part of the State. In most of our large cities, there are associations of mechanics, who legislate out of their society colored men. And in many cases where our young men have learned trades, they have had to come to low employments, for want of encouragement in those trades.

It must be a matter of rejoicing to know that in this vicinity colored fathers and mothers have the privileges of education. It must be a matter of rejoicing, that in this vicinity colored parents can have their children trained up in schools. —At present, we find the colleges barred against them.

I will say nothing about the inconvenience which I have experienced myself, and which every man of color experiences, though made in the image of God. I will say nothing about the inconvenience of travelling; how we are frowned upon and despised . . . we find embarrassments every where.

But sir, this prejudice goes farther. It debars men from heaven. While sir, slavery cuts off the colored portion of the community from religious privileges, men are made infidels. What, they demand, is your Christianity? How do you regard your brethren? How do you treat them at the Lord's table? Where is your consistency in talking about the heathen; traversing the ocean to circulate the Bible every where, while you frown upon them at the door? These things meet us and weigh down our spirits.

And, sir, the constitution of society, moulded by this prejudice, destroys souls. I have known extensively, that in revivals which have been blessed and enjoyed, in this part of the country, the colored population were overlooked. I recollect an instance. The Lord God was pouring out His Spirit. He was entering every house, and sinners were converted. I asked, Where is the colored man? where is my brother? where is my sister? who is feeling for him or her? who is weeping for them? who is endeavoring to pull them out of the fire? No reply was made. —I was asked to go round with one of the elders, and visit them. We went and they humbled themselves. The Church commenced efficient efforts, and God blessed them as soon as they began to act for these people as though they had souls.

SLAVERY IN THE CHURCH

And sir, the manner in which our churches are regulated destroys souls. Whilst the church is thrown open to every body, and one says, come, come in and share the blessings of the sanctuary, this is the gate of heaven—he says to the colored man, be careful where you take your stand. I KNOW an efficient church in this State, where a respectable colored man went to the house of God, and was going to take a seat in the gallery, and one of the officers contended with him, and says—"you cannot go there sir."

In one place the people had come together to the house of the Lord. The sermon was preached—the emblems were about to be administered—and all at once the person who managed the church, thought the value of the pews would be diminished, if the colored people sat in them[.] They objected to their sitting there, and the colored people left and went into the gallery, and that too when they were thinking of handling the memorials of the broken body and shed blood of the Saviour! And, sir, this prejudice follows the colored man everywhere, and depresses his spirits.

A WORD OF ENCOURAGEMENT

Thanks be to God, there is a buoyant principle which elevates the poor downtrodden colored man above all this:—It is that there is society which regards man according to his worth; It is the fact, that when he looks up to Heaven, he knows that God treats him like a moral agent, irrespective of caste, or the circumstances in which he may be placed . . . he is cheered by the hope that he will be disenthralled, and soon, like a bird set forth from its cage, wing his flight to Jesus, where he can be happy, and look down with pity on the man who despises the poor slave for being what God made him, and who despises him, because he is identified with the poor slave. Blessed be God for the principles of the Gospel. Were it not for these, and for the fact that a better day is dawning, I would not wish to live. —Blessed be God for the anti-slavery movement. Blessed be God that there is a war waging with slavery, that the granite rock is about to be rolled from its base. But as long as the colored man is to be looked upon as an inferior caste, so long will they disregard his cries, his groans, his shrieks.

I rejoice, sir, in this Society; and I deem the day when I joined this Society, as one of the proudest days of my life. And I know I can die better, in more peace to-day, to know there are men who will plead the cause of my children.

Let me, through you, sir, request this delegation to take hold of this subject. This will silence the slave-holder, when he says, where is your love for the slave? Where is your love for the colored man who is crushed at your feet? Talking to us about emancipating our slaves when you are enslaving them by your feelings, and doing more violence to them by your prejudice, than we are to our slaves by our treatment? They call on us to envince our love for the slave, by treating man as man, the colored man as a man, according to his worth.

Source: Theodore S. Wright, *Colored American,* July 8, 1837, found in the University of Detroit Mercy Black Abolitionist Archive.

ALBERT BARNES

An Inquiry into the Scriptural Views of Slavery, 1846

Albert Barnes (1798–1870) was born in New York, graduated from Hamilton College in 1820 and Princeton Theological Seminary in 1824, and ordained in 1825. He began his promising ministerial career as pastor of a congregation in Morristown, New Jersey. In addition to honing his strong homiletical skills, Barnes was a social reformer successfully leading prohibition efforts in Morristown. But as a proponent of New School Presbyterianism, Barnes moved away from the doctrines of original sin and substitutionary atonement in his preaching and writing. He underwent church disciplinary processes twice under the charges of breaking his ordination vows by promulgating erroneous doctrines "contrary to the Standards of the Presbyterian Church." Barnes appealed to the Adopting Act of 1729 to argue that his scruples with the Westminster Confession of Faith did not contradict the Confession's essential and necessary articles. Barnes was ultimately vindicated in the church judicatories and served as pastor of First Presbyterian Church in Philadelphia from 1830 to 1867. Barnes continued to integrate social justice in his pastoral ministry. His biblical interpretations of slavery contributed to the abolition movement through the precise and rigorous contrasts he presented between scriptural notions of slavery and the unjust ways in which the practice in the United States regarded enslaved African Americans as property instead of human beings.

The precepts addressed to masters, as such, in the New Testament, are two, and two only: Eph. vi. 9, "And ye, masters, do the same things unto them, forbearing threatening, knowing that your master also is in heaven; neither is there respect of persons with him;" and Col. iv. 1, "Masters, render unto your servants that which is just and equal, knowing that ye also have a master in heaven." There are no other passages in the New Testament which can be considered as directly addressed to the owners of slaves; and if a slaveholder can take shelter under any such address to himself, as sanctioning his claim, it must be found in these two verses. Let us inquire, then, whether an owner of slaves could find a sanction for continuing this relation in these passages of the New Testament. To determine this, it is necessary to look at them in connection with certain other declarations of the New Testament, which the owners of slaves could not but regard as demanding their attention.

(a) What do these passages really prove? What sanction do they give to slavery? What right do they give to the master to continue the relation? They simply inculcate on masters the duty of treating their slaves as they would wish to be treated, and to remember that they have a master in heaven. Do they say that the master has a right to hold them in bondage; to regard them as property; to sell them to whom he pleases; to avail himself of their unrequited labour; to make all their religious privileges and rights dependent only on his will? They say no such thing; they imply no such thing; fairly interpreted, they would go against any such claim.

And yet it is on such passages as these that the master must ground his right to continue to hold his fellow-men in bondage, if he founds that right on the precepts addressed to him in the New Testament; for there are no other. It is implied in the argument which is derived from these passages, that they sanction the whole system of domestic slavery, and grant a universal permission to establish and maintain it at all times, and in all lands, and are proof that it was the intention of the Author of the Christian religion that the system should be perpetuated. They are supposed to sanction the right of one man, who has the power, to compel a human being, a fellow-creature, a man redeemed by the blood of Christ, and an heir of salvation, to labour for him, without his own consent, and to be subject wholly to his will. They are supposed to sanction all the claim which is set up by the master over such a man—the right to withhold from him the Bible; to forbid his marrying the object of his affections; to regulate his food and clothing and mode of living; to control his children; and to give him a right, when he pleases, to sunder his connection with his wife and children for ever, and to sell him, or her, or them, to any one whom he pleases. They are supposed to sanction the right to all that such a man can earn, and all by which he can in any way contribute to the wealth, the ease, or the luxurious indulgence of the master. Every thing that enters essentially into the system of slavery; all the claims which a master asserts over his slaves; all the laws which go to uphold the system,—all these are supposed to be sanctioned by these two injunctions. . . .

(b) But in order to see the exact bearing of these precepts, and to understand whether they could properly be regarded by a Christian master as sanctioning his claim over a human being, they should be considered in connection with other things, in which he would feel himself to be concerned, and certain representations made in the New Testament which he could not but regard as having an important bearing on him, and on the question of his duty to his slaves. The object now is to obtain a just view of the attitude in which a master would be placed, with all the statements of the New Testament before his mind that could be considered to relate to his duty to his slaves. What would he do, or how would he esteem this system, under the influence of all the doctrines and precepts laid down in the New Testament that could be regarded as applicable to him in this relation? To see this, let the following things be borne in mind:

(1.) The right of the master to the slave, as already observed, is never once recognised, either in so many words, or in any expressions which fairly imply it. It is not found in any statement of his right in general, or in detail. It is never said that he is the lawful owner of the slave, or that the relation is good and desirable, or that it is contemplated by Christianity that it should be continued; nor is it anywhere said that he has the right to avail himself of the labour of the slave, or to interfere with his relations to his wife or children, or to prescribe the time or the mode in which he shall worship God. There is not one thing which enters essentially into the nature of slavery, for which an explicit precept of the New Testament can be pleaded. It is not said that he has a right to enforce obedience, or even to require it of his slaves. It is indeed enjoined on servants that they be obedient to their masters, as it was on subjects to be obedient to the laws of Nero; but there is no authority given to masters to require or enforce such obedience, any more than there is to Nero, or any other bloody tyrant. What was the duty of the servant in the premises, and what were the obligations of the master, are different questions, and the one throws no light on the other. When a man strikes me, it is my duty to receive the blow with a proper spirit; but this furnishes no sanction for his conduct.

Now this undeniable fact, that the right of the master over the person and the services of the slave is never recognised at all in the New Testament, is a most important fact, and in the circumstances of the case could not but have an important bearing on the whole subject in the view of the early Christians. How could it be that he would not be led to ask the question, as already remarked, whether the apostles regarded it as right? If an owner of slaves in the United States were now to appeal to the New Testament to justify what is actually done, to what part of the New Testament would he look? Where would he find a distinct precept, giving him a right to buy a fellow being? Or to hold him as property? Or to sell him? Or to separate him from his wife and children? Or to withhold from him the Bible? Or to feed him on coarse fare, and to clothe him in coarse raiment, in order that he himself and his family might be supported in indolency and luxury? For not one of these things will he find a direct precept or permission in the New Testament; and yet all of them are things which are unlawful without such a precept or permission.

(2.) The New Testament lays down the doctrine, in terms so plain that a holder of slaves could not be ignorant of it, that all men are by nature equal in regard to their rights; that there is no distinction of blood, or caste, or complexion that can justify such an institution as that of slavery. It is one of the fundamental doctrines of Christianity—a doctrine on which the whole system is based, and which sends its influence into every portion of the system—that God "hath made of one blood all nations of men for to dwell on all the face of the earth." Acts xviii. 26. They are descended from the same earthly ancestors, and are children alike of the same heavenly Parent. Whatever distinction of complexion there may be, it is a doctrine of the Bible that all belong to one and the same great family, and that in the most important matters pertaining to their existence they are on a level. By nature, one is no more the favourite of Heaven than another; one has no rights over another. Now, this doctrine, which lies everywhere on the face of the Bible, could not but be seen by a conscientious Christian master in the times of the apostles, to strike at one of the fundamental conceptions on which slavery is based—the essential superiority of one class of men over another. It was on this ground professedly that Aristotle advocated slavery; and if it were not for this conception, slavery could not long exist at all. I need not say that extensively at the South now in our own country, it is maintained that the negro belongs to a race essentially inferior to the white man, and that by his physical incapacity it may be demonstrated that he was designed by his Creator to be in a condition of servitude; nor need I say that this idea of essential inferiority contributes much, even among good men, though often unconsciously to themselves, to perpetuate the system. All over the world it would probably be found that one of the essential things on which the institution of servitude rests, is this supposition of the natural inferiority of one class to another, and the moment when that shall be made to disappear, and the conception shall fully enter the mind, that, whatever difference of complexion or physical characteristics of any kind there may be, there is essential equality; that all are the children of God alike; that the same blood flows in all human veins; that every human being is a brother—that moment a death blow will be given to slavery, from which it will never recover. I need not say that whatever support the system was supposed to derive among the ancients from the inequality of men, or the inferiority of one class to another, or whatever it may be supposed to derive from the same consideration now, this receives no countenance from the New Testament. It would be impossible for a Christian master to derive the least sanction to his claim to the service of others, from any intimation of the kind in that book.

(3.) The New Testament lays down the doctrine that all are alike in a more important respect than in the equality of natural rights, and their being of the same family. All are redeemed by the same blood, and are heirs of the same glorious immortality. The same great sacrifice has been made for the slave which has been made for his master; and so far as the purchase made by redemption affixes any stamp of value on the human soul, it proclaims that the soul of the slave is worth as much as that of the master. In every respect as a redeemed sinner; as an heir of heaven; as a child of God, the slave is on a level with his master. He has the same right to worship God; to partake of the ordinances of religion; to pray; to read the Bible. In the highest of all senses they are brethren—ransomed in the same way, and destined, if they are Christians, to live in the same heaven. It is unnecessary to attempt to prove this from the New Testament, for it lies on the face of the volume, and no one can call it in question.

Yet it is impossible not to see what would be the bearing of this truth on the mind of a Christian master, and on the whole question of slavery. In spite of all reasoning to the contrary, the feeling must cross the mind of such a master that he has no right to hold a Christian brother in bondage; to regard him as property; to sell him to others; to break up his domestic relations; to interfere with any of his rights as a husband, a father, a son, or a Christian. The feeling will cross the mind that, as a redeemed man, he has the same rights as any other redeemed man; that as Christ died for him, he is to be treated in every way as an heir of life; that as all hope for the same heaven, no one has a right to rivet the fetters of bondage on another. A Christian master, in order to his having perfect peace in asserting his claims over a redeemed man as a slave, must feel that there ought to be some explicit warrant for this in the New Testament; and if there is any thing for which such a plain, unequivocal warrant should be adduced, it is for the asserted right of holding a Christian brother,—a fellow-heir of life—a candidate for heaven,—as property; the right to sell him or to keep him; to alienate him by contract or by will; to appropriate all the avails of his labour to our own use; to regulate exactly his manner of living; to separate him from wife, and children, and home; and to determine the times and seasons, if any, when he may worship God. And when we ask for this explicit warrant, this unambiguous authority in the case, we are referred to two texts of the New Testament, enjoining on masters 'to do the same things to them, forbearing threatening, knowing that they have a master in heaven;' and 'to render to their servants that which is just and equal.' And this is all. This is the whole authority which is or can be adduced for reducing one for whom Christ died to bondage, and holding a Christian brother in the chains of perpetual servitude. Verily, a Christian master should be able to refer to some more explicit authority than this. . . .

Now, suppose a man to be fairly under the influence of these undoubted principles of Christianity. Let him be imbued with the conviction that God has made of one blood all the human race; that all are by nature equal before him; that all have been redeemed by the same great sacrifice on the cross, showing no respect to colour, caste, or rank; that all true Christians are brethren—belonging to the same family and fellow-heirs of the grace of life; and that it is a duty to render to all that which is just and equal; and to these things let him add the golden rule of the Saviour, and what sanction would these two passages (Eph. vi. 9, and Col. iv. 1) really give to the system of slavery? What would be the fair influence of all the precepts of Christianity which the master could regard as appropriate to him, and bearing on his duty? Would it be—could it be, to satisfy his conscience that the apostles meant to teach that it was right for him as a Christian man to hold his brother—his fellow Christian—as property; and to regard him as, in any sense, a 'chattel' or a 'thing?' Could he feel this—when it is never said, and when it is never even implied? No! no man under the full and fair influence of these principles could feel thus.

Source: Albert Barnes, *An Inquiry into the Scriptural Views of Slavery* (Philadelphia: Perkins & Purves, 1846), 308–14, 317–18.

GEORGE D. ARMSTRONG

The Christian Doctrine of Slavery, 1857

George D. Armstrong (1813–1899) was born in New Jersey, graduated from the College of New Jersey (now Princeton University) in 1832, and studied at Union

Theological Seminary in Virginia from 1836 to 1838. He spent the early part of his career teaching chemistry and mechanics at Washington College (now Washington and Lee University). Armstrong resigned from higher education in 1851 to serve as pastor of First Presbyterian Church in Norfolk, Virginia, and helped to plant several other churches in Virginia until he retired in 1891. He was a prolific writer with published works on a broad range of topics, such as the doctrine of baptism, a history of yellow fever, evolution, higher criticism, religious conversion, and slavery. This excerpt from Armstrong's The Christian Doctrine of Slavery *includes his refutation of antislavery movements (namely, Albert Barnes's biblical arguments in favor of abolition) and outlines his own hermeneutic that differentiates between the essential nature of slavery found in the biblical witness and the incidental evils of slavery that must be reformed in the practice of slavery in the United States.*

WHERE God has appointed a work for his Church, he has generally appointed the way also in which that work is to be done. And where this is the case, the Church is as much bound to respect the one appointment as the other. . . . In the case of a race of men in slavery, the work which God has appointed his Church—as we learn it, both from the example and the precepts of inspired men—is to labor to secure in them a Christian life on earth and meetness for his heavenly kingdom. The African slave, in our Southern States, may be deeply degraded; the debasing effects of generations of sin may, at first sight, seem to have almost obliterated his humanity, yet is he an immortal creature; one for whom God the Son died; one whom God the Spirit can re-fashion, so as to make him a worthy worshipper among God's people on earth, and a welcome worshipper among the ransomed in heaven; one whom God the Father waiteth to receive as a returning prodigal to his heart and to his home. And the commission of the Church, "go ye into all the world and preach the Gospel to every creature," sends her a messenger of glad tidings to him as truly as to men far above him in the scale of civilization. On this point there can be no difference of opinion among God's people, North or South, who intelligently take the word of God as their "only rule of faith and obedience." This is the work of God, assigned by him to his Church, in so far as the slave race among us is concerned.

In what way is this work to be done? We answer, [b]y preaching the same Gospel of God's grace alike to the master and the slave; and when there is credible evidence given that this Gospel has been received in faith, to admit them, master and slave, into the same Church—the Church of the Lord Jesus Christ, in which "there is neither bond nor free" —and to seat them at the same table of the Lord, that drinking of the same cup, and eating of the same loaf, they may witness to the world their communion in the body and blood of the same Saviour. And having received them into the same Church, to teach them the duties belonging to their several "callings" out of the same Bible, and subject them to the discipline prescribed by the same law, the law of Christ. And this, the teaching of the Church, is to be addressed not to her members only, but to the world at large; and her discipline of her members is to be exercised not in secret, but before the world, that the light which God has given her may appear unto all men. This is just the way in which Christ and his Apostles dealt with slavery. The instructions they have given us in their life and in their writings prohibit any other.

In this way must the Church labor to make "good masters and good slaves," just as she labors to make "good husbands, good wives, good parents, good children, good rulers, good subjects.["] With the ultimate effect of this upon the civil and political condition of the slave the Church has nothing directly to do. If the ultimate effect of it be the emancipation of the slave—we say—in God's name, "let it come." "If it be of God, we cannot" —and we would not if we could— "overthrow it, lest haply we be found even to fight against God." If the ultimate effect be the perpetuation of slavery divested of its incidental evils—a slavery in which the master shall be required, by the laws of man as well as that of God, "to give unto the slave that which is just and equal," and the slave to render to the master a cheerful obedience and hearty service—we say, let slavery continue. It may be, that such a slavery, regulating the relations of capital and labor, though implying some deprivation of personal liberty, will prove a better defense of the poor against the oppression of the rich, than the too great freedom in which capital is placed in many of the free States of Europe at the present day. . . .

It is comparatively an easy matter to devise a scheme of emancipation in which all the just rights and the well-being of the master shall be provided for. But how shall we, as God-fearing men, provide for the just rights and well-being of the emancipated slave? To leave the partially civilized slave race, in a state of freedom, in contact with a much more highly civilized race, as all history testifies, is inevitable destruction to the former. Their writ of enfranchisement is their death-warrant. To remove one hundredth part of the annual increase of the slave race to Liberia, year by year, would soon quench for ever that light of Christian civilization which a wise philanthropy has kindled upon the dark coast of Africa. How shall we provide for the well-being of the enfranchised slave? Here is the real difficulty in the problem of emancipation.

We mean to express no opinion respecting the feasibility of the future emancipation of the slave race among us. As we stated in the outset, our purpose is to introduce no question on which the Bible does not give us specific instruction. And we have referred to the question of emancipation —a question which it belongs to the State, and not the Church, to settle—simply that the reader may see how completely God's word and God's providence are "at one," in so far as the present duty of the Church is concerned. Is slavery to continue? We want the best of Christian masters and the best of Christian slaves, that it may prove a blessing to both the one and the other. We want the best of Christian masters to devise and carry out the scheme by which it shall be effected, and the best of Christian slaves, that their emancipation may be an enfranchisement indeed. And this is just what the Bible plan of dealing with slavery aims at. The future may be hidden from view in "the clouds and darkness" with which God oft veils his purposes; but there is light—heaven's light—upon the present. And it is with the present alone we have immediately to do.

This is one way of dealing with slavery, and so firmly convinced are we that it is God's way for his Church that we cannot abandon it.

Another way proposed is—confounding the distinction between slavery itself and the incidental evils which attach to it in our country, and at the present day, under the guise of dealing with "AMERICAN SLAVERY." . . . To all this we object—

FIRST. —There is a radical fallacy involved in the use which is made of the expression, "AMERICAN SLAVERY."

By American Slavery, Dr. Barnes means—and the same is true of all anti-slavery writers whose works we have seen—the aggregate of, 1. Slavery itself; and, 2. The incidental evils which attach to it in this country and at this day, considered as inseparable—an indivisible unit. This treatment of the subject is—

1. Unphilosophical. Nothing is more real than the distinction, as set forth in the writing of Paul. . . . The fact that Dr. B. can write about Jewish slavery, and Roman slavery, and American slavery, as different the one from the others, shows that there must be something common to them all, to which we give the common name, Slavery; and something peculiar to each, which we designate by the adjuncts Jewish, Roman, American. Dr. B. admits that Roman slavery, as encountered by the Apostles in their day, was far more cruel and oppressive than American slavery now is—that is, that much of the incidental evil which once attached to slavery has disappeared. If much has already disappeared, why may not all that remains disappear in like manner? The change that has taken place, has been effected under the benign influence of Christianity. And just as certainly as we believe that Christianity is from God, and is destined to a final triumph in the world, just so certainly do we believe that slavery—if it is to continue to exist—must continue to be modified by it, until all its incidental evils disappear.

2. It is unscriptural. By this we mean, 1. It is an essentially different way of approaching the subject of slavery from that adopted by the Apostles. Paul never wrote a line respecting Jewish slavery—meaning thereby, slavery itself

and the incidental evils which attached to it in his day and among the Jews—or Roman slavery; nor does he give the Churches any directions couched in any such language as this. He writes about slavery, which he treats as neither a sin nor an offence; and about certain evils attaching to slavery as he encountered it, which he treats as sinful, and requires the Church, in her own proper sphere, to labor to correct. 2. It ignores the very ground upon which the whole method of dealing with slavery prescribed in the Word of God, is predicated. . . .

We take slavery, and the whole of slavery, just as it exists among us, and, after Paul's example, we separate it into—1. That which is essential, i.e., that which must continue if slavery continues; and, 2. That which is incidental, i.e., that which may disappear and slavery yet remain. Having done this, we then, in discussion, deal with both parts. We prove from the Word of God, that the first is not in violation of his law; and show, just as clearly, that much of the second is in violation of that law. And in our practical dealing with it, as a Church, we deal with both parts. The first we treat as not sinful, and require both the parties to conform to its obligations; much of the second—and just so much of it as is in violation of God's law—we prohibit, with all the authority given by Christ to his church over her members, and in every proper way, we seek to remove from the world at large. If this is not dealing with slavery in its entirety, we ask, [w]hat is? If this is dealing with slavery in the abstract, we ask, [w]hat have we abstracted?

We remarked that there was "a radical fallacy involved in the use which is made of the expression, American slavery," as used by Dr. B. and other writers of the same school. The reader will now see just what was meant by that remark.

The only meaning which can properly attach to the expression American slavery, is that of slavery as it exists in these United States of America. In this sense of the expression, we are dealing with American slavery, just as truly, and just as fully, and with far more of practical wisdom, we think, than Dr. B. is. The real difference between us is, that we distinguish between that which is essential and that which is incidental, as Paul did, and we deal with each as it deserves, as Paul did. Whilst Dr. B., neglecting this distinction, and thus, practically, treating all as essential, deals with it as an indivisible unit; and he does this under the guise of dealing with "American slavery," foisting upon that phrase, in addition to its proper meaning, the idea of the indivisible unity of the mass. To take such a course as this, when the issues in question are such as they are, is nothing more nor less than "a begging of the question."

SECOND. —We object to the course proposed by Dr. B. and others, for dealing with slavery, because it requires the Church to obtrude herself into the province of the State, and this, in direct violation of the ordinance of God. A course which has never been taken in times past, without disastrous consequences to the Church which did the wrong, as well as to the State which permitted the wrong to be done. Many a thing which it is right and proper, and even the duty of the Christian citizen, in this our free country, to do, the Church, as such, has not right to intermeddle with. It is, doubtless, the duty of the Christian citizen, for example, to use all proper means to inform himself respecting the qualifications of candidates for office, and having thus informed himself, to vote for the one whom he believes will best discharge the duties of the office. But will any Christian man, hence contend that it is right for the preacher, in the pulpit and on the Sabbath, to discuss the claims of rival candidates, and the Church, in her councils to direct her members how to vote? The Church and State has each its own appropriate sphere of operation assigned it of God, and neither can innocently intrude herself into the province of the other.

THIRD. —It leads to tampering with God's truth, and "wresting the Scripture," as Dr. B. has done in his Notes, by the application to them of principles and methods of interpretation, which destroy all certainty in human language. In order to make the Bible declare that slave-holding is a sin, when it plainly teaches just the contrary; and to teach in the Church doctrines which we are forbidden to teach under the most solemn sanctions. . . . This course has led not a few, once fair and promising members of the Church, and even ministers, into open "blasphemy;" and Paul teaches us, that such is its natural tendency, (1 Tim. VI. 4.)[.] We have no desire to walk in their way, or to meet their doom.

FOURTH. —It requires us to quit a method of dealing with slavery which has worked well in time past—all of real advantage to the slave that has ever been done by the Church has been done in this way—and to substitute for it a method which, to say the least of it, is a mere experiment, and an experiment which has wrought nothing but harm to the slave thus far—and we say this, after watching its operation during a ministry of twenty years, all of it, in God's providence, spent in a slave-holding state.

Source: George D. Armstrong, *The Christian Doctrine of Slavery* (New York: Charles Scribner, 1857), 131–40, 142–47.

CHARLES HODGE

"The General Assembly," 1865

Charles Hodge (1797–1878) was born in Philadelphia, Pennsylvania, graduated from the College of New Jersey (now Princeton University) in 1815 and Princeton

Theological Seminary in 1819, and ordained in 1821. After discerning his vocation was in the academy and not in congregational ministry, Hodge began teaching at Princeton Seminary in 1822. He studied Semitic languages and theology in Europe (Paris, Halle, and Berlin) from 1826 to 1828 but otherwise spent the rest of his career at Princeton Seminary. He published numerous works and edited The Biblical Repertory and Princeton Review, *one of the most prominent nineteenth-century theological journals. Hodge emerged as the chief architect of the "Princeton Theology," a method of Christian thought blending scriptural authority, Scottish Common Sense philosophy, systematic Reformed theology, and attention to religious experience that deeply informed Presbyterianism in the United States. In addition to constructing new modes to interpret the Bible and articulate Christian doctrine, Hodge advanced his ideas through critical appraisals of the religious developments in his era, such as the modifications to Calvinism emerging from the "New Haven Theology" and Charles Grandison Finney's "new measures" of revivalism. Like many Presbyterian theologians in his day, Hodge was involved in ecclesiastical matters. He began writing an annual report of the General Assembly in 1835. In this excerpt from 1865, Hodge delineates the reasons for his opposition to overtures that demanded southern Presbyterians publically repent for the sin of seceding from the United States.*

This subject occupied a large portion of the time of the Assembly, and gave rise to protracted and excited debates. It was not introduced incidentally in the discussion of other subjects, but was formally presented in three different ways. First, a memorial was laid before the house, signed by some forty names of members of the Assembly, and other ministers and elders of our church, calling for the following action on the part of the Assembly, viz.

I. An order to all the presbyteries and church sessions under its care, requiring them to examine every minister and member (and take testimony, if need be) who may apply for reception into any presbytery or church from any presbytery or church in any of the said "Confederate States," or which may have been claimed as such by the so-called "Confederate authorities" on the following points:

1. Whether he has in any way, directly or indirectly, of his own free will and consent, and without external constraint, been concerned at any time in aiding or countenancing the authority claimed by the said "Confederate States," or in aiding or countenancing the war which they have waged against the government of the United States; and if it be found from his own confession, or from sufficient testimony, that he has been so concerned in one or both these respects, that he be required to acknowledge and forsake his sin in this regard before he shall be received. . . .

It is an axiom in our Presbyterianism that the General Assembly can make no law to bind the conscience. It cannot alter by adding thereto or detracting therefrom the constitutional terms of ministerial or Christian fellowship. Those terms are laid down in express words in our Form of Government, which we are all bound to obey. Assent to the truth or propriety of the deliverances or testimonies of the Assembly is not one of the terms prescribed. If the Assembly may make agreement in their testimony on slavery a term of communion, they may make their deliverances on temperance, colonization, or any other subject such a term. This was often attempted during the temperance excitement. We have seen a minister rise in one of our synods and say that the time had come when the church would not tolerate any man in the ministry who refused to take the pledge of total abstinence from intoxicating liquors. This was done by a man who, if not at that time secretly a drunkard, soon became notorious for his addiction to that vice. We have no security for liberty of conscience, no protection from the tyranny of casual majorities, if the principle be once admitted that the Assembly can make anything beyond what the constitution prescribes, a condition either of admission into the ministry of our church or of continuance in it. This is too plain to be questioned. Yet this plain principle is obviously violated in the minute adopted on the Report of the Committee of Bills and Overtures. . . .

It may be said however that the action of the Assembly virtually amounts to nothing more than a declaration, that taking part in the rebellion and dissent from the deliverances of the Assembly respecting slavery, are moral offences, which are proper grounds of exclusion from church privileges until confessed and repented of. The Assembly of course has the right to express its judgment and give instructions on all points of truth and duty. So has every presbytery and every minister or Christian. But such judgments and instructions have only the authority due to the advice or opinions of those from whom they proceed. They have no legal force on any man's conscience or conduct. If a presbytery should admit a minister who had favoured the rebellion, or dissented from the Assembly's deliverance on slavery, and any one should bring the matter before the higher court by a complaint, the Assembly would have the right to give a judgment which would be binding on all the lower courts. But every man would be entitled to his opinion as to the correctness of that judgment, and the next Assembly would have a perfect right to pronounce a decision of a directly opposite character. The Popish doctrine of the infallibility of church courts does not suit Americans. It is high time that these simple principles of religious liberty should be clearly announced and openly asserted. It is no new thing that the greatest advocates of liberal doctrines should become intolerant and tyrannical when invested with power. If a man makes up his mind always to go with the majority, it will be a miracle if he do[es] not often go wrong.

It is, moreover, very obvious that the action of the Assembly with regard to the Southern churches is founded on a disregard of two plain distinctions. The one is the difference between political offences and ordinary crimes. As this point has been considered in a previous article of this number of our journal, we shall not dwell upon it here. It is enough to repeat, what no one can deny, that a man's taking the wrong side in a civil war, is no proof that he is not a Christian. His course may be determined by a wrong political theory, or by a regard for those actually in authority over him. We are bound to obey a de facto government, although it be that of a usurper. The apostle in enjoining submission to the "powers that be," meant those in actual possession of the authority of the state, whether a Nero or any one else. This obligation is, of course, limited by the higher obligation to obey God rather than man. But it is not necessary that every man should investigate the title of a ruler's authority before believing in its validity. The present inhabitants of France are bound to recognize Louis Napoleon as emperor, whatever they may think of the revolution which placed him in power. The fact, therefore, that a man or minister supported the late wicked rebellion, is not to be assumed as a proof that he is unworthy of Christian fellowship, even if that support was voluntary on his part.

The other distinction to which we referred, is that between sin and ecclesiastical offences. Every day sad exhibitions are made by those whom we are obliged to regard as Christians, of the imperfection which belongs to our present state. How often do we see manifestations of pride, covetousness, maliciousness, arrogance, to say nothing of idleness, sloth, lukewarmness, and worldly-mindedness in ministers and church members? It is seldom that a meeting of the General Assembly itself occurs without some exhibition of unholy temper. All these things are great sins. They are heinous in the sight of God, and offensive to all good people. Yet they are not matters for formal church discipline. We may, therefore, see and feel that the conduct of the Southern ministers and members has been exceeding wrong; that the spirit of pride, contempt, and animosity which they have in so many cases exhibited towards their Northern brethren and fellow-citizens, are great sins in the sight of God; but so also are the evil tempers, the worldly-mindedness, avarice, and other sins which we have so much reason to lament in ourselves and others. Church courts cannot visit all kinds of sin with ecclesiastical censure. We are obliged to receive all into the fellowship of the church who give evidence that they are true Christians, however imperfect they may be; otherwise the best of us would be excluded. . . .

Again, it is hard to see why, if favouring the rebellion is a crime calling for confession and repentance, it should not be visited upon Northern as well as Southern offenders. The fact is undeniable that thousands of men, many of them members and officers in our own church, have sympathized with the

South in this whole conflict. They openly rejoiced when our armies were defeated, and mourned over our successes. Many faithful pastors have been driven from their churches, because they felt in conscience bound to pray for the President and the success of our national arms, and to give thanks over our victories. If these are overlooked, and if the Assembly refused to direct their being made the grounds of church censure, with what consistency can Southern men be rejected for the same thing. If there be a difference in the case, it is in favour of Southern men who espoused the Southern cause which they regarded as the cause of their country, and not of Northern men who sided against what they knew to be their country, and took part with those who were seeking its destruction. We are bound by our ordination vows to promote the peace and unity of the church, to endeavour to bring into harmony and Christian fellowship, both external and inward, all who agree with us in the adoption of the same faith and discipline.

Source: Charles Hodge, "The General Assembly," in *The Biblical Repertory* and *Princeton Review* vol. 37, no. 3 (Philadelphia: Peter Walker, 1865), 496–97, 508, 510–13.

6

The Rising Tides and Crashing Waves of Theological Controversy

ROBERT LEWIS DABNEY

"The Public Preaching of Women," 1879

Robert Lewis Dabney (1820–1898) was born and raised in Louisa County, Virginia. He studied at Hampden-Syndey College, the University of Virginia, and Union Theological Seminary in Virginia. He was ordained in 1847 and served as the pastor of a rural congregation in Augusta County, Virginia, until joining the faculty at his alma mater, Union Theological Seminary, in 1853. During the Civil War, Dabney left the seminary to enlist in the Confederate Army, beginning his service as a chaplain in 1861 and then as an officer on the staff of his close friend, General Thomas (Stonewall) Jackson in 1862. He became ill during the war and returned to his seminary post, where he taught theology, church history, and polity until 1883. He subsequently moved to Texas to help establish the Austin School of Theology (now Austin Presbyterian Theological Seminary) in 1884. Dabney was a strong proponent of theological conservatism and engaged in many intellectual debates covering a myriad of subjects, such as biblical inerrancy, natural science, and women in ministry. In "The Public Preaching of Women," Dabney combats the increasing number of female preachers in American religion as well as broader feminist movements advocating for women's rights in American culture with his interpretations of Scripture on gender and order in the church and larger society.

In this day innovations march with rapid strides. The fantastic suggestion of yesterday, entertained only by a few fanatics, and then only mentioned by the sober to be ridiculed, is to-day the audacious reform, and will be to-morrow the recognized usage. Novelties are so numerous and so wild and rash, that in even conservative minds the sensibility of wonder is exhausted and the instinct of righteous resistance fatigued. A few years ago the public preaching of women was universally condemned among all conservative denominations of Christians, and, indeed, within their bounds, was totally unknown. Now the innovation is brought face to face even with the Southern churches, and female preachers are knocking at our doors. We are told that already public opinion is so truckling before the boldness and plausibility of their claims that ministers of our own communion begin to hesitate, and men hardly know whether they have the moral courage to adhere to the right. These remarks show that a discussion of woman's proper place in Christian society is again timely.

The arguments advanced by those who profess reverence for the Bible, in favor of this unscriptural usage, must be of course chiefly rationalistic. They do indeed profess to appeal to the sacred history of the prophetesses, Miriam, Deborah, Huldah, and Anna, as proving that sex was no sufficient barrier to public work in the Church. But the fatal answer is: that these holy women were inspired. Their call was exceptional and supernatural. There can be no fair reasoning from the exception to the ordinary rule. Elijah, in his civic relation to the kingdom of the ten tribes, would have been but a private citizen without his prophetic afflatus. By virtue of this we find him exercising the highest of the regal functions (1 Kings xviii.), administering the capital penalty ordained by the law against seducers into idolatry, when he sentenced the priests of Baal and ordered their execution. But it would be a most dangerous inference to argue hence, that any other private citizen, if moved by pious zeal, might usurp the punitive functions of the public magistrate. It is equally bad logic to infer that because Deborah prophesied when the supernatural impulse of the Spirit moved her, therefore any other pious woman who feels only the impulses of ordinary grace may usurp the function of the public preacher. It must be remembered, besides, that all who claim a supernatural inspiration must stand prepared to prove it by supernatural works. If any of our preaching women will work a genuine miracle, then, and not until then, will she be entitled to stand on the ground of Deborah or Anna. . . .

But the rationalistic arguments are more numerous and are urged with more confidence. First in natural order is the plea that some Christian women are admitted to possess every gift claimed by males: zeal, learning, piety, power of utterance; and it is asked why these are not qualifications for the ministry in the case of the woman as well as of the man. It is urged that there is a mischievous, and even a cruel impolicy in depriving the church of the accessions, and souls of the good, which these gifts and graces might procure when exercised in the pulpit. Again, some profess that they have felt the spiritual and conscientious impulse to proclaim the gospel which crowns God's call to the ministry. They "must obey God rather than men;" and they warn us against opposing their impulse, lest haply we be "found even to fight against God." They argue that the apostle himself has told us, in the new creation of grace "there is neither Jew nor Greek, circumcision nor uncircumcision, barbarian, Scythian, bond nor free." In Christ "there is neither Jew nor Greek, there is neither bond nor free, there is neither male nor female" (Col. iii. 11; Gal. iii. 28). But if the spiritual kingdom thus levels all social and temporal distinctions, its official rights should equally be distributed in disregard of them all. And last, it is claimed that God has decided the question by setting the seal of his favor on the preaching of some blessed women, such as the "Friend," Miss Sarah Smiley. If the results of her ministry are not gracious, then all the fruits of the gospel may as reasonably be discredited. And they ask triumphantly, [w]ould God employ and honor an agency which he himself makes unlawful?

We reply, yes. This confident argument is founded on a very transparent mistake. God does not indeed honor, but he does employ, agents whom he disapproves. Surely God does not approve a man who "preaches Christ for envy and strife" (Phil. i. 15), yet the apostle rejoices in it, and "knows that it shall result in salvation through his prayers and the supply of the Spirit of Jesus Christ." Two very simple truths, which no believer disputes, explode the whole force of this appeal to results. One is, that a truly good person may go wrong in one particular; and our heavenly Father, who is exceedingly forbearing, may withhold his displeasure from the misguided efforts of his child, through Christ's intercession, because, though misguided, he is his child. The other is, that it is one of God's clearest and most blessed prerogatives to bring good out of evil. Thus, who can doubt but it is wrong for a man dead in sins to intrude into the sacred ministry? Yet God has often employed such sinners to convert souls: not sanctioning their profane intrusion, but glorifying his own grace by overruling it. This experimental plea may be also refuted by another answer. If the rightfulness of actions is to be determined by their results, then it ought evidently to be by their whole results. But who is competent to say whether the whole results of one of these pious disorders will be beneficial or mischievous? A zealous female converts or confirms several souls by her preaching? Grant it. But may she not, by this example, in the future introduce an amount of confusion, intrusion, strife, error and scandal which will greatly overweigh the first partial good? This question cannot be answered until time is ended, and it will require an omniscient mind to judge it. Thus it becomes perfectly clear that present seeming good results cannot [ever] be a sufficient justification of conduct which violates the rule of the Word. This is our only sure guide. Bad results, following a course of action not commanded in the Word, may present a sufficient, even an imperative reason for stopping, and good results following such action may suggest some probability in its favor. This is all a finite mind is authorised to argue in these matters of God's service; and when the course of action transgresses the commandment, such probability becomes worthless.

Pursuing the arguments of the opposite party in the reverse order, we remark next, that when the apostle teaches the equality of all in the privilege of redemption, it is obvious he is speaking in general, not of official positions in the visible Church, but of access to Christ and participation in his blessings. The expository ground of this construction is, that thus alone can we save him from self-contradiction. For his exclusion of women from the pulpit is as clear and emphatic as his assertion of the universal equality in Christ. Surely he does not mean to contradict himself! Our construction is established also by other instances of a similar kind. The apostle expressly excludes "neophytes" from office. Yet no one dreams that he would have made the recency of their engrafting a ground of discrimination against their equal privileges in Christ. Doubtless the apostle would have been as ready to assert that in Christ there is neither young nor old, as that in him there is neither male nor female. So every sane man would exclude children from office in the Church, yet no one would disparage their equal interest in Christ. So the apostle inhibited Christians who were implicated in polygamy from office, however sincere their repentance. So the canons of the early Church forbade slaves to be ordained until they had legally procured emancipation, and doubtless they were right in this rule. But in Christ there is "neither bond nor free." If, then, the equality of these classes in Christ did not imply their fitness for public office in the Church, neither does the equality of females with males in Christ imply it. Last, the scope of the apostle in these places proves that he meant no more; for his object in referring to this blessed Christian equality is there seen to be to infer that all classes have a right to church membership, if believers, and that Christian love and communion ought to embrace all.

When the claim is made that the church must concede the ministerial function to the Christian woman who sincerely supposes she feels the call to it, we have a perilous perversion of the true doctrine of vocation. True, this vocation is spiritual, but it is also scriptural. The same Spirit who really calls the true minister also dictated the Holy Scriptures. When even a good man says that he thinks the Spirit calls him to preach, there may be room for doubt; but there can be no doubt whatever that the Spirit calls no person to do what the Word dictated by him forbids. The Spirit cannot contradict himself. No human being is entitled to advance a specific call of the Spirit for him individually to do or teach something contrary to or beside the Scriptures previously given to the church, unless he can sustain his claim by miracle. Again, the true doctrine of vocation is that the man whom God has designed and qualified to preach learns his call through the Word. The Word is the instrument by which the Spirit teaches him, with prayer, that he is to preach. Hence, when a person professes to have felt this call whom the Word distinctly precludes from the work, as the neophyte, the child, the penitent polygamist, the female, although we may ascribe her mistake to an amiable zeal, yet we absolutely know she is mistaken: she has confounded a human impulse with the Spirit's vocation. Last, the scriptural vocation comes not only through the heart of the candidate, but of the brotherhood; and the call is never complete until the believing choice of the brethren has confirmed it. But by what shall they be guided? By the "say so" of any one who assumes to be sincere? Nay, verily. The brethren are expressly commanded "not to believe every spirit, but to try the spirits whether they are of God." They have no other rule than Scripture. Who can believe that God's Spirit is the agent of such anarchy as this, where the brotherhood hold in their hands the Word, teaching them that God does not call any woman, and yet a woman insists, against them, that God calls her? He "is not the author of confusion, but of peace, as in all the churches of the saints." It is on this very subject of vocation to public teaching that the apostle makes this declaration. . . .

In Titus ii. 4, 5, women who have not reached old age are to be "affectionate to their husbands, fond of their children, prudent, pure, keepers at home, benevolent, obedient to their own husbands, that the word of God may not be reviled." And the only teaching function hinted even for the aged women is, verse 4, that they should teach these private domestic virtues to their younger sisters. Does not the apostle here assign the home as the proper sphere of the Christian woman? That is her kingdom, and neither the secular nor the ecclesiastical commonwealth. Her duties in her home are to detain her away from the public functions. She is not to be a ruler of men, but a loving subject to her husband. . . .

Every true believer should regard the scriptural argument as first, as sufficient, and as conclusive by itself. But as the apostle said in one place, that his task was "to commend himself to every man's conscience in God's sight," so it is proper to gather the teachings of sound human prudence and experience which support God's wise law. The justification is not found in any disparagement of woman as man's natural inferior, but in the primeval fact: "Male and female made he them." In order to ground human society God saw it necessary to fashion for man's mate, not his exact image, but his counterpart. Identity would have utterly marred their companionship, and would have been an equal curse to both. But out of this unlikeness in resemblance it must obviously follow that each is fitted for works and duties unsuitable for the other. And it is no more a degradation to the woman that the man can best do some things which she cannot do so well, than to the man that woman has her natural superiority in other things. But it will be cried: "Your Bible doctrine makes man the ruler, woman the ruled." True. It was absolutely necessary, especially after sin had entered the race, that a foundation for social order should be laid in a family government. This government could not be made consistent, peaceful or orderly by being made double-headed; for human finitude, and especially sin, would ensure collision, at least at some times, between any two human wills. It was essential to the welfare of both husband and wife and of the offspring, that there must be an ultimate human head somewhere. . . .

The case is the same in this respect with his ordinance restraining the most gifted woman from publicity. But there is a more obvious answer. God has assigned to her a private sphere sufficiently important and honorable to justify the whole expenditure of angelic endowments: the formation of the character of children. This is the noblest and most momentous work done on earth. . . . Again, the instrumentality of the mother's training in the salvation of her children is mighty and decisive; the influence of the minister over his hundreds is slight and non-essential. If he contributes a few grains, in numerous cases, to turn the scales for heaven, the mother contributes tons to the right scales in her few cases. The one works more widely on the surface, the other more deeply; so that the real amount of soil moved by the two workmen is not usually in favor of the preacher. The woman of sanctified ambition has nothing to regret as to the dignity of her sphere. She does the noblest work that is done on earth. Its public recognition is usually more through the children and beneficiaries she ennobles than through her own person. True; and that is precisely the feature of her work which makes it most Christ-like. It is precisely the feature at which a sinful and selfish ambition takes offence...

This common movement for "women's rights" and women's preaching must be regarded then as simply infidel. It cannot be candidly upheld without attacking the inspiration and authority of the Scriptures. We are convinced that there is only one safe attitude for Christians, presbyters, and church courts to assume towards it. This is utterly to discountenance it, as they do any other assault of infidelity on God's truth and kingdom.

Source: Robert Lewis Dabney, "The Public Preaching of Women," in *The Southern Presbyterian Review*, vol. 30, no. 4 (October 1879), 689–95, 700, 705–6, 708–9, 712.

6.1　Robert Lewis Dabney, 1885 (Presbyterian Historical Society, Philadelphia, PA)

SHALL

WOMAN PREACH?

OR

THE QUESTION

ANSWERED,

BY

MRS. LOUISA M. WOOSLEY.

———o———

CANEYVILLE, KY.
1891.

6.2　Louisa M. Woosley, 1891 (Presbyterian Historical Society, Philadelphia, PA)

LOUISA M. WOOSLEY

Shall Woman Preach? Or the Question Answered, 1891

Louisa M. Woosley (1862–1952) was born and raised in Grayson County, Kentucky. As a teenager, Woosley converted to Christianity at a Baptist revival meeting and immediately aspired to become a preacher in 1874. She encountered opposition to her call to ministry and began poring over the pages of Scripture to study the roles of women in the church. This intense study confirmed her belief in 1883 that God desired to use women as preachers no less than men. Four years later, when the minister of her small Cumberland Presbyterian church did not appear to lead worship on a Sunday morning, the elders selected a reluctant Woosley to lead the service. The session's affirmation inspired Woosley to deliver her first sermon that day, and she never stopped preaching. In the next two years, she proclaimed over five hundred sermons as an evangelist, and her ministry added approximately three hundred members to the Cumberland Presbyterian Church. The Nolin Presbytery made her the first ordained female Presbyterian teaching elder in 1889. In 1890, the Kentucky Synod ordered Woosley's presbytery to remove her name from its roster of ministers. The following year, Woosley published a book that employed meticulous analysis of the relevant biblical passages and the regnant biblical interpretations of her day to demonstrate the validity and necessity of women preaching.

The objections to woman's preaching and ordination, are very numerous, and as frivolous as numerous. Our object in this chapter is to investigate these objections carefully, and to answer them biblically, and in the light of reason.

1. Some say women ought not to preach, because Paul condemns it (or rather, forbids it). "Let your women keep silence in the churches: for it is not permitted unto them to speak."— I. Cor. 14: 34. Well, then, if we are to obey this injunction strictly, and to compel our women to keep silence in the churches, see what follows. We take all the women out of our choirs, and oh! what music we would have with our male voices and our bass singers! But you insist that nothing is said against their singing, but against their speaking. Very well, then, women are not to speak in the church courts at all. If that is what is meant, it does seem that, either we have been dull of comprehension, or very rebellious. In many of our church courts the voice of woman has been heard, and is still being heard. For example, we refer to the General Assembly, which met at Union City, Tenn., May, 1890. In the presence of a large audience, and right in the midst of the transaction of business by that intelligent body, a woman (Mrs. Louisa Ward) was called for. She mounted the rostrum, and we all heard her voice, as she stood for forty minutes defending

her own cause. All this was in opposition, too, to what Paul said, as some would have us believe.

If we are to give Paul a literal interpretation, then women may not even pray or talk in church, for they are not permitted to speak. Where then is the authority for their testifying for Christ at all? If those persons, who insist on a literal interpretation of these passages of Scripture, are consistent, and want our confidence, they will never call upon another woman to take part in a praise-meeting: since it is impossible for a woman to praise the Lord, or testify for Jesus, without speaking. Just as long as they allow women to talk in these meetings, we will be constrained to believe they are acting in bad faith: for Paul says they are not permitted to speak, but to be in silence. Then why allow her even to sing? [T]his breaks the silence. It is indeed a good thing to practice what we preach; and if we fail to do so, there is a contradiction. If these objectors want our confidence, they must change either their practice or their preaching. They must not allow their women to pray, talk, or even sing in churches: since Paul says "Let your women keep silence."

Has it been the experience of these objectors, that the prayers, songs, and admonitions of godly women, have done them, or the cause of Christ an injury? Who can say he has been harmed by the talk of a good Christian woman? Many, who shall read these pages, have been led to accept Christ through the instrumentality of woman. Many hearts have overflowed with love, and have swelled with thankfulness to God for her prayers and testimonies. Why then (how can any one object?) object when women speak or pray? Why invite them to come to Christ, or seek salvation at all? [S]ince they are forbidden to tell it if the Lord blesses them. It is like inviting them to your house, and then forbidding them to speak to you; or, to your table, and not allowing them to eat; or, like asking a thirsty, way-worn traveler to your well, and then refusing him drink.

If it is a shame for a woman to speak in the church, why ask her to give evidence of a change of heart, or to relate her Christian experience, when she comes forward and asks membership in the church? If a woman were to come forward to join the church, and the pastor should say, ["]Well, my sister, tell us what the Lord has done for you.["] She makes no reply, and we think it very strange. Then we fancy the preacher says, ["]Do you feel that your sins have been pardoned?["] She sits like a padlock was upon her mouth. Then he says, ["]Do you want to join the church?["] And still she sits as mute as a mummy. You say, well there is something wrong; that woman must be crazy. Whereupon Paul rises up and says, oh no; that is all right: "For it is a shame for women to speak in the church."

. . . But we will give our objectors all the rope, and admit that it is meant that there are certain times and circumstances when women ought to keep silence—when it would be a shame for them to speak publicly in the church. Cumberland Presbyterians teach, in accordance with the Bible, that the bad are gathered with the good into the Church. "They are not all Israel which are of Israel," and sometimes these give us a great deal of trouble. Being guilty of very grave offenses, such as, dancing, gambling, horse-racing, drinking, and even adultery. These parties must be dealt with, and after complying with certain prescribed rules, if we fail to gain them, we are to tell it to the church. Of course under these circumstances, it is a shame for a woman to speak in the church. Hence the admonition, "Let all things be done decently and in order." According to Presbyterian polity, a committee may be appointed to see after these matters privately, and so the shame from having such offenses brought before the public, may be avoided, at least to some extent.

The very same record that says, let the women keep silence in the churches, also says let the men (and that too in the very same church) keep silence in the church (see I. Cor. 14: 28). So according to Paul, there is a time when men should keep silence in the church, as well as the women. But this is a church in confusion, and he admonishes the men to keep silence in such churches; and common sense itself teaches us, that under such circumstances, "It is a shame for women to speak in the church." "For God is not the author of confusion, but of peace, as in all churches of the saints." (verse 33).

It is evident that the scripture referred to in verse 34, applies solely to married women, and it has no reference to religious worship of any kind. If it does, then a woman must sit in church as mute as a mummy. If she even sings she breaks the silence, and thereby becomes disobedient. God has made no distinction in his kingdom between matron and maid. They all have the same happy privileges. There is no such thing as one gospel for the matron and another for the maid. In the law referred to (Gen. 3: 16), "Thy desire shall be to thy husband, and he shall rule over thee," the obedience spoken of has no reference to worship of any kind, and surely not to public meetings, but to the obedience that is due from wife to husband. If worship is meant, the husband is lord over the wife's conscience, and the only one to whom she must give an account. Can he answer for her in judgment? Has she been left out of the covenant of grace? Is she in the world without any sure light to guide her? [A]menable to no law, human or divine, except that of her husband, to which she must render perfect obedience? Is her husband to be her only teacher, from whom she must learn in silence with all subjection?

. . . Notice that Paul said, "I suffer not a woman to teach, nor to usurp authority over the man." He did not say usurp authority over the Church, but over the man. Is it possible that a woman cannot sing, pray, or teach a Sunday-school class, or preach the gospel, without usurping authority over the man? Have you ever heard of any woman who felt that she was called of God to preach, who tried to force herself upon the Church, or upon the public? Does she try to usurp authority by putting restrictions upon the mouths of men? We are sure that the women are not trying to take the gospel, or any church privileges from the men; neither do they desire to rule over them. Their object is rather to stand by his side—where God intended she should stand—as an helpmeet.

It seems that this subject, as all others, has two extremes. Those who are so bitter against woman's usurping authority, are in danger of becoming usurpers themselves, by passing over the line and going to the other extreme. As a Church, we claim to occupy a medium ground. Then we should not cast the woman down below man, nor raise her up above him. Side by side shall they stand, sharing in the responsibilities of life, and bearing together the heat and burden of the day. Let neither usurp authority over the other, as both are raised from a dead level in sin, to a living perpendicular in Christ. . . .

These objectors must remember that the Twelve were commissioned by the crucified, dead, buried, and risen Christ, to preach through him as their living head, repentance and remission of sins: in other words, to disciple all nations. In doing this, they preach a risen Savior; for it is the living Christ that saves. We to-day preach him as, "the way, the truth, and the life;" as "the end of the law for righteousness to every one that believeth." But the Twelve were not the first ones commissioned to preach a risen Lord. The world's Redeemer saw fit, in his wisdom, to bestow this honor upon woman. To her he first manifested himself, and spoke words of cheer, quieting her fears, and drying up her tears. When she recognized him, she drew near to worship him, but "Jesus saith unto her, Touch me not; for I am not yet ascended to my Father; but go to my brethren, and say unto them, I ascend unto my Father, and your Father, and to my God, and your God."—Jno. 20: 17. "Go tell my brethren that they go into Galilee, and there shall they see me."—Matt. 28: 10.

The women returned from the sepulcher, and told these things to the eleven and to all the rest—yea, they departed with great joy, and did run to bring the disciples word. But it is said, "Their words seemed to them as idle tales, and they believed them not." We do not know how many women there were, neither can we give all their names, for they are not revealed. To say the least of it, there could not have been less than five (see Luke 24: 10). . . .

So we find in both the Old and the New Testaments' times, that men and women prophesied, spoke to the people, as the call of God and the occasion required. God saw fit in his wisdom to use women as judges, as leaders, as prophets, and as teachers under "the Law." Where is the authority for taking those privileges from them under the Gospel? It has been the prevailing opinion that under the New Testament dispensation, their privileges have been enlarged, and their liberties increased. Why this should not be, and why they should not preach, is a thought difficult of conception. It is true that Miriam was not admitted to the priesthood (neither were Moses and Joshua allowed to offer sacrifices), but that she was recognized a leader by Israel, cannot be denied. And no one doubts but that she was faithful in the performance of her duties, and in the work God assigned her. Deborah was called of God to be Israel's fourth judge; her song of praise is still ringing in our ears; it ranks with that of Moses and Miriam; she should be held up before the eyes of the world, and especially of all Bible readers. Surely no one would strike the record of this great woman from the sacred canon.

Huldah was chosen of God to adorn the sacred record, and to expound the law. In fact the whole tenor of the Scriptures proves that it was nothing unusual for a woman to teach the people, and there is not a single word of reproof or prohibition in the Old Testament Scriptures against woman's preaching. So, whatever may be said against her now, it is certain that she did preach and teach under the Law, and even administered the sacrament of Circumcision. . . .

Surely the tide is upon us, seeing that God had so great an army of women, who by his authority proclaimed his truth, came at his calling, and went at his bidding. . . . Clothed with official authority, Phebe visited the church at Rome under the sanction of the apostle, who instructed the church to render her all the assistance she needed. The business committed to her was certainly the work of the Lord, and of course she could not make it known unless she had a right to speak in the church, else such business would not have been intrusted to her. Strange that the apostle should instruct them to assist her in this business, if it were a shame for a woman to speak in the church—since it is a fact that they must hear her (for she must deliver her message before they could possibly understand the nature of that business) in order to give the assistance needed. The conclusion is, that when Phebe visited the church at Rome that she went as a legally authorized delegate or commissioner, to counsel with that body on matters pertaining to the interest of the church. We, as Cumberland Presbyterians, have a form of commission, and it is similar to that used by the apostle in the case of Phebe (see Confession of Faith, 133, secs. 10, 11). And now "I [Paul] commend unto you Phebe [Smith, Jones, or Henry], which is a servant [pastor] of the church at Cenchrea [Denver]; that ye receive her [him] in the Lord as becometh saints, and that ye assist her [him] in whatsoever business she [he] hath need of you." That is, that you give her [him] a place or seat or a voice in the council or Assembly. Given by order of the church at Cenchrea, and signed by Paul, A. D. 60. "What I have written, I have written."

Source: Louisa M. Woosley, *Shall Woman Preach? Or the Question Answered* (Caneyville, KY: Louisa M. Woosley, 1891), 11–14, 16–18, 21–22, 24–25, 159–60, 164–66.

ARCHIBALD A. HODGE AND BENJAMIN B. WARFIELD

"Inspiration," 1881

Archibald A. Hodge (1823–1886) and Benjamin B. Warfield (1851–1921) collaborated to write on the doctrine of biblical inspiration. The authors both graduated from Princeton Theological Seminary, studying under Charles Hodge, and taught at the institution. Archibald A. Hodge was also the son of Charles Hodge. Before succeeding his father as a theology professor at the seminary in 1877, Hodge was a missionary in India for three years, a pastor of Presbyterian congregations in Virginia and Pennsylvania, and a professor at Western Theological Seminary in Pennsylvania (now Pittsburgh Theological Seminary). After graduating from Princeton Seminary, Warfield spent a year studying in Leipzig, Germany, and then returned to the United States to serve as a pastor at First Presbyterian Church in Baltimore, Maryland. He then taught the New Testament at Western Seminary for approximately nine years before following Archibald A. Hodge as professor of didactic and polemic theology at Princeton Seminary in 1887. This article responds to the rise of historical criticism with a robust conservative argument outlining the inerrancy of the Scriptures as the inspired words of God in the ipsissima verba ("the very words") of the original autographs.

During the entire history of Christian theology the word Inspiration has been used to express either some or all of the activities of God, cooperating with its human authors in the genesis of Holy Scripture. We prefer to use it in the single sense of God's continued work of superintendence, by which, His providential, gracious, and supernatural contributions having been presupposed, He presided over the sacred writers in their entire work of writing, with the design and effect of rendering that writing an errorless record of the matters He designed them to communicate, and hence constituting the entire volume in all its parts the Word of God to us.

While we have restricted the word Inspiration to a narrower sphere than that in which it has been used by many in the past, nevertheless we are certain that the above statement of the divine origin and infallibility of Scripture accurately expresses the faith of the Christian Church from the first. Still several points remain to be more particularly considered, concerning which, some difference of opinion at present prevails.

1st. Is it proper to call this Inspiration "plenary"? This word, which has often been made the occasion of strife, is in itself indefinite, and its use contributes nothing, either to the precision or the emphasis of the definition. The word means simply "full," "complete," perfectly adequate for the attainment of the end designed, whatever that might have been. There ought not to be on any side any hesitancy to affirm this of the books of the Bible.

2d. Can this Inspiration be properly said to be "verbal"? The objection to the application of this predicate to Inspiration is urged upon three distinct grounds:

(I). We believe that the great majority of those who object to the affirmation that Inspiration is verbal, are impelled thereto by a feeling, more or less definite, that the phrase implies that Inspiration is, in its essence, a process of verbal dictation, or that, at least in some way, the revelation of the thought, or the inspiration of the writer, was by means of the control which God exercised over his words. And there is the more excuse for this misapprehension because of the extremely mechanical conceptions of Inspiration maintained by many former advocates of the use of this term "verbal." This view, however, we repudiate as earnestly as any of those who object to the language in question. At the present time the advocates of the strictest doctrine of Inspiration, in insisting that it is verbal, do not mean that, in any way, the thoughts were inspired by means of the words, but simply that the divine superintendence, which we call Inspiration, extended to the verbal expression of the thoughts of the sacred writers, as well as to the thoughts themselves, and that, hence, the Bible considered as a record, an utterance in words of a divine revelation, is the Word of God to us. Hence, in all the affirmations of Scripture of every kind, there is no more error in the words of the original autographs than in the thoughts they were chosen to express. The thoughts and words are both alike human, and, therefore, subject to human limitations, but the divine superintendence and guarantee extends to the one as much as the other. . . .

It is evident, therefore, that it is not clearness of thought which inclines any of the advocates of a real inspiration of the Holy Scriptures to deny that it extends to the words. Whatever discrepancies or other human limitations may attach to the sacred record, the line (of inspired or not inspired, of infallible or fallible) can never rationally be drawn between the thoughts and the words of Scripture.

3d. It is asked again: In what way, and to what extent, is the doctrine of Inspiration dependent upon the supposed results of modern criticism, as to the dates, authors, sources, and modes of composition of the several books? To us the following answer appears to be well founded, and to set the limits within which the Church doctrine of inspiration is in equilibrium with the results of modern criticism fairly and certainly:

The doctrine of Inspiration, in its essence and, consequently, in all its forms, presupposes a supernatural revelation and a supernatural providential guidance, entering into and determining the genesis of Scripture from the beginning. Every naturalistic theory, therefore, of the evolution of Scripture, however disguised, is necessarily opposed to any true version of the Catholic doctrine of Inspiration. It is, also, a well-known matter of fact that Christ himself is the ultimate witness on whose testimony the Scriptures, as well as their doctrinal contents, rest. We receive the Old Testament just as Christ handed it to us, and on His authority. And we receive as belonging to the New Testament all, and only those books which an apostolically instructed age testifies to have been produced by the Apostles or their companions, i.e., by the men whom Christ commissioned, and to whom He promised infallibility in teaching. It is evident, therefore, that every supposed conclusion of critical investigation which denies the apostolical origin of a New Testament book, or the truth of any part of Christ's testimony in relation to the Old Testament and its contents, or which is inconsistent with the absolute truthfulness of any affirmation of any book so authenticated, must be inconsistent with the true doctrine of Inspiration. On the other hand, the defenders of the strictest doctrine of Inspiration should cheerfully acknowledge that theories as to the authors, dates, sources, and modes of composition of the several books, which are not plainly inconsistent with the testimony of Christ or His Apostles as to the Old Testament, or with the apostolic origin of the books of the New Testament, or with the absolute truthfulness of any of the affirmations of these books so authenticated, cannot in the least invalidate the evidence or pervert the meaning of the historical doctrine of Inspiration.

4th. The real point at issue between the more strict and the more lax views of Inspiration maintained by believing scholars remains to be stated. It is claimed and admitted equally on both sides that the great design and effect of Inspiration is to render the sacred Scriptures in all their parts a divinely infallible and authoritative rule of faith and practice; and hence that in all their elements of thought and expression concerned in the great purpose of conveying to men a revelation of spiritual doctrine or duty, the Scriptures are absolutely infallible. But if this be so, it is argued by the more liberal school of Christian scholars, that this admitted fact is not inconsistent with other facts which they claim are matters of their personal observation; to wit, that in certain elements of Scripture which are purely incidental to their great end of teaching spiritual truth, such as history, natural history, ethnology, archaeology, geography, natural science, and philosophy, they, like all the best human writings of their age, are, while for the most part reliable, yet limited by inaccuracies and discrepancies. While this is maintained, it is generally at the same time affirmed, that when compared with other books of the same antiquity, these inaccuracies and discrepancies of the Bible are inconsiderable in number, and always of secondary importance, in no degree invalidating the great attribute of Scripture, its absolute infallibility and its divine authority as a rule of faith and practice.

The writers of this article are sincerely convinced of the perfect sound- ness of the great Catholic doctrine of Biblical Inspiration, i.e., that the Scriptures not only contain, but ARE THE WORD OF GOD, and hence that all their elements and all their affirmations are absolutely errorless, and binding the faith and obedience of men. Nevertheless we admit that the question between ourselves and the advocates of the view just stated, is one of fact, to be decided only by an exhaustive and impartial examination of all the sources of evidence, i.e., the claims and the phenomena of the Scriptures themselves. There will undoubtedly be found upon the surface many apparent affirmations presumably inconsistent with the present teachings of science, with facts of history, or with other statements of the sacred books themselves. Such apparent inconsistencies and collisions with other sources of information are to be expected in imperfect copies of ancient writings; from the fact that the original reading may have been lost, or that we may fail to realize the point of view of the author, or that we are destitute of the circumstantial knowledge which would fill up and harmonize the record. Besides, the human forms of knowledge by which the critics test the accuracy of Scripture are themselves subject to error. In view of all the facts known to us, we affirm that a candid inspection of all the ascertained phenomena of the original text of Scripture will leave unmodified the ancient faith of the Church. In all their real affirmations these books are without error.

It must be remembered that it is not claimed that the Scriptures any more than their authors are omniscient. The information they convey is in the forms of human thought, and limited on all sides. They were not designed to teach philosophy, science, or human history as such. They were not designed to furnish an infallible system of speculative theology. They are written in human languages, whose words, inflections, constructions, and idioms bear everywhere indelible traces of human error. The record itself furnishes evidence that the writers were in large measure dependent for their knowledge upon sources and methods in themselves fallible; and that their personal knowledge and judgments were in many matters hesitating and defective, or even wrong. Nevertheless the historical faith of the Church has always been, that all the affirmations of Scripture of all kinds, whether of spiritual doctrine or duty, or of physical or historical fact, or of psychological or philosophical principle, are without any error, when the ipsissima verba of the original autographs are ascertained and interpreted in their natural and intended sense. There is a vast difference between exactness of statement, which includes an exhaustive rendering of details, an absolute literalness, which the Scriptures never profess, and accuracy, on the other hand, which secures a correct statement of facts or principles intended to be affirmed. It is this accuracy and this alone, as distinct from exactness, which the Church doctrine maintains of every affirmation in the original text of Scripture without exception. Every statement accurately corresponds to truth just as far forth as affirmed. . . .

A proved error in Scripture contradicts not only our doctrine, but the Scripture claims and, therefore, its inspiration in making those claims. It is, therefore, of vital importance to ask: can phenomena of error and untruth be pointed out?

There is certainly no dearth of "instances" confidently put forward. But it is abundantly plain that the vast majority of them are irrelevant. We must begin any discussion of them, therefore, by reasserting certain simple propositions, the result of which will be to clear the ground of all irrelevant objections. It is to be remembered, then, that: 1. We do not assert that the common text, but only that the original autographic text was inspired. No "error" can be asserted, therefore, which cannot be proved to have been aboriginal in the text. 2. We do not deny an everywhere-present human element in the Scriptures. No mark of the effect of this human element therefore—in style of thought or wording—can be urged against inspiration, unless it can be shown to result in untruth. 3. We do not erect inspiration into an end, but hold it to be simply a means to an end, viz, the accurate conveyance of truth. No objection, therefore, is valid against the form in which the truth is expressed, so long as it is admitted that that form conveys the truth. 4. We do not suppose that inspiration made a writer false to his professed purpose; but rather that it kept him infallibly true to it. No objection is valid, therefore, which overlooks the prime question: what was the professed or implied purpose of the writer in making this statement? These few simple and very obvious remarks set aside the vast majority of the customary objections. The first throws out of court numbers of inaccuracies in the Old and New Testaments as either certainly or probably not parts of the original text, and therefore not fit evidence in the case. The second performs the same service for a still greater number, which amount simply to the discovery of individual traits, modes of thought or expression, or forms of argumentation in the writings of the several authors of the biblical books. The third sets aside a vast multitude, drawn from pressure of language, misreading of figures, resurrection of the primary sense of idioms, etc., in utter forgetfulness of the fact that no one claims that Inspiration secured the use of good Greek in Attic severity of taste, free from the exaggerations and looseness of current speech, but only that it secured the accurate expression of truth, even (if you will) through the medium of the worst Greek a fisherman of Galilee could write, and the most startling figures of speech a peasant could invent. Exegesis must be historical as well as grammatical, and must always seek the meaning intended, not any meaning that can be tortured out of a passage. The fourth in like manner destroys the force of every objection which is tacitly founded on the idea that partial and incomplete statements cannot be inspired, no documents can be quoted except verbatim, no conversations reported unless at length, etc., and which thus denies the right of an author to speak to the present purpose only, appeal to the sense, not wording of a document, give abstracts of discourses, and apply, by a true exegesis, the words of a previous writer to the present need. The sum of the whole matter is simply this: no phenomenon can be validly urged against verbal inspiration which, found out of Scripture, would not be a valid argument against the truth of the writing. Inspiration securing no more than this—truth, simple truth—no phenomenon can be urged against verbal inspiration which cannot be proved to involve an indisputable error. . . .

The wonderful accuracy of the New Testament writers in all, even the most minute and incidental details of their historical notices, cannot, however, be made even faintly apparent by a simple answering of objections. Some sort of glance over the field as a whole is necessary to any appreciation of it. There are mentioned in the New Testament some thirty names—Emperors, members of the family of Herod, High-priests, Rabbis, Roman Governors, Princes, Jewish leaders—some mention of which might be looked for in contemporary history or on contemporary monuments. All but two of these—and they the insignificant Jewish rebels, Theudas and Barabbas—are actually mentioned; and the New Testament notices are found, on comparison, to be absolutely accurate in every, even the most minute, detail. Every one of their statements has not, indeed, passed without challenge, but challenge has always meant triumphant vindication. Some examples of what is here meant have been given already; others may be added in a note for their instructiveness. Now, the period of which these writers treat is absolutely the most difficult historical period in which to be accurate that the world has ever seen. Nothing was fixed or stable;—vacillation, change, was everywhere. The province which was senatorial to-day was imperial to-morrow,—the boundaries that were fixed to-day were altered to-morrow. That these writers were thus accurate in a period and land wherein Tacitus failed to attain complete accuracy means much.

We reach the same conclusion if we ask after their geographical accuracy. In no single case have they slipped here, either; and what this means may be estimated by noting what a mass of geographical detail has been given us. Between forty and fifty names of countries can be counted in the New

Testament pages; every one is accurately named and placed. About the same number of foreign cities are named, and all equally accurately. Still more to the purpose, thirty-six Syrian and Palestinian towns are named, the great majority of which have been identified, and wherever testing is possible the most minute accuracy emerges. Whether due to inspiration or not, this unvarying accuracy of statement is certainly consistent with the strictest doctrine of Inspiration.

Source: Archibald A. Hodge and Benjamin B. Warfield, "Inspiration," in *The Presbyterian Review*, vol. 2, no. 6 (April 1881), 232–33, 235–38, 245–46, 250–52.

CHARLES AUGUSTUS BRIGGS

"The Authority of Holy Scripture," 1891

Charles Augustus Briggs (1841–1913) was born in New York City and studied at the University of Virginia, Union Theological Seminary in New York, and the University of Berlin. After returning from his studies in Germany, Briggs first served as pastor of a Presbyterian congregation in New Jersey from 1870 to 1874 and then taught at his alma mater, Union Seminary, from 1874 until his death. He became one of the most influential scholars of his day with his published works defending and implementing historical-critical approaches to the Bible. Upon his promotion to the Edward Robinson Chair of Biblical Theology at Union Seminary, he delivered this address in 1891. Although his title suggested an orthodox lecture, Briggs used the occasion to sharply debunk existing Presbyterian doctrines on biblical authority, inerrancy, and inspiration. Briggs argued that the doctrine of biblical inerrancy was not found in the Scriptures and touted historical criticism as a divine gift to enable Christians to better understand biblical truths. He was found guilty of heresy at the General Assembly two years later and suspended from his validated ministry at Union Seminary. The seminary's board of directors refused to abide by the assembly's action and left the denomination in order to retain Briggs.

The Bible is the book of God, the greatest treasure of the Church. Its ministry are messengers to preach the Word of God, and to invite men to His presence and government. It is pharisaic to obstruct their way by any fences or stumbling-blocks whatever. It is a sin against the divine majesty to prop up divine authority by human authority, however great or extensive. The sun is shining in noontide splendor. Lest men, by looking at it, should quench the light of the great luminary, let us build walls so high that they cannot see the sun, and let us guard its light by reflecting mirrors. The grace of God is the true elixir of life to all mankind. Lest indiscriminate use of it should vitiate may not come to men directly, but only through a succession of safe hands. How absurd, you say. And yet this is the way men have been dealing with the Bible, shutting out the light of God, obstructing the life of God, and fencing in the authority of God.

(1.) Superstition. —The first barrier that obstructs the way to the Bible is superstition. We are accustomed to attach superstition to the Roman Catholic Mariolatry, Hagiolatry, and the use of images and pictures and other external things in worship. But superstition is no less superstition if it take the form of Bibliolatry. It may be all the worse if it concentrate itself on this one thing. But the Bible has no magical virtue in it, and there is no halo enclosing it. It will not stop a bullet any better than a mass-book. It will not keep off evil spirits any better than a cross. It will not guard a home from fire half so well as holy water. If you desire to know when and how you should take a journey, you will find a safer guide in an almanac or a daily newspaper. The Bible is no better than hydromancy or witchcraft, if we seek for divine guidance by the chance opening of the Book. The Bible, as a book, is paper, print, and binding,—nothing more. It is entitled to reverent handling for the sake of its holy contents, because it contains the divine word of redemption for man, and not for any other reason whatever.

(2.) Verbal Inspiration. —The second barrier, keeping men from the Bible, is the dogma of verbal inspiration. The Bible in use in our churches and homes is an English Bible. Upon the English Bible our religious life is founded. But the English Bible is a translation from Hebrew, Aramaic, and Greek originals. It is claimed for these originals by modern dogmaticians that they are verbally inspired. No such claim is found in the Bible itself, or in any of the creeds of Christendom. And yet it has been urged by the common opinion of modern evangelicalism that there can be no inspiration without verbal inspiration. But a study of the original languages of the Bible finds that they are languages admirably fitted by divine Providence for their purpose, but still, languages developing in the same way essentially as other human languages. The text of the Bible, in which these languages have been handed down, has shared the fortunes of other texts of other literature.

We find there are errors of transmission. There is nothing divine in the text,—in its letters, words, or clauses. There are those who hold that thought and language are as inseparable as body and soul. But language is rather the dress of thought. A master of many languages readily clothes the same thought in half a dozen different languages. The same thought in the Bible itself is dressed in different literary styles, and the thought of the one is as authoritative as the other. The divine authority is not in the style or in the words, but in the concept, and so the divine power of the Bible may be transferred into any human language. The divine authority contained in the Scriptures speaks as powerfully in English as in Greek, in Choctaw as in Aramaic, in Chinese as in Hebrew. We force our way through the language and the letter, the grammar and the style, to the inner substance of the thought, for there, if at all, we shall find God.

(3.) Authenticity. —The third barrier is the authenticity of the Scriptures. The only authenticity we are concerned about in seeking for the divine authority of the Scriptures is divine authenticity, and yet many theologians have insisted that we must prove that the Scriptures were written by or under the superintendence of prophets and apostles. Refusing to build on the authority of the living Church, they have sought an authority in the dead Church; abandoning the authority of institutional Christianity, they have sought a prop in floating traditions. These traditions assign authors to all the books of the Bible, and on the authority of these human authors, it is claimed that the Bible is divine. These theologians seem altogether unconscious of the circle of reasoning they are making. They prove the authority of the Bible from the authority of its authors. But what do we know of the authors apart from the Bible itself? Apart from the sacred writings,—Moses and David, Paul and Peter, would be no more to us than Confucius or Sakya Muni. They were leaders of men, but how do we know that they were called of God to speak divine words to us? The only way in which we can prove their authority is from their writings, and yet we are asked to accept the authority of the writings on the authority of these authors. When such fallacies are thrust in the faces of men seeking divine authority in the Bible, is it strange that so many turn away in disgust? It is just here that the Higher Criticism has proved such a terror in our times. Traditionalists are crying out that it is destroying the Bible, because it is exposing their fallacies and follies. It may be regarded as the certain result of the science of the Higher Criticism that Moses did not write the Pentateuch or Job; Ezra did not write the Chronicles, Ezra, or Nehemiah; Jeremiah did not write the Kings or Lamentations; David did not write the Psalter, but only a few of the Psalms; Solomon did not write the Song of Songs or Ecclesiastes, and only a portion of the Proverbs; Isaiah did not write half of the book that bears his name. The great mass of the Old Testament was written by authors whose names or connection with their writings are lost in oblivion. If this is destroying the Bible, the Bible is destroyed already. But who tells us that these traditional names were the authors of the Bible? The Bible itself? The creeds of the Church? Any reliable historical testimony? None of these! Pure, conjectural tradition! Nothing more! We are not prepared to build our faith for time and eternity upon such uncertainties as these. We desire to know whether the Bible came from God, and it is not of any great importance that we should know the names of those worthies chosen by God to mediate His revelation. It is possible that there is a providential purpose in the withholding of these names, in order that men might have no excuse for building on human authority, and so should be forced to resort to divine authority. It will ere long become clear to the Christian people that the Higher Criticism has rendered an inestimable service to this generation and to the generations to come. What has been destroyed has been the fallacies and conceits of theologians; the obstructions that have barred the way of literary men from the Bible. Higher Criticism has forced its way into the Bible itself and brought us face to face with the holy contents, so that we may see and know whether they are divine or not. Higher Criticism has not contravened any decision of any Christian council, or any creed of any Church, or any statement of Scripture itself. It has rather brought the long-neglected statement of the Westminster Confession into prominence: "The authority of the Holy Scripture, for which it ought to be believed and obeyed, dependeth not upon the testimony of any man or church, but wholly upon God (who is truth itself), the author thereof; and therefore it is to be received, because it is the word of God. . . ."

(4.) Inerrancy. —The fourth barrier set up by theologians to keep men away from the Bible is the dogma of the inerrancy of Scripture. This barrier confronts Historical Criticism. It is not a pleasant task to point out errors in the sacred Scriptures. Nevertheless Historical Criticism finds them, and we must meet the issue whether they destroy the authority of the Bible or not. It has been taught in recent years, and is still taught by some theologians, that one proved error destroys the authority of Scripture. I shall venture to affirm that, so far as I can see, there are errors in the Scriptures that no one has been able to explain away; and the theory that they were not in the original text is sheer assumption, upon which no mind can rest with certainty. If such errors destroy the authority of the Bible, it is already destroyed for historians. Men cannot shut their eyes to truth and fact. But on what authority do these theologians drive men from the Bible by this theory of inerrancy? The Bible itself nowhere makes this claim. The creeds of the Church nowhere sanction it. It is a ghost of modern evangelicalism to frighten children. The Bible has maintained its authority with the best scholars of our time, who with open minds have been willing to recognize any error that might be pointed out by Historical Criticism; for these errors are all in the circumstantials and not in the essentials; they are in the human setting, not in the precious jewel itself; they are found in that section of the Bible that theologians commonly account for from the providential superintendence of the mind of the author, as distinguished from divine revelation itself. It may be that this providential superintendence gives infallible guidance in every particular; and it may be that it differs but little, if at all, from the providential superintendence of the fathers and schoolmen and theologians of the Christian Church. It is not important for our purpose that we should decide this question. If we should abandon the whole field of providential superintendence so far as inspiration and divine authority are concerned and limit divine inspiration and authority to the essential contents of the Bible, to its religion, faith, and morals, we would still have ample room to seek divine authority where alone it is essential, or even important, in the teaching that guides our devotions, our thinking, and our conduct. Whether divine authority extends to the circumstantials of this divine teaching or not, it is unwise and it is unchristian to force men to accept the divine authority of the Bible or reject it, on the question of its inerrancy in the circumstantials and the details of every passage.

(5.) Violation of the Laws of Nature. —The fifth obstruction to the Bible has been thrown up in front of modern science. It is the claim that the miracles disturb, or violate, the laws of nature and the harmony of the universe; and so the miracles of the Bible have become to men of science sufficient evidence that the Bible is no more than other sacred books of other religions. But the theories of miracles that have been taught in the Christian Church are human inventions for which the Scriptures and the Church have no responsibility whatever.

The miracles of the Bible are confined to the life of Christ and His apostles and to the ministry of Moses, Elijah, and Elisha, with very few exceptions. The Biblical writers do not lay so much stress upon them as modern apologists. Moses and Jesus both warn their disciples against miracles that would be wrought in the interest of false prophets and false messiahs. The tests that they gave to discriminate the true from the false were not their marvellous character, their violation of the laws of nature, their suspension of the uniformity of law, or the comprehension of extraordinary laws with ordinary laws in higher laws—nothing of the kind; but the simple test whether they set forth the holy character and the gracious teaching of God and His Messiah. The miracles of the Bible are miracles of redemption. They exhibit the love of God and the compassion of the Messiah for the needy, the suffering and the lost. These divine features of Biblical miracles have been obscured by the apologists, who have unduly emphasized their material forms. The miracles of the Bible were the work of God either by direct divine energy or mediately through holy men, energized to perform them; but there is no reason why we should claim that they in any way violate the laws of nature or disturb its harmonies. We ought not to be disturbed by the efforts of scholars to explain them under the forms of divine law, in accordance with the order of nature. If it were possible to resolve all the miracles of the Old Testament into extraordinary acts of Divine Providence, using the forces and forms of nature in accordance with the laws of nature; and if we could explain all the miracles of

Jesus, His unique authority over man and over nature, from His use of mind cure, or hypnotism, or any other occult power,—still I claim that nothing essential would be lost from the miracles of the Bible; they would still remain the most wonderful exhibition of loving purpose and redemptive acts of God and of the tenderness and grace of the Messiah's heart. . . .

I rejoice at the age of Rationalism, with all its wonderful achievements in philosophy. I look upon it as preparing men to use their reasons in the last great age of the world. Criticism will go on with its destruction of errors, and its verification of truth and fact. The human mind will learn to know its powers and to use them. The forms of the reason, the conscience, the religious feeling, the aesthetic taste—all the highest energies of our nature, will exert themselves as never before. God will appear in their forms, and give an inward assurance and certainty greater than that given in former ages. These increased powers of the human soul will enable men to search those higher mysteries of Biblical Theology that no theologian has yet mastered, and those mysteries that are wrapt up in the institutions of the Church, to all who really know them. It is impossible that the Bible and the Church should ever exert their full power until the human Reason, trained and strained to the uttermost, rise to the heights of its energies and reach forth after God and His Christ with absolute devotion and self-renouncing love. Then we may expect on the heights of theological speculation, and from the peaks of Christian experience, that those profound doctrines that now divide Christendom by their antinomies will appear as the two sides of the same law, or the foci of a divine ellipse, which is itself but one of the curves in that conic section of God's dominion, in which, in loving wisdom, He has appointed the lines of our destiny.

Source: Charles Augustus Briggs, "The Authority of Holy Scripture: An Inaugural Address, Second Edition" (New York: Charles Scribner's Sons, 1891), 29–38, 65–66.

7

Emerging Understandings of Mission and Ministry at the Turn of the Twentieth Century

JOHN HENRY BARROWS

An Address at the World's Parliament of Religions, 1893

John Henry Barrows (1847–1902) was born in Michigan, studied at Olivet College, Yale Divinity School, Union Theological Seminary in New York, and Andover Theological Seminary, and ordained as a Congregationalist minister in 1875. Six years later, he accepted a call to become the pastor of First Presbyterian Church in Chicago. He rose to prominence as a gifted preacher and spoke at religious meetings across the United States. Barrows was also one of the chief organizers of the inaugural World's Parliament of Religions in Chicago. The Parliament, which took place over two weeks in 1893, was the first significant interreligious event that encompassed representatives of different world religions, such as Buddhism, Christianity, Confucianism, Hinduism, Islam, and Judaism, from Eastern and Western nations. Barrows resigned from his pastoral ministry to continue the interfaith work initiated at the Parliament and traveled around the world until he was elected president of Oberlin College in 1898. This excerpt of Barrows's opening address at the Parliament highlights the aspirations and impositions liberal Presbyterians held when engaging other world religions and foreign cultures.

Welcome, most welcome, O wise men of the East and of the West! May the star which has led you hither be like that luminary which guided the sages of old, and may this meeting by the inland sea of a new continent be blessed of heaven to the redemption of men from error and from sin and despair.

I wish you to understand that this great undertaking, which has aimed to house under one friendly roof in brotherly council the representatives of God's aspiring and believing children everywhere, has been conceived and carried on through strenuous and patient toil, with an unfaltering heart, with a devout faith in God, and with most signal and special evidences of his divine guidance and favor. . . .

I do not forget—I am glad to remember—that devout Jews, lovers of humanity, have cooperated with us in this Parliament; that these men and women representing the most wonderful of all races and the most persistent of all religions, who have come with good cause to appreciate the spiritual freedom of the United States of America—that these friends, some of whom are willing to call themselves Old Testament Christians, as I am willing to call myself a New Testament Jew, have zealously and powerfully cooperated in this good work. But the world calls us, and we call ourselves, a Christian people. We believe in the gospels and in Him whom they set forth as "the light of the world," and Christian America, which owes so much to Columbus and Luther, to the Pilgrim Fathers and to John Wesley, which owes so much to the Christian church and the Christian college and the Christian school, welcomes to-day the earnest disciples of other faiths and the men of all faiths who, from many lands, have flocked to this jubilee of civilization. . . .

It is perfectly evident to illuminated minds that we should cherish loving thoughts of all peoples and humane views of all the great and lasting religions, and that whoever would advance the cause of his own faith must first discover and gratefully acknowledge the truths contained in other faiths.

This Parliament is likely to prove a blessing to many Christians by marking the time when they shall cease thinking that the verities and virtues of other religions discredit the claims of Christianity or bar its progress. It is our desire and hope to broaden and purify the mental and spiritual vision of men. Believing that nations and faiths are separated in part by ignorance and prejudice, why shall not this Parliament help to remove the one and soften the other? Why should not Christians be glad to learn what God has wrought through Buddha and Zoroaster—through the sage of China, and the prophets of India and the prophet of Islam?

We are met together to-day as men, children of one God, sharers with all men in weakness and guilt and need, sharers with devout souls everywhere in aspiration and hope and longing. We are met as religious men, believing even here in this capital of material wonders, in the presence of an Exposition which displays the unparalleled marvels of steam and electricity, that there is a spiritual root to all human progress. We are met in a school of comparative theology, which I hope will prove more spiritual and ethical than theological. We are met, I believe, in the temper of love, determined to bury, at least for the time, our sharp hostilities, anxious to find out wherein we agree, eager to learn what constitutes the strength of other faiths and the weakness of our own. And we are met as conscientious and truth-seeking men, in a council where no one is asked to surrender or abate his individual convictions, and where, I will add, no one would be worthy of a place if he did.

We are met in great conference, men and women of different minds, where the speakers will not be ambitious for short-lived, verbal victories over others, where gentleness, courtesy, wisdom and moderation will prevail far more than heated argumentation. I am confident that you appreciate the peculiar limitations which constitute the peculiar glory of this assembly. We are not here as Baptists and Buddhists, Catholics and Confucians, Parsees and Presbyterians, Methodists and Moslems; we are here as members of a Parliament of Religions, over which flies no sectarian flag, which is to be stampeded by no sectarian war-cries, but where for the first time in a large council is lifted up the banner of love, fellowship, brotherhood. We all feel that there is a spirit which should always pervade these meetings, and if anyone should offend against this spirit let him not be rebuked publicly or personally; your silence will be a graver and severer rebuke. . . .

Welcome, one and all, thrice welcome to the world's first Parliament of Religions! Welcome to the men and women of Israel, the standing miracle of nations and religions! Welcome to the disciples of Prince Siddartha, the many millions who cherish in their heart Lord Buddha as the light of Asia! Welcome the high priest of the national religion of Japan! This city has every reason to be grateful to the enlightened ruler of the sunrise kingdom. Welcome to the men of India and all faiths! Welcome to all the disciples of Christ, and may God's blessing abide in our council and extend to the twelve hundred millions of human beings whose representatives I address at this moment.

It seems to me that the spirits of just and good men hover over this assembly. I believe that the spirit of Paul is here, the zealous missionary of Christ whose courtesy, wisdom and unbounded tact were manifest when we preached Jesus and the resurrection beneath the shadows of the Parthenon. I believe the spirit of the wise and humane Buddha is here, and of Socrates the searcher after truth, and of Jeremy Taylor and John Milton and Roger Williams and Lessing, the great apostles of toleration. I believe that the spirit of Abraham Lincoln, who sought for a church founded on love for God and man, is not far from us, and the spirit of Tennyson and Whittier and Phillips Brooks, who all looked forward to this Parliament as the realization of a noble idea.

Source: John Henry Barrows, ed. *The World's Parliament of Religions: An Illustrated and Popular Story of the World's First Parliament of Religions, Held in Chicago in Conjunction with the Columbian Exposition of 1893,* vol. 1 (Chicago: The Parliament Publishing Company, 1893), 73–75, 78–79.

LUCY CRAFT LANEY

"The Burden of the Educated Colored Woman," 1899

Lucy Craft Laney (1854–1933) was born to free black parents in Georgia and among the first graduates of the Higher Normal Department of Atlanta University (now Clark Atlanta University) in 1873. Her father, David Laney, was born a slave and purchased his freedom through his earnings from carpentry work. He moved from South Carolina to Georgia in 1836 and served as pastor of African American Presbyterian congregations in Macon and Savannah. When the Hopewell Presbytery ordained him in 1866, they instructed Laney to restrict his ministry to African Americans. Lucy Craft Laney taught in several African American public schools in Georgia for ten years before founding her own school in Augusta in 1883. Dissatisfied with the limited educational opportunities for African American students in her context, Laney designed a more diverse curriculum that integrated a wide range of liberal arts subjects with the vocational training offered in the other public schools. The enrollment at Laney's school, which initially met in one room of Christ Presbyterian Church, grew, and she traveled to Minneapolis to appeal for financial aid from the Presbyterian Church in the U.S.A. General Assembly in 1886. She addressed the General Assembly but only received prayer support. But there she met Francine E. H. Haines, an affluent white woman serving as secretary of the Women's Executive Committee of Home Missions, who became a strong benefactor for Laney's school. Laney used the funds to develop a school with over thirty teachers and approximately nine hundred students by 1912. She was also a pioneer who established the first kindergarten and the first nursing training program for African American women in Augusta. Her essay addresses the perils of racial injustice and the promises of education for African American children and youth.

If the educated colored woman has a burden,—and we believe she has—what is that burden? How can it be lightened, how may it be lifted? What it is can be readily seen perhaps better than told, for it constantly annoys to irritation; it bulges out as did the load of Bunyan's Christian— ignorance—with its inseparable companions, shame and crime and prejudice.

That our position may be more readily understood, let us refer to the past; and it will suffice for our purpose to begin with our coming to America in 1620, since prior to that time, we claim only heathenism. During the days of training in our first mission school—slavery—that which is the foundation of right training and good government, the basic rock of all true culture—the home, with its fire-side training, mother's moulding, woman's care, was not only neglected but utterly disregarded. There was no time in the institution for such teaching. We know that there were, even in the first days of that school, isolated cases of men and women of high moral character and great intellectual worth, as Phillis Wheatley, Sojourner Truth, and John Chavers, whose work and lives should have taught, or at least suggested to their instructors, the capabilities and possibilities of their dusky slave pupils. The progress and the struggles of these for noble things should have led their instructors to see how the souls and minds of this people then yearned for light—the real life. But alas! these dull teachers, like many modern pedagogues and school-keepers, failed to know their pupils—to find out their real needs, and hence had no cause to study methods of better and best development of the boys and girls under their care. What other result could come from such training or want of training than a conditioned race such as we now have?

. . . In the old institution there was no attention given to homes and to home-making. Homes were only places in which to sleep, father had neither responsibility nor authority; mother, neither cares nor duties. She wielded no gentle sway nor influence. The character of their children was a matter of no concern to them; surroundings were not considered. It is true, house cleaning was sometimes enforced as a protection to property, but this was done at stated times and when ordered. There is no greater enemy of the race than these untidy and filthy homes; they bring not only physical disease and death, but they are very incubators of sin; they bring intellectual and moral death. The burden of giving knowledge and bringing about the practice of the laws of hygiene among a people ignorant of the laws of nature and common decency, is not a slight one. But this, too, the intelligent women can and must help to carry.

The large number of young men in the state prison is by no means the least of the heavy burdens. It is true that many of these are unjustly sentenced; that longer terms of imprisonment are given Negroes than white persons for the same offences; it is true that white criminals by the help of attorneys, money, and influence, oftener escape the prison, thus keeping small the number of prisoners recorded, for figures never lie. . . . This fact remains, that many of our youth are in prison, that large numbers of our young men are serving out long terms of imprisonment, and this is a very sore burden. Five years ago while attending a Teacher's Institute at Thomasville, Ga., I saw working on the streets in the chain gang, with rude men and ruder women, with ignorant, wicked, almost naked men, criminals, guilty of all the sins named in the decalogue, a large number of boys from ten to fifteen years of age, and two young girls between the ages of twelve and sixteen. It is not necessary that prison statistics be quoted, for we know too well the story, and we feel most sensibly this burden, the weight of which will sink us unless it is at once made lighter and finally lifted.

Last, but not least, is the burden of prejudice, heavier in that it is imposed by the strong, those from whom help, not hindrance, should come. They are making the already heavy burden of their victims heavier to bear, and yet they are commanded by One who is even the Master of all: "Bear ye one another's burdens, and thus fulfil the law." This is met with and must be borne everywhere. In the South, in public conveyances, and at all points of race contact; in the North, in hotels, at the baptismal pool, in cemeteries; everywhere, in some shape or form, it is to be borne. No one suffers under the weight of this burden as the educated Negro woman does; and she must help to lift it.

Ignorance and immorality, if they are not the prime causes, have certainly intensified prejudice. The forces to lighten and finally to lift this and all of these burdens are true culture and character, linked with that most substantial coupler, cash. We said in the beginning that the past can serve no further purpose than to give us our present bearings. It is a condition that confronts us. With this we must deal, it is this we must change. The physician of today inquires into the history of his patient, but he has to do especially with diagnosis and cure. We know the history; we think a correct diagnosis has often been made—let us attempt a cure. We would prescribe: homes—better homes, clean homes, pure homes; schools—better schools; more culture; more thrift; and work in large doses; put the patient at once on this treatment and continue through life. Can woman do this work? She can; and she must do her part, and her part is by no means small.

Nothing in the present century is more noticeable than the tendency of women to enter every hopeful field of wage-earning and philanthropy, and attempt to reach a place in every intellectual arena. Women are by nature fitted for teaching very young children; their maternal instinct makes them patient and sympathetic with their charges. Negro women of culture, as kindergartners and primary teachers have a rare opportunity to lend a hand to the lifting of these burdens, for here they may instill lessons of cleanliness, truthfulness, loving kindness, love for nature, and love for Nature's God. Here they may daily start aright hundreds of our children; here, too, they may save years of time in the education of the child; and may save many lives from shame and crime by applying the law of prevention. In the kindergarten and primary school is the salvation of the race.

For children of both sexes from six to fifteen years of age, women are more successful as teachers than men. This fact is proven by their employment. Two-thirds of the teachers in the public schools of the United States are women. It is the glory of the United States that good order and peace are maintained not by a large, standing army of well trained soldiers, but by the sentiment of her citizens, sentiments implanted and nourished by her well trained army of four hundred thousand school teachers, two-thirds of whom are women.

The educated Negro woman, the woman of character and culture, is needed in the schoolroom not only in the kindergarten, and in the primary and the secondary school; but she is needed in high school, the academy, and the college. Only those of character and culture can do successful lifting, for she who would mould character must herself possess it. Not alone in the schoolroom can the intelligent woman lend a lifting hand, but as a public lecturer she may give advice, helpful suggestions, and important knowledge that will change a whole community and start its people on the upward way. . . . The refined and noble Negro woman may lift much with this lever. Women may also be most helpful as teachers of sewing schools and cooking classes, not simply in the public schools and private institutions, but in classes formed in neighborhoods that sorely need this knowledge. Through these classes girls who are not in school may be reached; and through them something may be done to better their homes, and inculcate habits of neatness and thrift. To bring the influence of the schools to bear upon these homes is the most needful thing of the hour. . . .

As a teacher in the Sabbath school, as a leader in young people's meetings and missionary societies, in women's societies and Bible classes our cultured women are needed to do a great and blessed work. Here they may cause many budding lives to open into eternal life. Froebel urged teachers and parents to see to the blending of the temporal and divine life when he said, "God created man in his own image; therefore man should create and bring forth like God." The young people are ready and anxiously await intelligent leadership in Christian work. The less fortunate women already assembled in churches, are ready for work. Work they do and work they will; that it may be effective work, they need the help and leadership of their more favored sisters. . . .

There is plenty of work for all who have the proper conception of the teacher's office, who know that all men are brothers, God being their common father. But the educated Negro woman must teach the "Black Babies;" she must come forward and inspire our men and boys to make a successful onslaught upon sin, shame, and crime. . . . Today not only the men on top call, but a needy race,—the whole world, calls loudly to the cultured Negro women to come to the rescue. Do they hear? Are they coming? Will they push?

Source: Lucy C. Laney, "The Burden of the Educated Colored Woman," in *Hampton Negro Conference Number III, July 1899* (Hampton, VA: Hampton Institute Press, 1899), 37–43.

7.1 Miss Lucy Craft Laney, n.d. (Presbyterian Historical Society, Philadelphia, PA)

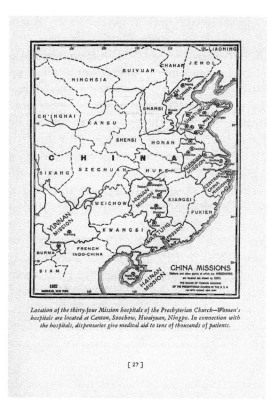

Location of the thirty-four Mission hospitals of the Presbyterian Church—Women's hospitals are located at Canton, Soochow, Hwaiyuan, Ningpo. In connection with the hospitals, dispensaries give medical aid to tens of thousands of patients.

[27]

7.2 Presbyterian Church in the U.S.A. Map of China Missions, 1932
(Presbyterian Historical Society, Philadelphia, PA)

ARTHUR JUDSON BROWN

The Foreign Missionary: An Incarnation of a World Movement, 1907

Arthur Judson Brown (1856–1963) was born in Massachusetts, graduated from Wabash College in 1880, and then enrolled at Lane Theological Seminary in Cincinnati, Ohio. Presbyterians founded Lane Seminary in 1829, and Lyman Beecher was the school's president from 1832 to 1850. In 1932, the seminary became part of McCormick Theological Seminary in Chicago. After graduating from Lane Seminary in 1883, Brown served as the pastor of Presbyterian congregations in Wisconsin, Illinois, and Oregon. Brown became a secretary of the Board of Foreign Missions of the Presbyterian Church in the U.S.A. in 1895 and worked as a board executive until his retirement at seventy-two years of age in 1929. Brown was also involved in ecumenical endeavors, helping to organize the Ecumenical Missionary Conference in New York in 1900 and the World Missionary Conference in Edinburgh in 1910. American Presbyterians across various ecclesial bodies were committed to foreign missions at the turn of the twentieth century. In 1915, the Presbyterian Church in the U.S.A. supported 1,276 foreign missionaries all over the world. The countries with the highest numbers of missionaries were China (429), India (195), and Korea (127). This excerpt from Brown's book, which prioritizes evangelism as the primary motivation for world mission, encapsulates Presbyterian approaches to and attitudes toward the persons they encountered in Africa, Asia, Latin America, and Oceania.

It is difficult to understand how those who profess to serve Christ can be indifferent to the most important work which Christ has committed to His followers, or how they can expect His blessing while they neglect His specific injunction! "If a man love Me, he will keep My words," said Christ (John 14:20), and the word is "go—preach." If we believe in Christ, we must believe in foreign missions.

Foreign missions, therefore, is not a side issue, the object of an occasional "collection"; it is the supreme duty of the Church, the main work of the Church. So the first disciples understood it, for they immediately went forth as missionaries. It is interesting to note that the word "apostle" is derived from a Greek word which means one sent forth, a messenger, and that the word "missionary" comes from an original which is simply the Latin equivalent of the Greek apostle. Therefore the modern apostle is the missionary, and while men at home are disputing over apostolic succession, the foreign missionaries, who are the real apostles of the present, are doing what their lineal predecessors did—"going away" from home to preach the gospel to the scattered nations of the earth. . . .

Christ did not say: "Teach all nations save those that you deem beneath you"; nor did He say: "Preach to every creature, except the Hindu and the Buddhist and Mohammedan, who have religions of their own." He made the scope of His command absolutely universal. . . . Christianity is not a life-boat sent out to a sinking ship to rescue a few passengers and let the rest go to the bottom. It will save all the passengers, unless they refuse to be saved, and it will save the ship. The Bible looks to a redeemed earth. Let us hope and pray and work for nothing short of that stupendous consummation. Limiting the grace of God, doubting its adequacy for all men, acting as if it were for America and not for Africa and the islands of the sea, are sins against the Holy Ghost.

These are and ever must remain the primary motives of the missionary enterprise. There are others, however, of a secondary character, which are influential with many people and which may be briefly enumerated:

(a) The Philanthropic Motive. —This is stirred by the consciousness of human brotherhood and the natural desire to relieve the appalling suffering and ignorance which prevail throughout the heathen world. Christ is the Great Physician now as of old. As we see the prevalence of disease and misery, the untended ulcers, the sightless eyes to which the surgeon's skill could bring light, the pain-racked limbs pierced with red-hot needles to kill the alleged demon that causes the suffering, and the fevered bodies that are made ten times worse by the superstitious and bungling methods of treatment, our sympathies are profoundly moved and we freely give and labour that such agony may be alleviated. Medical missions with their hospitals and dispensaries strongly appeal to this motive, as do also the educational missions with their teaching of the principles of better living. The gospel itself is sometimes preached and supported from this motive, for it is plain that the sufferings of men are diminished and the dignity and the worth of life increased by the application of the principles of Christianity to human society.

(b) The Intellectual Motive. —Missionaries have vastly increased the world's store of useful knowledge. They have opened vaguely known lands. They have probably done more than any other class of men to extend a knowledge of the earth's surface and its inhabitants. Geography and ethnology, entomology and zoology, botany and kindred sciences gratefully enroll the names of missionaries among their most successful explorers, and many thoughtful men appreciate this and give their sympathy to the cause which the missionaries represent.

(c) The Commercial Motive. —The missionary is the representative of a higher civilization. His teaching and his manner of living incidentally, but none the less really, create wants and introduce goods. He lights his house with a lamp, and straightaway thousands of the natives become dissatisfied with a bit of rag burning in a dish of vegetable oil. So foreign lamps are being used by millions of Chinese, Japanese, and Siamese and East Indians. The missionary marks time with a clock, and German, English and American firms suddenly find a new and apparently limitless market for their products. He rides a bicycle on his country tours, and the result is that today the bicycle is as common in the cities and many of the villages of Siam and Japan as it is in the United States. His wife makes her own and her children's dresses on a sewing-machine, and ten thousand curious Chinese, Japanese, and Laos are not satisfied till they have sewing-machines. And so the missionary opens new markets and extends trade. He has been one of the most effective agents of modern commerce, not because he intended to be, not because he reaped any personal profit from the goods that he introduced, but because of the inevitable tendencies that were set in motion by the residence of an enlightened family among unenlightened people. And this appeals to some minds as a motive of missionary interest. It begets hundreds of addresses on the reflex influence of foreign missions and it undoubtedly secures some support for the cause from those who might not be responsive to the other arguments.

(d) The Civilizing Motive. —This is closely allied to the preceding motives. In the ways that have been indicated and in others that might be specified, the missionary is "the advance agent of civilization." As the product of centuries of Christian civilization with all its customs and ideals, he appears in a rude village in Africa. He opposes slavery, polygamy, cannibalism and infanticide. He teaches the boys to be honest, sober and thrifty; the girls to be pure, intelligent and industrious. He induces the natives to cover their nakedness, to build houses and to till the soil. He inculcates and exemplifies the social and civic virtues. His own home and his treatment of his wife and daughters are object lessons in a community which had always treated woman as a slave. The inertia of long-established heathenism is hard to overcome, but slowly it yields to the new power and the beginning of civilized society gradually appears. Volumes might be filled with the testimonies of statesmen, travellers, military and naval officers to the value of missionary work from this viewpoint. Ask almost any public man to speak at a missionary meeting, and he will probably respond with an address in which he enlarges upon this aspect of missionary effort. . . .

(e) The Historical Motive. —With many people of the utilitarian type, the argument from results is the most decisive. They want to see that their money accomplishes something, to know that their investment is yielding some tangible return. They eagerly scan missionary reports to ascertain how many converts have been made, how many pupils are being taught, how many patients are being treated. To tell them of successes achieved is the surest method of inducing them to increase their gifts. Mission boards often find it difficult to sustain interest in apparently unproductive fields, but comparatively easy to arouse enthusiasm for fields in which converts are quickly made. The churches are eager and even impatient for results. Fortunately, in many lands results have been achieved on such a scale as to satisfy this demand. But in other lands not less important, weary years have had to be spent in preparing the soil and sowing the seed, and hardworking missionaries have been half disheartened by the insistent popular demand for accounts of baptisms before the harvest time has fairly come.

There is, apparently, a growing disposition to exalt this whole class of motives. The basis of the missionary appeal has noticeably changed within the last generation. Our humanitarian, commercial and practical age is more impressed by the physical and temporal, the actual and the utilitarian. The idea of saving men for the present world appeals more strongly than the idea of saving them for the next world, and missionary sermons and addresses give large emphasis to these motives. We need not and should not undervalue them. They are real. It is legitimate and Christian to seek the temporal welfare of our fellow men, to alleviate their distresses, to exalt woman and to purify society. It is, moreover, true and to the credit of the missionary enterprise that it widens the area of the world's useful knowledge, introduces the conveniences and necessities of Christian civilization, and promotes wealth and power, while it is certainly reasonable that those who toil should desire to see some results from their labour and be encouraged and incited to renewed diligence by the inspiring record of achievements.

But these motives are nevertheless distinctly secondary. They are effects of the missionary enterprise rather than causes of it, and the true Christian would still be obliged to give and pray and work for the evangelization of the world even if not one of these motives existed. . . .

There may be questions as to method, but no objection lies against the essential enterprise that does not lie with equal force against the fundamental truths of the Christian religion. Through all the tumult of theological strife, the one figure that is standing out more and more clearly and commandingly before men is the figure of the Son of Man, the Divine and Eternal Son of the Ever-Living God. In Him is the true unity of the race and around Him cluster its noblest activities. No matter how much Christians may differ as to other things, they will be more and more agreed as to the imperative duty and inspiring privilege of preaching Jesus Christ to the whole world.

Source: Arthur Judson Brown, *The Foreign Missionary: An Incarnation of a World Movement* (New York: Fleming H. Revell, 1907), 20–25, 28.

7.3 United Presbyterian Church of North America Women's General Missionary Society Board of Directors, 1889 (Presbyterian Historical Society, Philadelphia, PA)

7.4 Seal of the Woman's Board of Home Missions of the Presbyterian Church in the U.S.A., n.d. (Presbyterian Historical Society, Philadelphia, PA)

CHARLES STELZLE

The Call of the New Day to the Old Church, 1915

Charles Stelzle (1869–1941) was born and raised in an impoverished neighborhood on the Lower East Side of New York City. He began working in a sweatshop at eight years of age and became a machinist during his teens. His organizational skills were cultivated though his participation in the International Association of Machinists. But because he did not possess a formal education, Princeton Theological Seminary and Union Theological Seminary in New York rejected his application for admission. After studying at the Moody Bible Institute for two years and serving as a lay assistant for congregations in Minneapolis and New York City, he was ordained and installed as pastor of the Markham Memorial Church in St. Louis in 1900. Three years later, the Presbyterian Board of Home Missions commissioned Stelzle to a new ministry that would address urban poverty and labor conditions. In 1906, Stelzle became the superintendent of the Department of Church and Labor, which was the first denominational agency in the United States committed to implementing social gospel teachings. Stelzle's direct experiences with working class movements gave him penetrating insight into how Presbyterians could more effectively meet the religious and social needs of the urban poor. This excerpt reveals how Stelzle challenged and directed Presbyterians to new understandings of ministry that must work toward economic justice ("social salvation") alongside gospel proclamation ("individual salvation").

Throughout the entire Church there is a growing restlessness among its ministers, especially among the younger men who have been brought into touch with present-day problems. This restlessness is due less to theological considerations than it is to sociological conditions. Many of these ministers have resigned their charges to become leaders in social work, either local or national, while hundreds of strong men who might otherwise have entered the Christian ministry have become allied with broader sociological movements. Some of these men have taken this step after having experienced keen disappointment because they felt that they could not carry on their life's work through the Church. They have not lost faith in the Church as an institution, but they no longer have confidence in certain institutions of the Church.

The reactionary element which is now in control in the Church has sneeringly said that men of this type are "socialists" or "anarchists," and that the Church is better off without them. They said the same thing about Jesus two thousand years ago. It has often happened that men have been driven into radical positions because of the intolerance of this reactionary group, which, apparently, hasn't the remotest idea what socialism or anarchy mean.

But the real menace to the Church of Jesus Christ to-day is not the radical, whether his radicalism be theological or sociological. The real menace is the smug, self-satisfied person who is quite content with things as they are, and who wants no change of any kind which will compel him to readjust himself to meet the modern need.

Jesus Christ was a Revolutionist. He disregarded altogether the ecclesiastical aristocracy of His day and the social aristocracy of His period. Neither had they any use for Him. The latter scorned Him because of His poverty and lowly origin, while the former crucified Him because He dared tell the truth. His message was disturbing. It unsettled things. When His disciples preached it they were brought before the Sanhedrin upon the charge that they were proclaiming a doctrine which was turning the world upside down. These accusers were right. This Gospel which Jesus gave the world will continue to turn the world upside down until it is turned right side up.

To keep the Church clear-eyed and open-minded is a great necessity. Were the Church to insist that God has ceased to reveal Himself and His purposes for the world, it would at once mean stagnation. God is revealing Himself anew day by day, in His dealings with men and with nations. There are prophets of God in the twentieth century just as surely as there were in the first or the centuries preceding it. It cannot be that the Bible is a closed book, and that God has ceased to speak through men simply because a church council decreed it. God is writing new chapters every day. . . .

The appeal of the average evangelist is too narrow. If he were more sympathetic towards a larger, fuller gospel, which might be preached by those who stay after he goes, it would make the task less difficult, but usually the evangelist goes out of his way to ridicule and completely discredit a social message which would really make his own work more effective. He makes it almost impossible for the minister to discuss with the new converts the social aspects of the Gospel, with the result that many of the men and women who were enthusiastic for service when they came into the Church soon drift out, because they cannot all teach Sunday-school classes, or serve as deacons or elders, or remain inactive in Bible classes. If the evangelist cannot himself preach a full-orbed gospel, he should not object to others preaching the message that he neglects.

The Church is being severely tested in the cities. From 1900 to 1910 the cities of 25,000 and over increased fifty-five per cent. Can it be said that church membership in these cities also increased fifty-five per cent? By no juggling of figures can this increase be established. The tendency of the population to move towards the city is one of the marvels of modern times. One-tenth of the population in the United States lives in the three cities of New York, Philadelphia, and Chicago. One-half the population of New York state lives in New York City. One-fourth the population of this country lives upon one four-hundredth of the total land area. The cities of agricultural Canada are growing even more rapidly than those in the United States. The cities of Europe and Asia are also swelling their population figures in phenomenal fashion.

But as populations and problems in the city increase, the churches move steadily out. We contend that the Church has the only solvent of the social problem, but in a situation which demands its direct and immediate application, we seem to grow suddenly pessimistic regarding its actual effectiveness, or we quickly deny that our Gospel was intended to be used to cure modern social ills, except by indirection.

Without the slightest compunction we sell down-town church property, made valuable by reason of what the neighbors did through the payment of taxes and the general improvement of property, and appropriate it for the building of fine churches in other parts of the city. We seem to forget that the community has a stake in the church which never paid taxes and scarcely made an attempt to benefit the people in the neighborhood in any practical way. We fail to recall that a church is relieved from paying taxes on the principle that it is performing services to the state which is at least equivalent to the amount of the taxes it should pay. We talk about the problem of "the down-town church," whereas the emphasis should be placed upon the down-town problem of the Church. For the problems that face us here must not become the concern of a single church, nor of the churches which happen to be situated in the down-town district. They must be attacked by the entire Church. . . .

The industrial situation is becoming increasingly complex. The development of Socialism in every part of the world is full of significance. There are to-day about 30,000,000 Socialists in Europe and America. In 1888 the Socialists in the United States polled 2,000 votes. In 1914 they polled over a million votes. Socialism cannot be bluffed out or laughed out. The only way to eradicate Socialism is to wipe out the conditions which have given rise to Socialism. To many men and women Socialism has become a religion. They are ready to sacrifice as much for "the cause" as is the case with Christian missionaries. . . .

What should be the attitude of the church towards these movements? Let it be said with definiteness—the Church must not become the advocate of any particular social system. It is the business of the Church to preach the fundamental principles of Jesus, applying them to present-day problems in a perfectly fair but fearless fashion. But the Church must be broad enough to include all those whose lives are dominated by the Spirit of Jesus, and who are seeking to bring in the Kingdom of God, no matter what their economic beliefs may be. There are many men outside the Church to-day who would be within, had they not been made to feel uncomfortable because of their personal convictions regarding the economic situation and its permanent betterment. They are Christian men. There is no doubt of this, if one may judge them by their fruits and their spirit. And these must be the final test. . . .

The Church has been emphasizing the importance of individual salvation. It is time that we talked more about social salvation. We have been saying that we must "build up the Church." We ought to be more deeply interested in "building up the people." It is well to declare that the individual must be saved. But the individual can be saved only as he helps save society.

The time has come for a great new crusade in the name of the Church—a crusade which will have as its slogan these words: "He that saveth his life shall lose it, and he that loseth his life for My sake shall find it." Some of us have been thinking only of what we could get out of our religion. Jesus thought only of what He could put into it. This is the basis of His teaching. This is the philosophy of His religion. He came "not to be ministered unto, but to minister." He came to give His life a sacrifice for me. "As the Father hath sent Me, even so send I you," He told the disciples. This commission is also given to twentieth century Christians. The social message of Jesus means sweat and blood and sacrifice and suffering.

Institutional work is a very small part of the social gospel. Mere sociability is even less typical of what it implies. The social gospel includes economic justice. It means that underfed women and overworked men must get a square deal. It means that there shall be a more equitable distribution of profits in industry. It carries with it the spirit of true brotherhood and democracy.

The Church must not remain in ignorance of vile sanitary conditions and bad economic relationships. It must study these questions with an open mind and then strike at them with a closed fist. The Church must find out why so many people die of contagious but preventable disease. In former days men said that great epidemics were visitations of divine Providence. To-day they charge it up to the Board of Health. The Church cannot remain out of the fight for health and life. It is too late for the church to say that it has nothing to do with men's bodies—that it is its business simply to save men's souls. If the Church does not care for men's bodies, which it has seen, how can it care for men's souls[,] which it has not seen? If Jesus thought it worth His time to heal men's diseases, isn't it worth our while to prevent diseases? And doesn't this mean an interest in sanitation and pure food and good housing? One does not get very far along in the study of social problems before one runs upon a moral principle. Such work is religious. It isn't a thing separate and apart. It is vitally related to the deepest spiritual experience. . . . The deepest meaning of the cross finds its expression in unselfish devotion to all the needs of men.

This is the creed of the social worker. It must increasingly become that of the Church.

Source: Charles Stelzle, *The Call of the New Day to the Old Church* (New York: Fleming H. Revell, 1915), 14–17, 21–23, 31, 33, 44–46, 48.

J. GRESHAM MACHEN

"Liberalism or Christianity?," 1922

J. Gresham Machen (1881–1937) was born in Maryland and graduated from Johns Hopkins University in 1901 and Princeton Theological Seminary in 1905. After a year of graduate study in Germany, he returned to the United States to teach New Testament at his alma mater, Princeton Seminary. Machen emerged as a leading voice in the theological controversies that embroiled Presbyterians (and other Protestants) in the early twentieth century. He argued for the fundamentalist cause against modernists and moderates. In an essay published in The Princeton Theological Review, *Machen criticized liberal Protestants for espousing views antithetical to scriptural authority and charged them with betraying the essential tenets of the Christian faith in their promotion of social progressivism. In 1923, Machen elaborated on these points in his book* Christianity and Liberalism, *explaining that the theological disputes between fundamentalists and modernists did not represent competing Christian perspectives. Instead, Machen defined his liberal Protestant opponents as "un-Christian" and warned that the application of their principles constituted an attack on orthodoxy that would ultimately destroy the Presbyterian Church. His uncompromising stance toward modernists and moderates led to his resignation from Princeton Seminary in 1929 after the school adopted a more inclusive identity. He helped to found Westminster Theological Seminary in Philadelphia the same year and a new Presbyterian denomination (now the Orthodox Presbyterian Church) in 1936.*

The chief modern rival of Christianity is "liberalism." An examination of the teachings of liberalism will show that at every point the liberal movement is in opposition to the Christian message. . . .

In the Christian view of God as set forth in the Bible, there are many elements. But one attribute of God is absolutely fundamental in the Bible; one attribute is absolutely necessary in order to render intelligible all the rest. That attribute is the awful transcendence of God. From beginning to end the Bible is concerned to set forth the awful gulf that separates the creature from the Creator. It is true, indeed, that according to the Bible God is immanent in the world. Not a sparrow falls to the ground without Him. But he is immanent in the world not because He is identified with the world, but because He is the free Creator and Upholder of it. Between the creature and the Creator a great gulf is fixed.

In modern liberalism, on the other hand, this sharp distinction between God and the world is broken down, and the name "God" is applied to the mighty world process itself. We find ourselves in the midst of a mighty process, which manifests itself in the indefinitely small and in the indefinitely great—in the infinitesimal life which is revealed through the microscope and in the vast movements of the heavenly spheres. To this world-process, of which we ourselves form a part, we apply the dread name of "God." God, therefore, it is said in effect, is not a person distinct from ourselves; on the contrary our life is a part of His. Thus the Gospel story of the Incarnation, according to modern liberalism, is sometimes thought of as a symbol of the general truth that man at his best is one with God.

It is strange how such a representation can be regarded as anything new, for as a matter of fact, pantheism is a very ancient phenomenon. And modern liberalism, even when it is not consistently pantheistic, is at any rate pantheizing. It tends everywhere to break down the separateness between God and the world, and the sharp personal distinction between God and man. Even the sin of man on this view ought logically to be regarded as part of the life of God. Very different is the living and holy God of the Bible and of Christian faith.

Christianity differs from liberalism, then, in the first place, in its conception of God. But it also differs in its conception of man.

Modern liberalism has lost all sense of the gulf that separates the creature from the Creator; its doctrine of man follows naturally from its doctrine of God. But it is not only the creature limitations of mankind which are denied. Far more important is another difference. According to the Bible, man is a sinner under the just condemnation of God; according to modern liberalism, there is really no such thing as sin. At the very root of the modern liberal movement is the loss of the consciousness of sin.

The consciousness of sin was formerly the starting-point of all preaching; but to-day it is gone. Characteristic of the modern age, above all else, is a supreme confidence in human goodness; the religious literature of the day is redolent of that confidence. Get beneath the rough exterior of men, we are told, and we shall discover enough self-sacrifice to found upon it the hope of society; the world's evil, it is said, can be overcome with the world's good; no help is needed from outside the world. . . .

The fundamental fault of the modern Church is that she is busily engaged in an impossible task—she is busily engaged in calling the righteous to repentance. Modern preachers are trying to bring men into the Church without requiring them to relinquish their pride; they are trying to help men avoid the conviction of sin. The preacher gets up into the pulpit, opens the Bible, and addresses the congregation somewhat as follows: "You people are very good," he says; "you respond to every appeal that looks toward the welfare of the community. Now we have in the Bible—especially in the life of Jesus—something so good that we believe it is good enough even for you good people." Such is modern preaching. It is heard every Sunday in thousands of pulpits. But it is entirely futile. Even our Lord did not call the righteous to repentance, and probably we shall be no more successful than He.

Modern liberalism, then, has lost sight of the two great presuppositions of the Christian message—the living God, and the fact of sin. The liberal doctrine of God and the liberal doctrine of man are both diametrically opposite to the Christian view. But the divergence concerns not only the presuppositions of the message, but also the message itself.

According to the Christian view, the Bible contains an account of a revelation from God to man, which is found nowhere else. . . . The way was opened, according to the Bible, by an act of God, when, almost nineteen hundred years ago, outside the walls of Jerusalem, the eternal Son was offered as a sacrifice for the sins of men. To that one great event the whole Old Testament looks forward, and in that one event the whole of the New Testament finds its centre and core. Salvation then, according to the Bible, is not something that was discovered, but something that happened. Hence appears the uniqueness of the Bible. All the ideas of Christianity might be discovered in some other religion, yet there would be in that other religion no Christianity. For Christianity depends, not upon a complex of ideas, but upon the narration of an event. Without that event, the world, in the Christian view, is altogether dark, and humanity is lost under the guilt of sin. There can be no salvation by the discovery of eternal truth, for eternal truth brings naught but despair, because of sin. But a new face has been put upon life by the blessed thing that God did when he offered up his only begotten Son. . . .

Very different is the view of modern liberalism. The modern liberal rejects the unique authority of the Bible. But what is substituted for the Christian doctrine? What is the liberal view as to the seat of authority in religion?

The impression is sometimes produced that the modern liberal substitutes for the authority of the Bible the authority of Christ. He cannot accept, he says, what he regards as the perverse moral teaching of the Old Testament or the sophistical arguments of Paul. But he regards himself as being the true Christian because, rejecting the rest of the Bible, he depends upon Jesus alone. . . .

As a matter of fact, however, the modern liberal does not hold fast even to the authority of Jesus. Certainly he does not accept the words of Jesus as they are recorded in the Gospels. For among the recorded words of Jesus are to be found just those things which are most abhorrent to the modern liberal Church, and in His recorded words Jesus also points forward to the fuller revelation which was afterwards to be given through His apostles. Evidently, therefore, those words of Jesus which are to be regarded as authoritative by modern liberalism must first be selected from the mass of the recorded words by a critical process. The critical process is certainly very difficult, and the suspicion often arises that the critic is retaining as genuine words of the historical Jesus only those words which conform to his own preconceived ideas. But even after the sifting process has been completed, the liberal scholar is still unable to accept as authoritative all the sayings of Jesus; he must finally admit that even the historical Jesus said some things that are untrue. . . .

The truth is that the life-purpose of Jesus discovered by modern liberalism is not the life-purpose of the real Jesus, but merely represents those elements in the teaching of Jesus—isolated and misinterpreted—which happen to agree with the modern program. It is not Jesus, then, who is the real authority, but the modern principle by which the selection within Jesus' recorded teaching has been made. Certain isolated ethical principles of the Sermon on the Mount are accepted, not at all because they are teachings of Jesus, but because they agree with modern ideas. . . .

Such is the present situation. It is a great mistake to suppose that liberalism is merely a heresy—merely a divergence at isolated points from true Christian teaching. On the contrary it proceeds from a totally different root. It differs from Christianity in its view of God, of man, of the seat of authority, of Christ, and of the way of salvation. Christianity is being attacked from within by a movement which is anti-Christian to the core.

What is the duty of laymen at such a time? What is the duty of the ruling elders in the Presbyterian Church?

. . . Laymen, as well as ministers, should return, in these trying days, with new earnestness, to the study of the Word of God. If the Word of God be heeded, the Christian battle will be fought both with love and with faithfulness. Party passions and personal animosities will be put away, but on the other hand, even angels from heaven will be rejected if they preach a gospel different from the blessed gospel of the Cross. Every man must decide upon which side he will stand. God grant that we may decide aright! God grant that instead of directing men, as modern liberalism does, to the village of Morality, where dwells a gentleman whose name is Legality, said to have skill in easing men of their burdens, we may direct them on the old, old way, through the little wicket gate, to a place somewhat ascending, where they shall really see the Cross, that when at that sight the burden of their sin has fallen away, they may press on past the Hill Difficulty, past the Valley of Humiliation and the Valley of the Shadow of Death, past the allurements of Vanity Fair, up over the Delectable Mountains, and so, at length, across the last river, into the City of God.

Source: J. Gresham Machen, "Liberalism or Christianity?," in *The Princeton Theological Review*, vol. 20, no. 1 (January 1922), 97–100, 103–7, 114, 117.

8

Denominational Reunions, Divisions, and Differing Ecclesial Emphases

"In Unity—For Mission: A Message to All Congregations from the Uniting General Assembly of The United Presbyterian Church in the United States of America," 1958*

In the early 1950s, representatives from the different Presbyterian denominations began plans for reconciliation and reunion. Two northern denominations, the United Presbyterian Church of North America, consisting largely of members in western Pennsylvania and Ohio with Scots and Scots-Irish roots, and the Presbyterian Church in the U.S.A., a larger and more diverse group with members across the country (except from the southern states), agreed to merge into The United Presbyterian Church in the United States of America (UPCUSA) in 1958. Although some progressives in the southern body, the Presbyterian Church U.S. (also known as the Presbyterian Church in the United States), advocated for union, conservatives led a vote against the merger in 1954 over concerns about northern actions supporting desegregation and ordaining women as clergy. When southern Presbyterians revived merger plans in 1969, conservatives split to form the Presbyterian Church in America (PCA) in 1973. The following two documents are the introductory messages from the reuniting General Assembly of the UPCUSA in Pittsburgh, Pennsylvania, and the first General Assembly of the PCA (initially called the National Presbyterian Church) in Birmingham, Alabama. They aptly capture the enduring ecclesial unity of Presbyterians on some crucial elements and the escalating tensions over differing positions on other significant matters during the second half of the twentieth century.

*Scripture quotations in this article are from the Revised Standard Version of the Bible and are copyright © 1946, 1952 by the Division of Christian Education of the National Council of the Churches of Christ in the U.S.A.

I

The Church Is God's Servant.

By the gracious providence of Almighty God, we who formerly were two Churches of the same tradition are no longer two but one. We give heartfelt thanks to God for those who have prayed and labored for this day, many of whom, having died, saw its fulfillment only from afar. We are strengthened by the contemplation of our heritage, but God forbid that reflection upon it should engender false pride or create complacency. It is all too easy for the Church to become a venerated but sterile institution in the society in which it exists. Neither the Church itself nor any of its achievements, whether its structure or its doctrine, its unity or its work, can ever be mere ends in themselves; all are but means to serve the ongoing purpose and redemptive love of God.

We look forward, in faith, to the unfolding of God's purpose for our new Church. As The United Presbyterian Church in the United States of America, the largest body in the world-wide Presbyterian family, we must understand our Reformed tradition and relate it to our day.

The Church is truly the Church when it serves God, when God's sons and daughters joyously become their Father's servants. God gave a mission to his people: "You are my servant, Israel, in whom I will be glorified . . . I will give you as a light to the nations, that my salvation may reach to the end of the earth." The Christian Church is the new Israel, God's new servant, the fellowship of those for whom Jesus Christ is Lord. The Church exists to glorify God, to make Him manifest to men, to reflect the splendor of His nature, and to serve His eternal purpose in Jesus Christ, who is the sole Head of the Church.

To the Church united in this purpose, the Holy Spirit gives power. Unity is Christian unity only when all the members of the Body of Christ are one in their obedience to Him. As Christians we are fellow workers with God. Let us, therefore, in comradeship with one another, be heralds of God's glory and so fulfill the church's mission for our time.

II

It Is the Church's Mission to Radiate the Light of God

The Church is called to radiate the light of God in every society and in every age. In this day when Christian ideas are widely rejected or distorted, the Church is called to point our generation to the fountain of Truth and Goodness, to God Himself as He is revealed through Holy Scripture in Jesus Christ the Word made flesh. In the light of Jesus Christ, and only in that light, does man's thought become luminous and relevant.

Our Lord Jesus Christ lays upon us an inescapable obligation to "discern this time," to examine the life of man in the light of God. Like our ancestors, we must zealously search for truth, truth about God and the world, truth about man and his destiny, truth about the Church and its responsibility toward the nation and toward mankind.

In our day, revolutionary unrest is rampant. Nations are tragically divided. This is a time of judgment. Mankind journeys through dread. The world is in the darkness of nuclear despair, but Christians need not lose their calm. We believe God. He reigns. He is sovereign over men and nations, over all the forces of nature and of history. God and His righteousness, not the falsehood and villainy of men, shall have the final word.

We must discern the Word of God in the Bible. God's wrath falls upon nations whose rulers willfully and openly deny Him, but He may use them to execute His purpose and chastise His own people. Against Israel, He used the imperial power of Assyria as the rod of His anger and the staff of His fury. He may in our time use Communist or other godless powers to chastise privileged, nominally Christian nations who forget God and ignore their indebtedness to Him. Our nation, favored by God, stands in the same jeopardy as ancient Israel. Are we subtly yet surely dethroning God in our national life? Are we patronizing God and ceasing to serve Him? Are we trying to fit the Almighty into our own little schemes, instead of fitting ourselves into His great plan for the world?

A nation, as well as an individual, can lose its soul. We Americans are in danger of rejecting the heritage which made us what we are. With penitence let us confess that as a people we are becoming less interested in righteousness than in national security and international superiority. Relations between us and other peoples are no longer primarily determined by moral principles or by considerations of human need. The ancient words justice and righteousness, emptied of their true content, are used as weapons in international politics. Self-interest is becoming the great absolute. Even baptizing self-interest with the adjective enlightened does not make it Christian.

Our fathers' concept of freedom is also being debased. For them, freedom flowed from obedience to God. We must be deeply disturbed by the contemporary myth of the free world. This nation counts among its allies some nations which are in no sense free. By our actions we proclaim to the world that lands where human freedom is utterly dead can qualify for membership in the free world simply by supplying military bases or strategic commodities. This kind of international hypocrisy should be abhorrent to Christians, and in its presence the Church dare not keep silent. In the effort to achieve a posture of power, our nation must not ignore the suppression of God-given human rights in any land. We call, therefore, for a reappraisal of the current concepts of freedom and the free world.

Today, as always, "the fear of the Lord is the beginning of wisdom." Wisdom stems from a spiritual relationship between God and man which, in turn, transforms relations among men. Wisdom's supreme expression is a ministry of reconciliation, the bringing of estranged and alienated people to God through the Gospel. Thus a human society becomes possible in which the reality of brotherhood prevails between nation and nation, between class and class, between race and race.

Wisdom teaches that in the pursuit of human understanding there can be no substitute for personal encounter. Estranged people must meet one another; they must talk with one another and strive to understand one another. They must probe the causes of their alienation. They must overcome enmity and distrust by the sharing of goods, knowledge, and human resources for the welfare of mankind. When men who profess the Christian religion make no adequate provision for a face-to-face encounter with their enemies, they betray the religion which they profess. Yet in human tensions today, nations continue to talk at one another and about one another, instead of talking with one another. This is one of our greatest perils. When men talk solely in declamatory tones, they only add clamor to disorder.

Neither is there any substitute for forgiveness. Civilization at its best stands in need of divine forgiveness. While some nations are greater sinners than others, there is no righteous nation upon earth. We as a people should, therefore, be ready to admit our faults to other nations as a prelude to seeking a basis of understanding. Contrition for our own sins will do more to create an atmosphere conducive to peace than press releases denouncing the sins of others.

Two things we must remember. First, all persons and peoples are loved by God and live under His sovereign governance. Second, the command "Love your enemies" is our Lord's command. We must explore the implications of this command for international relations. Statesmen may be completely sincere, perfectly well-intentioned, eminently patriotic, but if their policies have no place for the command to love one's enemies, the consequences of those policies will be disastrous.

Another tragic error is the deification of scientific knowledge. The theologian and the scientist agree that man and the universe are to be understood as fully and as accurately as possible, but the irrational cry for intensified education in technological science arises from man's failure to understand man. To put our faith in science, not as a partner in the search for truth but as a fabricator of weapons, is to worship the graven image of technology. The glorification of technology can make men, even churchmen, skilled barbarians; it cannot produce spiritually creative men and women. Technology, enshrined, creates both physical power and spiritual terror. It can only accelerate the race toward disaster.

Scientists dedicated to the search for truth are needed. But the greater need is for enlightened men and women, including scientists, educated in human relations and the social sciences, in the arts of understanding, and communicating with, peoples of all nations and cultures. With God's help such men and women can do much to terminate this present peril.

To accept the inevitability of increasing hostility between Communism and the West reveals our loss of faith in God and in the power of truth and goodness, as well as our ignorance of the sobering lessons of history. We need instead, to ask some serious questions. What gave birth to Communism? What are the things that make its progress possible and its peril real in many parts of the world? Communism can be met in a positive way only by the promotion of truth and the practice of goodness. People will not be convinced that we are interested in them for their own sakes, unless, indeed, we are. Selfish ends do not foster friendship among men or nations, nor can friendship be faked or purchased.

It is imperative that the voice of history echoing the wisdom of the Christian ages be heard. A false and baneful doctrine is being persistently proclaimed, namely, that in the present world situation there are only two alternatives, either victory over the new Communistic powers, or the annihilation of the traditional democracies. There was a time when Christians and Moslems fervently held that one group or the other had to be totally vanquished by force. But eventually they learned to live in the same world. At a later period in history, Protestants and Roman Catholics thought that one side or the other had to be wiped out. But the time came when they, too, learned to co[e]xist as they do today. In neither situation, however, does coexistence imply the compromise of Christian convictions and the abatement of evangelistic zeal. Persuasion rather than force is the true means of conversion. So, also, while still striving for freedom of all men, we today must co[e]xist with Communist nations. In this nuclear age, the only alternative to coexistence is coextinction.

III

It Is the Church's Mission to Mediate the Love of God.

The supreme mission of the Church is redemptive in character. We are loyal to the Church's redemptive mission when we proclaim to all men the Gospel of Christ and when we love all men with the affection of Christ.

Christian truth is personal truth. It centers in a Person, Jesus Christ. It expresses itself in the lives of persons who become Christ's followers, whose lives bear His likeness, and who live under His leadership in church and society. The Lordship of Christ in the Church and in the world begins in individual persons.

The Lordship of Christ illuminates the contemporary concern: "What is the purpose and meaning of life?" This question is identical with our historic question: "What is the chief end of man?" The answer we learned in our childhood has even more relevance today: "Man's chief end is to glorify God, and to enjoy Him for ever."

Man is truly man when in his personality he displays the character of God, when in his behavior he serves the purpose of God, and when in his life he enjoys communion with God. True human freedom is born when a man becomes God's captive. Saints in the Biblical sense are God's men and women. They are sons and daughters of God who, with joyous abandon and a sense of privilege, make themselves His loyal and devoted servants. The Church exists to bring such men and women into being and to mobilize them for Christ's missionary service.

For the first time in history there exists a world Christian community. This community is, in great part, the result of Christian missionary effort. In every land today there are groups of Christians who gather together to worship God in the name of Jesus Christ. In the comradeship of Churches that are the fruit of a century's missionary devotion, and in cooperation with older Churches, in this and other lands, we are pledged to mediate the love of God, by word and deed, to the uttermost bounds of human habitation.

IV

The Church's Mission Is on the Frontier

To radiate the light of God and mediate the love of God, the Church must be a pilgrim Church. God summons us to pilgrimage, to life on the missionary road. We must journey not only along desert paths and jungle trails, but in the teeming alleys of our cities. God commands us to be missionaries not only in the community where we live, not alone in the national environment of our home church, but to the ends of the earth. The Church's place is the frontier. But for the Church in the discharge of its God-given mission, the frontier is more than a location. It is wherever any sector of thought or life has to be occupied in the name of Jesus Christ.

Only as church members become Christ's missionaries in their several vocations, in government and diplomacy, in industry and commerce, in the home and in the classroom, in the clinic and on the farm, will men perceive that Christ is the Way, the Truth, and the Life.

The world is no better than it is primarily because we Christians are no better than we are, and for the same reason the Church is no better than it is. We have not abandoned ourselves to God's will. We have not assumed a full measure of responsibility for the world in which we must continue to live. We are haunted by our Lord's own question, "What do ye more than others?" Our Lord calls the Church to unqualified obedience. The measure of our obedience is the measure of our power. Let the Church demonstrate by the consistency of its life the validity of its claims.

This we call upon our churches to do. Every congregation should be a reflection of the holy, catholic Church. "There is neither Jew nor Greek, there is neither slave nor free, there is neither male nor female; for you are all one in Christ Jesus." In Christ racial, cultural, social, economic, and sex distinctions become meaningless and are erased. As the Church is commissioned to make disciples of all nations, so each congregation is called upon to evangelize, and to welcome into its membership, all the unchurched people of its community without regard to their racial, economic, or cultural background and condition. To fail at this point is to deny the efficacy of the Atonement in our own lives and to betray the very Gospel we seek to proclaim.

Christ has called us friends. "You are my friends," he said, "if you do what I command you." Abraham, the Biblical example of a friend of God, showed his friendship by his obedience. At God's command, he embarked on an adventure into the unknown. Let us today dedicate ourselves as a Church to a new Abrahamic adventure. Let us be so constrained by the love of Christ that we shall show our love for Him by becoming channels of His love to others.

Let us, therefore, implore our Father in Heaven for a fresh outpouring of His Spirit upon us. We pray that this union will mark the beginning of that spiritual awakening which our Church, and all the Churches, and the whole human family, so sorely need in this hour.

Jesus promised his followers that he would be with them in holy companionship to the end of the road, to the close of the age. As we gird ourselves for our pilgrimage, our courage is in His pledge. And, as we journey, our strength is in the imperishable hope that the kingdoms of this world shall become the Kingdom of our Lord and of his Christ.

The grace of our Lord Jesus Christ be with us all.

Source: "In Unity—For Mission: A Message to all congregations from the Uniting General Assembly of The United Presbyterian Church in the United States of America," in Minutes of the General Assembly of The United Presbyterian Church in the

8.1 Presbyterians at Pittsburgh, 1958: Moderators Harold R. Martin and Robert N. Montgomery shake hands during march (photograph by Arthur M. Byers, image from Presbyterian Historical Society, Philadelphia, PA)

8.2 Presbyterians at Pittsburgh, 1958: Dr. Charles Leber and Dr. Martin Luther King, Jr. at the Overseas Breakfast (photograph by Arthur M. Byers, image from Presbyterian Historical Society, Philadelphia, PA)

United States of America, Part I: Journals and Supplement, Pittsburgh, Pennsylvania, May 27–June 4, 1958 (Philadelphia: Office of the General Assembly, 1958), 155–60.

"A Message to All Churches of Jesus Christ throughout the World from the General Assembly of the National Presbyterian Church," 1973*

Greeting: Grace, Mercy and Peace be multiplied upon you!

As the National Presbyterian Church takes her place among the family of Churches of the Lord Jesus Christ, we take this opportunity to address all Churches by way of a testimony.

We gather as a true branch of the Church of our Lord Jesus Christ. We affirm our allegiance to Him as the sole Head of the Church and the sole Law-giver in Zion. We remember that "the gates of hell shall not prevail" against His Church.

The constituency of this new denomination for the most part have separated themselves from the Presbyterian Church in the United States. The decision to separate has come only after long years of struggle and heartache on the part of many of us to return the Church to purity of faith and practice. Principle and conviction entered into that decision, reached only after much soul searching and earnest prayer. We have reluctantly accepted the necessity of separation, deeming loyalty to Christ to take precedence over relationship to any earthly institution, even to a visible branch of the Church of Christ.

In much prayer and with great sorrow and mourning we have concluded that to practice the principle of purity in the Church visible, we must pay the price of separation. We desire to elaborate upon those principles and convictions that have brought us to that decision.

We are convinced that our former denomination as a whole, and in its leadership, no longer holds those views regarding the nature and mission of the Church, which we accept as both true and essential. When we judged that there was no human remedy for this situation, and in the absence of evidence that God would intervene, we were compelled to raise a new banner bearing the historic, Scriptural faith of our forefathers.

First, we declare the basis of the authority for the Church. According to the Christian faith, the Bible is the Word of God written and carries the authority of its divine Author. We believe the Bible itself asserts that it has been given by inspiration, or, more literally, has been "God-breathed" (II Timothy 3:16). "No prophecy ever came by the will of man; but men spake from God, being moved by the Holy Spirit" (II Peter 1:21). We declare, therefore, that the

*Scripture quotations in this article are from the American Standard Version.

Bible is the very Word of God, so inspired in the whole and in all its parts, as in the original autographs, to be the inerrant Word of God. It is, therefore, the only infallible and all-sufficient rule of faith and practice.

This was the position of the founding fathers of the Presbyterian Church in the United States. We affirm with them in their "Address to All Churches" the application of this principle to the Church and her mission:

Let it be distinctly borne in mind that the only rule of judgment is the written Word of God. The Church knows nothing of the intuitions of reason or the deductions of philosophy, except those reproduced in the Sacred Canon. She has a positive constitution in the Holy Scriptures, and has no right to utter a single syllable upon any subject except as the Lord puts words in her mouth. She is founded, in other words, upon express revelation. Her creed is an authoritative testimony of God, and not speculation, and what she proclaims she must proclaim with the infallible certitude of faith, and not with the hesitating assent of an opinion.

We have called ourselves "Continuing" Presbyterians because we seek to continue the faith of the founding fathers of that Church. Deviations in doctrine and practice from historic Presbyterian positions as evident in the Presbyterian Church in the United States, result from accepting other sources of authority, and from making them coordinate or superior to the divine Word. A diluted theology, a gospel tending towards humanism, an unbiblical view of marriage and divorce, the ordination of women, financing of abortion on socio-economic grounds, and numerous other non-Biblical positions are all traceable to a different view of Scripture from that we hold and that which was held by the Southern Presbyterian forefathers.

Change in the Presbyterian Church in the United States came as a gradual thing, and its ascendancy in the denomination, over a long period of time. We confess that it should not have been permitted. Views and practices that undermine and supplant the system of doctrine or polity of a confessional Church ought never to be tolerated. A Church that will not exercise discipline will not long be able to maintain pure doctrine or godly practice.

When a denomination will not exercise discipline and its courts have become heterodox or disposed to tolerate error, the minority finds itself in the anomalous position of being submissive to a tolerant and erring majority. In order to proclaim the truth and to practice the discipline which they believe obedience to Christ requires, it then becomes necessary for them to separate. This is the exercise of discipline in reverse. It is how we view our separation.

Some of our brethren have felt that the present circumstances do not yet call for such a remedy. They remain in the Presbyterian Church in the United States. We trust they will continue to contend for the faith, though our departure makes their position more difficult. We express to them our hope that

God will bless their efforts, and that there may come a genuine spiritual awakening in the Presbyterian Church in the United States.

We trust that our departure may cause those who control and direct the programs and policies of the Presbyterian Church in the United States to reexamine their own position in the light of the Word. Our prayer is that God may use this movement to promote spiritual awakening, not only in the new Church, but also in that from which we have separated. If in the providence of God, such were to occur, we would gladly acknowledge that the grounds for separation and division would have to be reassessed.

We declare also that we believe the system of doctrine found in God's Word to be the system known as the Reformed Faith. We are committed without reservation to the Reformed Faith as set forth in the Westminster Confession and Catechisms. It is our conviction that the Reformed faith is not sectarian, but an authentic and valid expression of Biblical Christianity. We believe it is our duty to seek fellowship and unity with all who profess this faith. We particularly wish to labor with other Christians committed to this theology.

We further renew and reaffirm our understanding of the nature and mission of the Church. We have declared that Christ is King and only Law-giver in Zion. He has established the Church. His Church is a spiritual reality. As such it is made up of all the elect from all ages. This spiritual entity is manifested visibly upon the earth.

The Church visible is found wherever there are those who profess the true faith together with their children. As an assembly of those who do so profess this faith, we have established this denomination in the belief that it is a true branch of the Christian Church.

We believe the Church in its visible aspect is still essentially a spiritual organism. As such, its authority, motivation and power come from Christ, the Head, who is seated at the right hand of God. He has given us His rulebook for the Church, namely, the Word of God written. We understand the task of the Church to be primarily declarative and ministerial, not legislative or magisterial. It is our duty to set forth what He has given us in His Word and not to devise our own message or legislate our own laws.

We declare that the ultimate purpose of the Church is to glorify God. We believe this includes giving top priority to Christ's Great Commission. We reaffirm the substance of the position taken by the founding fathers of our former Church regarding the mission of the Church:

We desire distinctly and deliberately to inscribe on our Church's banner, as she now unfurls it to the world, in immediate subservience to the authority of our Lord as Head and King of the Church His last command: "Go ye therefore, and make disciples of all nations, baptizing them into the name of the Father, and of the Son, and of the Holy Spirit: teaching them to observe all things whatsoever I commanded you, and lo, I am with you always, even unto the end of the world." We regard this as the great end of our organization, and obedience to it, as the indispensable condition of our Lord's promised presence. It is the one great comprehensive objective, a proper conception of whose grandeur and magnitude is the only thing which, under the constraining love of Christ, can ever sufficiently arouse our energies and develop our resources so as to cause us to carry on with that vigor and efficiency, which true loyalty to our Lord demands, those other agencies necessary to our internal growth and prosperity at home."

As a Church, we consciously seek to return to the historic Presbyterian view of Church government. We reaffirm in the words of that earlier "Address to All Churches" the following:

"The only thing that will be at all peculiar to us is the manner in which we shall attempt to discharge our duty. In almost every department of labor, except the pastoral care of congregations, it has been usual for the Church to resort to societies more or less closely connected with itself, and yet logically and really distinct. It is our purpose to rely upon the regular organs of our government, and executive agencies directly and immediately responsible to them. We wish to make the Church, not merely a superintendent, but an agent. We wish to develop the idea that the congregation of believers, as visibly organized is the very society or corporation which is divinely called to do the work of the Lord. We shall, therefore, endeavor to do what has never been adequately done—bring out the energies of our Presbyterian system of government. From the session to the Assembly, we shall strive to enlist all our courts, as courts, in every department of Christian effort. We are not ashamed to confess that we are intensely Presbyterian. We embrace all other denominations in the arms of Christian fellowship and love, but our own scheme of government we humbly believe to be according to the pattern shown in the Mount, and, by God's grace, we propose to put its efficiency to the test."

As this new member of the family of Churches of the Lord Jesus Christ comes into being, we necessarily profess the Biblical doctrine of the unity of all who are in Christ. We know that what happens in one portion of His Church affects all of the Body of Christ. We covet the prayers of all Christians that we may witness and serve responsibly. We desire to pursue peace and charity with love towards fellow Christians throughout the world.

To the Presbyterian Church in the United States, in particular, we express our continued love and concern. You are our spiritual mother, in your arms we were nurtured, under your ordinances we were baptized, in your courts we were ordained to serve our Lord and King, and to your visible organization we thought we had committed our lives. We sever these ties only with deepest regret and sorrow. We hope that our going may in some way recall you to that historic witness which we cherish as our common heritage.

We greet all believers in an affirmation of the bonds of Christian brotherhood. We invite into ecclesiastical fellowship all who maintain our principles of faith and order.

We now commend ourselves to God and the Word of His power. We devoutly pray that the Church catholic may be filled afresh with the Holy Spirit, and that she may speedily be stirred up to take no rest until the Lord accomplishes His Kingdom, making Zion a praise in the whole earth.

Source: "A Message to All Churches of Jesus Christ throughout the World from the General Assembly of the National Presbyterian Church," in Minutes of the First General Assembly of the Presbyterian Church in America, December 7, 1973.

EUGENE CARSON BLAKE AND MARTIN NIEMÖLLER

"The Open Door," 1965*

Eugene Carson Blake (1906–1985) and Martin Niemöller (1892–1984) met in 1965 to deliver a series of five sermon-dialogues at the (Episcopal) Church of the Holy Trinity in Philadelphia. For five consecutive days, the two preachers each gave an individual homily on a shared biblical text and then conversed together over additional questions and responses. At the time of this unique collaboration, Blake was the stated clerk of The United Presbyterian Church in the United States of America and Niemöller was one of the six presidents of the World Council of Churches. Blake was at the forefront of American Presbyterian engagement in national and global ecumenical movements, including the Consultation on Church Union, an effort to unite several major Protestant denominations in the United States, and served as general secretary of the World Council of Churches from 1966 to 1972. Niemöller was a prominent German theologian who was incarcerated from 1937 to 1945 for resisting state efforts to bring the German churches under Nazi control. After the Second World War, Niemöller helped to rebuild the Lutheran Church in his country and became an internationally renowned speaker advocating pacifism, world peace, and Christian unity.

*Scripture quotations in this article are from the Revised Standard Version of the Bible and are copyright © 1946, 1952 by the Division of Christian Education of the National Council of the Churches of Christ in the U.S.A.

TEXT: REVELATION 3:7–13 MONDAY, MARCH 15

DR. BLAKE BEGAN

. . . Now the question that I want you to ponder with me is this: What has happened in these five decades to put us together in this church, me with Martin Niemöller? For I was taught early to hate his nation, to ridicule his emperor, and to detest all that he was fighting for, and particularly to despise the "new barbarism" that the U-boat warfare symbolized, revealing, for all the world to see, the naked evil of the Huns, as we in those days described the German people. Had I been a little older, I too would doubtless have served this nation in its Armed Forces. One of us could have been put in the place to kill the other. What has happened to us, and to the church, and to the world, to make these dialogue sermons possible?

In a word, the answer is that the ecumenical movement has so transformed my Christian understanding that I am more interested to hear today what this German Lutheran Martin Niemöller will say to this my city of Philadelphia in the name of Jesus Christ than I would be to hear almost any other preacher or pastor in all the world. As an American Christian, I hope you will listen to him most carefully, for I believe we need here in the very churches of Philadelphia, and in all our nation, to hear and heed what God will say to us through this man.

Now, when the author of Revelation wrote his book, it was precisely at the moment that for the first time Christianity was moving out of the confines and limitations of one nation and one culture (that of Israel) into the Oikoumenē, "the whole inhabited world," with its many languages, its separate histories, and its varied faiths. The letters to the seven churches of Asia, which comprise the whole of the second and third chapters of this strange book, are in part at least symbolic of a new wholeness and a new transcendence that the author was pressing upon the new young churches then. And now, after nearly two millennia, what God said through the author of the book of Revelation to all the churches then is exactly what he is saying now to the churches, churches no longer new, churches, however, that are threatened with apostasy today, apostasy in forms caused sometimes by their ancient traditions and their root-age in separate and limited cultures. The open door about which we speak, the open door before our churches, is our opportunity to move with boldness in the name of Jesus Christ out into an open sea of an ecumenical movement in a frail craft with a cross for the mast, leaving the safe moorings in the protected harbors of our past.

The letter to the church in Philadelphia, a small city of Asia Minor, becomes the basic text of this series of dialogue sermons here in this Philadelphia of the new world. It begins: "And to the angel [or better, messenger] of the church in Philadelphia write: 'The words of the holy one, the true one, who has the key of David, who opens and no one shall shut, who shuts and no one opens. I know your works. Behold, I have set before you an open door, which no one is able to shut.'"

In these fifty years, the sovereign God of all the earth has set before the church—and all our churches—an open door. He has opened it. No man can shut it. He can shut it. He does not force our churches through it. The churches can, if they will, pretend that the door is closed. They can refuse to leave the cozy hearths of their household gods. But the ecumenical movement in our time is an open door. And it is not yet clear whether the churches of Philadelphia, or of any city in the world, quite dare to walk boldly through that door in faith. Nor is it clear how long that door will remain open to us, as it is today. For God, who is the God of history, the God of the history of ancient Israel (he has the key of David) and of all the separate histories of the varied peoples of the six continents, this God has opened the door in our times as earlier he opened it for Paul and Barnabas when they first embarked from Antioch consciously to share Jesus Christ, son of David and Son of God, with the whole inhabited world. At that time God opened the door by employing the given unity of the Greek language and culture and the given order of the Roman Empire.

Often the twentieth century has been described by disillusioned and discouraged men simply as a century of two great wars with another still greater threatening, and as a century of political, economic, moral, and social collapse. Our century may truly be so described. But not simply so. For in this shaking century, God has opened a door before his church, a door that has been blocked for millennia. The world has entered a new era of universal history. The church in Philadelphia, or in any city in the whole world, can no longer isolate herself from the Christian church of any nation. The church exists in Europe and in the Americas. The church lives and witnesses in Africa, Australia, Asia, and the islands of the sea. The church survives in China and in the U.S.S.R., in Eastern Europe, in Venezuela, Spain, and Cuba. . . .

One word more must be said to complete my part of this opening dialogue. So far I have spoken of this open door as if it were beckoning us simply across geographical lines and walls, across political and cultural differences, and so it is. But now I would remind you that God has been as active in his church as he has been active in his world in this half century. This action is symbolized by the fact I mentioned at the outset, that it is a Lutheran and a Presbyterian pastor who address you, members of our denominations but members, I am sure, of many others, and we address you in an Episcopal church. If our world has been shaken by God's action in these five decades of world history, no less has been the revolutionary shaking of the structures of the church of Jesus Christ itself. . . .

The ecumenical movement gives us opportunity then to move out boldly, if we will, through God's open door, not only across political and geographic divisions of a deeply divided world, but also across those sometimes higher walls, sharp-spiked, of the division of the church in all these local places, like Philadelphia, where Christians live, and work, and witness in their way to their Lord. . . .

DR. NIEMÖLLER CONTINUED

Surely, my Christian friends, the door behind which we Christians, as our Father's family, assemble and live in fraternal fellowship, in which Jesus the Christ spreads his Spirit as "the first-born among many brethren," is no longer barred. It never was; but when Jesus had left his disciples, they came together, and "the doors were shut . . . for fear of the Jews," as we are told in John's Gospel. Yet, we are told also that Jesus did not acknowledge their seclusion but that he "came . . . and stood in the midst," saying, "Peace be unto you." And there in the room that they had locked, he gave them his missionary mandate: "As my Father hath sent me, even so send I you." He opened the door!

Whenever and wherever the Christian church becomes aware of her weakness and her minority character, the temptation arises to shut and bar the doors to feel safe and—if possible at all—to save her life. This has happened in the history of the church quite a number of times; it always means a real and dangerous temptation; and in spite of the high valuation that the Christian church experiences and enjoys in certain parts of our world today, there is also this strong countercurrent of which most Christians are not even aware but which carries them—and maybe ourselves—along, when we thoughtlessly speak of people as "still going to church," "still having their children baptized," "still being Christians." "Still"—as if all this soon would be finished!

This being true, and I do think no one can deny it, we certainly ought to be on our guard when we become aware of "open doors." They may mean new chances for expanding Christian influence and effect in many, if not in all, parts of the world, and they may mean also a fruit-bearing exchange and communication among Christian communities and churches. The evolution of the ecumenical movement proceeds, to some extent at least, from this hope and expectation. But on the other hand, we know of Christian groups also who have their doubts and their hesitations with regard to these undeniably open doors, for they may be just as well open doors for the intrusion of adversaries and enemies, who intend and try to fight against, destroy, dissolve, and poison the body of Christ, to catch and to scatter the sheep. And we are warned of "false prophets, which come to you in sheep's clothing, but inwardly they are ravening wolves," or as it is expressed in our text, "the synagogue of Satan who say that they are Jews"—the people of God—"and are not, but lie." We must not pass by this problem. We have to face the decisive fact that the door before us has been opened wide so that we, the churches, can reach out and go to nearly "all people that on earth do dwell." We can associate with one another regardless of our traditional separations and still remaining differences in faith and order, and in doctrine and structure. As a church that wants to be genuinely Christian, we must face what this fact means to us, and what conclusions we have to draw from it. The answer is not just a matter of course, and the "open door" actually can be both a call to activity and action or a call to deliberation and cautiousness. Probably it must be both, for every chance has also a temptation with it, and it is up to us to take and to fulfill this chance and to resist and to reject the temptation. . . .

Christendom has had and has enjoyed the "open door" for many centuries, and the results of Christian activity and influence are obvious in what we call culture and civilization. We do think highly of what has been achieved in science and scholarship, in literature and arts, in learning and education, and in many other fields; and nearly everywhere in the "Christian world" the traces of Christian contribution in all fields of personal and social human life can be found and shown.

At the same time we cannot but admit that also the omissions and deficiencies are obvious in our "Christian world," that our fathers and we ourselves have not been able to "overcome" the tempting power of our own achievements. We Christians have gone out through the open door, we have paid our contribution, and then we have retired again and gone back through the open door into our own house of religious enjoyment and peace. The problem is: Do we, as Christians, in going out really keep the Master's word and not deny his name? Or do we go out on our own, handing over to others only those gifts and advices of the Lord which were accepted as agreeable and reasonable? In other words, did they then and do we now, in passing through the "open door," follow Jesus Christ; did they, and do we, walk and work in his presence and under his control and direction? For everything that the church does and that is not in concordance with his will and Spirit therefore will not find his approval and support. It will have no salutary effect, but instead will do harm or fade away. . . .

As we go through the open door and deal with our fellowmen and all their need and distress, we are being tempted to make plans and programs such as we, according to our own judgment, believe to be practicable.

Without any doubt we must do so, but we must also be mindful that these plans are nothing more than our contributions, and only meant to serve our fellows, to protect them from such harm as can be avoided, and to remove misfortune, grief, and pain. However, we must beware of mistaking our principles and actions for Christianity itself. The faith cannot be regarded as a system of principles in which we believe, principles that are nothing more than superstition. Christian faith means to belong to Jesus, the Christ and the Lord, to live in communion with him, to follow in his footsteps, and therefore to act in his spirit, to ask him what he wants us to do, and to receive from him what we need to fulfill his calling. . . .

THE DIALOGUE

. . . Dr. Blake posed the first question: "Martin, there are people who really feel that the ecumenical movement, if it is referred to at all in The Revelation to John, is the synagogue of Satan. They feel that the ecumenical movement presses against the truth that our several churches have received in the past. How do you, a Lutheran, a German Lutheran pastor of a church that is known for the sharp articulation of its faith in confessions, really work with us in the ecumenical movement without being drawn away from your faith, with all our Anglo-Saxon fuzziness and the American pragmatism—and I won't even mention some of the worst theologized variations that are even bad from my point of view?"

Dr. Niemöller replied: "I am not so deeply convinced that theology really answers those questions to which we must seek an answer. Theology and doctrine may be just as bad as what you call 'fuzziness' in American and English Christianity. To me, the point is quite different. As a son of the Westphalian diaspora—in my youth, Protestants were a minute minority in that part of Germany—I remained deeply opposed to any kind of Roman Catholicism until God brought me together in a concentration camp with three Roman Catholic priests. There it happened that each morning we prayed the breviary together, read the Protestant and Catholic Bibles together, and Greek and Hebrew in the afternoon. Finally, when we were freed after having lived thus together for two and one half years, we began corresponding with each other and signed these letters, 'Your Brother in Christ.' And so it came to me that their faith is not different from my faith.

"I really think that someone who believes in Jesus Christ and puts all his trust in him has a personal relationship to him, calls him 'My Lord,' and asks each and every day, 'What wilt thou have me to do; what shall I do? Do go with me through this day so that I do not go my own ways and wrong ways.' I believe that this is much more important for Christians who want to work together than any theological or psychological or otherwise seemingly important difference may be."

Dr. Blake said, with a smile: "I think I stimulated you to say what I wanted you to say. Isn't it true that one of the things that pulled you and the Roman Catholic priests together was your common use of the Scriptures? I have been to all kinds of Christian conferences from my boyhood until today, excepting, of course, a prison camp. In all of that experience there has been no place where we were not drawn together by the Scriptures. The Scriptures we do have in common! As I have sat and listened to representatives of the Eastern Orthodox churches and of the Anglicans and of all kinds and varieties of churches there was not one of them in the fellowship of the ecumenical movement who was willing to say, 'My place, my position, is not supported by the Word of God as we find it in the Bible.'"

Source: Marlene Maertens, ed., *The Challenge to the Church: The Niemöller-Blake Conversations* (Philadelphia: The Westminster Press), 31–40, 42–45.

TIMOTHY KELLER

"The Centrality of the Gospel," 2000*

Timothy Keller is the founding pastor of Redeemer Presbyterian Church in New York City. Before moving to New York in 1989, Keller served as the pastor of West Hopewell Presbyterian Church in Hopewell, Virginia, taught practical theology at Westminster Theological Seminary, and directed mercy ministries for the Presbyterian Church in America. Keller and a small ministry team, including his spouse, Kathy Keller, launched the church in a Seventh-day Adventist building and the attendance grew to six hundred over the first eighteen months. The church today is one of the largest Presbyterian congregations in the United States with over five thousand weekly worshipers. Keller is also the chairperson of Redeemer City to City, an organization that provides training and resources for new church developments in global cities, and author of several books on ecclesiology, theology, and culture. This essay demarcates Keller's understanding of the gospel from moralistic and relativistic interpretations of Christianity and outlines the implications of his gospel-centered ministry in the church and the world.

The gospel is the central element in the Christian life and continually renews the believer and the Church. Outlined in this article are fourteen ways in which the gospel impacts the believer and eight ways it nurtures the Church.

PRINCIPLE

In Galatians 2:14, Paul lays down a powerful principle. He deals with Peter's racial pride and cowardice by declaring that he was not living "in line with the truth of the gospel." From this we see that the Christian life is a process

*Scripture quotations are the author's own translation.

of renewing every dimension of our life—spiritual, psychological, corporate, social—by thinking, hoping, and living out the "lines" or ramifications of the gospel. The gospel is to be applied to every area of thinking, feeling, relating, working, and behaving. The implications and applications of Galatians 2:14 are vast.

PART 1: IMPLICATIONS AND APPLICATIONS

IMPLICATION #1—THE POWER OF THE GOSPEL

First, Paul is showing us that bringing the gospel truth to bear on every area of life is the way to be changed by the power of God. The gospel is described in the Bible in the most astounding terms. Angels long to look into it all the time (1 Peter 1:12). It does not simply bring us power, but it is the power of God itself, for Paul says, "I am not ashamed of the gospel, because it is the power of God for salvation" (Rom.1:16). It is also the blessing of God with benefits that accrue to anyone who comes near (1 Cor. 9:23). It is even called the very light of the glory of God itself: "they cannot see the light of the gospel of the glory of Christ . . . For God . . . [has] made his light shine in our hearts to give us the light of the knowledge of the glory of God in the face of Jesus Christ" (2 Cor. 4:4, 6).

After the gospel has regenerated us and we are converted, it is the instrument of all continual growth and spiritual progress: "All over the world this gospel is bearing fruit and growing, just as it has been doing among you since the day you heard it and understood God's grace in all its truth" (Col. 1:6). Here we learn several things: (1) The gospel is a living thing (cf. Rom 1:16), like a seed or a tree that brings more and more new life—bearing fruit and growing. (2) The gospel is "planted" in us so as to bear fruit only as we understand its greatness and implications deeply—understood God's grace in all its truth. (3) The gospel continues to grow in us and renew us throughout our lives—as it has been doing since the day you heard it. This text helps us avoid either an exclusively rationalistic or mystical approach to renewal. On the one hand, the gospel has a content—it is profound doctrine. It is truth, and specifically, it is the truth about God's grace. But on the other hand, this truth is a living power that continually expands its influence in our lives, just as a crop or a tree would grow and spread and increasingly dominate an area with roots and fruit.

IMPLICATION #2—THE SUFFICIENCY OF THE GOSPEL

Second, Paul is showing that in our Christian life we never "get beyond the gospel" to something more advanced. The gospel is not the first step in a stairway of truths; rather, it is more like the hub in a wheel of truth. The gospel is not just the ABCs but the A to Z of Christianity. The gospel is not the minimum required doctrine necessary to enter the kingdom but the way we make all progress in the kingdom.

We are not justified by the gospel and then sanctified by obedience; rather the gospel is the way we grow (Gal. 3:1–3) and are renewed (Col. 1:6). It is the solution to each problem, the key to each closed door, the power to take us through every barrier (Rom. 1:16–17). It is very common in the church to think as follows: "The gospel is for non-Christians. One needs it to be saved. But once saved, you grow through hard work and obedience." But Colossians 1:6 shows that this is a mistake. Both confession and "hard work" that is not arising from and in line with the gospel will not sanctify you—they will strangle you. All our problems come from a failure to apply the gospel. Thus when Paul left the Ephesians he committed them "to the word of his grace, which can build you up" (Acts 20:32).

The main problem in the Christian life, then, is that we have not thought out the deep implications of the gospel; we have not "used" the gospel in and on all parts of our life. Richard Lovelace says that most people's problems are just a failure to be oriented to the gospel—a failure to grasp and believe it through and through.[1] Luther says, "[The truth of the Gospel] is also the principal article of all Christian doctrine. . . . Most necessary is it therefore, that we should know this article well, teach it unto others, and beat it into their heads continually."[2] The gospel is not easily comprehended. Paul says that the gospel does its renewing work in us only as we understand it in all its truth. All of us to some degree live around the truth of the gospel but do not "get it." So the key to continual and deeper spiritual renewal and revival is continual rediscovery of the gospel. The discovery of a new implication or application of the gospel—seeing more of its truth—is an important stage of any renewal. This is true for either an individual or a church.

APPLICATIONS

The two "thieves" of the gospel

Since Paul uses the metaphor of being "in line" with the gospel, we can consider that gospel renewal occurs when we keep from walking "off line" either to the right or to the left. A key for thinking out the implications of the gospel is to consider the gospel a third way between two mistaken opposites. However, we must realize that the gospel is not a halfway compromise between

1. See Richard Lovelace. *Dynamics of Spiritual Life: An Evangelical Theology of Renewal* (Downers Grove, Ill: Inter-Varsity Press. 1979). p. 211: "Much that we have interpreted as a defect of sanctification in churchpeople is really an outgrowth of their loss of bearing with respect to justification."

2. Martin Luther. *A Commentary on St. Paul's Epistle to the Galatians* (London: James Duncan, 1830). Chapter 2, Verse 4, 5.

these two poles—it produces not something in the middle but something different from both.

Tertullian, a Christian writer in the second and third centuries, said, "Just as Christ was crucified between two thieves, so this doctrine of justification is ever crucified between two opposite errors." He meant that there were two basic false ways of thinking, each of which "steals" the power and the distinctiveness of the gospel from us by pulling us to one side or the other of the "gospel line." These two errors are very powerful, because they represent the natural tendency of the human heart and mind.

(The gospel is "revealed" by God [Rom. 1:17]—the unaided human mind cannot conceive it.) The "thieves" can be called moralism or legalism on the one hand and hedonism or relativism on the other hand. Another way to put it is: the gospel opposes both religion and irreligion (see Matt. 21:31; 22:10). On the one hand, moralism/religion stresses truth without grace, for it says that we must obey the truth in order to be saved. On the other hand, relativism/irreligion stresses grace without truth, for it says that we are all accepted by God (if there is a God) and we have to decide what is true for us. But "truth" without grace is not really truth, and "grace" without truth is not really grace. Jesus was "full of grace and truth" (John 1:14). Any religion or philosophy of life that deemphasizes or loses one or the other of these truths falls into legalism or license, and either way, the joy and power and release of the gospel are stolen.

THE MORALISM-RELIGION THIEF. HOW DOES MORALISM/RELIGION STEAL JOY AND POWER?

Moralism is the view that you are acceptable (to God, the world, others, yourself) through your attainments. Moralists do not have to be religious but often are. When they are, their religion is pretty conservative and filled with rules. Sometimes moralists have a view of God as very holy and just. This view will lead either to (a) self-hatred (because they can't live up to the standards) or (b) self-inflation (because they think they have lived up to the standards). It is ironic that inferiority and superiority complexes have the very same root. Whether the moralist ends up smug and superior or crushed and guilty just depends on how high the standards are and on his or her natural advantages such as family, intelligence, looks, willpower. Moralistic people can be deeply religious—but there is no transforming joy or power.

THE RELATIVISM-IRRELIGION THIEF. HOW DOES RELATIVISM STEAL JOY AND POWER?

Relativists are usually irreligious, or else they prefer what is called "liberal" religion. On the surface, they are more happy and tolerant than moralistic/

religious people. Although they may be highly idealistic in some areas (such as politics), they believe that everyone needs to determine what is right and wrong for themselves. They are not convinced that God is just and must punish sinners. Their beliefs in God will tend to picture him as loving or as an impersonal force. They may talk a great deal about God's love, but since they do not think of themselves as sinners, God's love for humankind costs him nothing. If God accepts us, it is because he is so welcoming or because we are not so bad. The gospel's concept of God's love is far richer and deeper and more electrifying.

WHAT DO BOTH RELIGIOUS AND IRRELIGIOUS PEOPLE HAVE IN COMMON?

They seem so different, but from the viewpoint of the gospel, they are really the same.

They are both ways to avoid Jesus as Savior and keep control of their lives.

Irreligious people seek to be their own saviors and lords through "worldly" pride. ("No one tells me how to live or what to do; I determine what is right and wrong for me!") But moral and religious people seek to be their own saviors and lords through "religious" pride. ("I am more moral and spiritual than other people, so God owes it to me to listen to my prayers and take me to heaven. God cannot let just anything happen to me—he owes me a happy life. I've earned it!") The irreligious person rejects Jesus entirely; the religious person uses Jesus as an example and helper and teacher—but not as a Savior. In her novel *Wise Blood*, Flannery O'Connor's main character Hazel thinks "that the way to avoid Jesus [is] to avoid sin." These are two different ways to do the same thing—control one's own life. (Note: Ironically, moralists, despite all the emphasis on traditional standards, are in the end self-centered and individualistic, because they have set themselves up as their own savior. Relativists, despite all their emphasis on freedom and acceptance, are in the end moralistic, because they still have to live up to [their own] standards or become desperate. And often they take great pride in their own open-mindedness and judge others who are not.)

They are both based on distorted views of the real God.

The irreligious person loses sight of the law and holiness of God, and the religious person loses sight of the love and grace of God; in the end they both lose the gospel entirely. For the gospel is that on the cross Jesus fulfilled the law of God out of love for us. Without a full understanding of the work of Christ, the reality of God's holiness will make his grace unreal, or the reality of God's love will make his holiness unreal. Only the gospel—that we are so sinful that we need to be saved utterly by grace—allows us to see God as he really is. The gospel shows us a God far more holy than the legalist can bear (he had to die because we could not satisfy his holy demands), and yet far more merciful than a humanist can conceive (he had to die because he loved us).

They both deny our sin—and therefore lose the joy and power of grace.

It is obvious that relativistic, irreligious people deny the depth of sin, and thus the message "God loves you" has no power for them. But although religious persons may be extremely penitent and sorry for their sins, they see sins as simply a failure to live up to standards by which they are saving themselves. They do not see sin as the deeper self-righteousness and self-centeredness through which they are trying to live lives independent of God. So when they go to Jesus for forgiveness, they go only as a way to cover over the gaps in their project of self-salvation. And when people say, "I know God is forgiving, but I cannot forgive myself," they mean that they reject God's grace and insist that they be worthy of his favor. So even religious people with "low self-esteem" are actually in their state because they will not see the depth of sin. They see it only as rule-breaking, not as rebellion and self-salvation.

A WHOLE NEW WAY OF SEEING GOD

Christians have adopted a whole new system of approach to God. They may have gone through both religious and irreligious phases in the past, but they have come to see that the reasons for both their irreligion and their religion were essentially the same, and essentially wrong! Christians come to see that both their sins and their best deeds have all been ways of avoiding Jesus as Savior. They come to see that Christianity is not fundamentally an invitation to become more religious. A Christian comes to say, "Though I have often failed to obey the moral law, the deeper problem was why I was trying to obey it. Even my efforts to obey it have been just ways of seeking to be my own savior. In that mindset, even if I obey or ask for forgiveness, I am really resisting the gospel and setting myself up as savior." To "get" the gospel is to turn from self-justification and rely on Jesus' record for a relationship with God. The irreligious don't repent at all, and the religious repent only of sins; Christians also repent of their righteousness. That is the distinction between the three groups—Christians, moralists (religious), and pragmatists (irreligious).

SUMMARY

Without a knowledge of our extreme sin, the payment of the cross seems trivial and does not electrify or transform us. But without a knowledge of Christ's completely satisfying life and death, the knowledge of sin would crush us or move us to deny and repress it. Take away either the knowledge of sin or the knowledge of grace and people's lives are not changed. They will either be crushed by the moral law or run from it in anger. So the gospel is not that we go from being irreligious to being religious but that we realize that our reasons for both our religiosity and our irreligiosity were essentially the same and essentially wrong. We were seeking to be our own savior and thereby keep control of our own life. When we trust in Christ as our Redeemer, we turn from trusting either self-determination or self-denial, either hedonism or moralism, for our salvation.

A WHOLE NEW WAY OF SEEING LIFE

Paul shows us, then, that we must not simply ask in every area of life, "What is the moral way to act?" but "What is the way that is in line with the gospel?" The gospel must be continually thought out to keep us from moving into our habitual moralistic or individualistic directions. We must bring everything in line with the gospel.

THE EXAMPLE OF RACISM

Since Paul applied the gospel to racism, let's use it as an example:

The moralistic approach to race. Moralists tend to be very proud of their culture. They easily fall into cultural imperialism and try to attach spiritual significance to their cultural norms, to make themselves feel morally superior to other peoples. This happens because moralistic people are very insecure, since they take the eternal law quite seriously and know deep down that they cannot keep it. Therefore they use cultural differences to buttress their sense of righteousness.

The relativistic approach to race. The opposite error from cultural imperialism is cultural relativism. This approach says, "Yes, traditional people were racists because they believed in absolute truth. But truth is relative. Every culture is beautiful in itself. Every culture must be accepted on its own terms."

The gospel approach to race. Christians know that intolerance does not stem so much from a belief in truth as from a lack of belief in grace. The gospel leads us (a) to be somewhat critical of all cultures, including our own (since there is truth), but (b) to realize that we can feel morally superior to no one; after all, we are saved by grace alone, and therefore a non-Christian neighbor may be more moral and wise than I. This gives the Christian a radically different posture from that of either moralists or relativists.

Note: Relativists (as noted above) are ultimately moralistic, and therefore they can be respectful only of other people who believe everything is relative! But Christians cannot feel morally superior to relativists.

PART II: THE KEY TO EVERYTHING

The gospel is the way that anything is renewed and transformed by Christ—whether a heart, a relationship, a church, or a community. It is the key to all doctrine and to our view of our lives in this world. Therefore, all our problems come from a lack of orientation to the gospel. Put positively, the gospel transforms our hearts and thinking and approaches to absolutely everything.

A. THE GOSPEL AND THE INDIVIDUAL

1. Approach to discouragement. When a person is depressed, the moralist says, "You are breaking the rules—repent." On the other hand, the relativist says, "You just need to love and accept yourself." Without the gospel, superficialities will be addressed instead of the heart. The moralist will work on behavior and the relativist will work on the emotions themselves. But (assuming there is no physiological basis for the depression) the gospel leads us to examine ourselves and say, "Something in my life has become more important than God, a pseudo-savior, a form of works righteousness." The gospel leads us to repentance, not to merely setting our will against superficial issues.

2. Approach to the physical world. Some moralists are indifferent to the physical world and see it as "unimportant." Other moralists are downright afraid of physical pleasure, and since they are seeking to earn their salvation, they prefer to focus on sins of a physical nature like a failure to discipline sex and the other appetites. These are easier to avoid than sins of the spirit like pride. Therefore, moralists prefer to see sins of the body as worse than other kinds. The legalism that results usually leads to a distaste of pleasure. On the other hand, the relativist is often a hedonist, someone who is controlled by pleasure and makes it an idol. The gospel leads us to see that God has created both body and soul and so will redeem both body and soul, although under sin both body and soul are broken. Thus the gospel leads us to enjoy the physical (and to fight against physical brokenness, such as sickness and poverty) yet to be moderate in our use of material things.

3. Approach to love and relationships. Moralism often makes relationships into a "blame game." This is because a moralist is traumatized by criticism that is too severe and maintains a self-image as a good person by blaming others. On the other hand, moralism can use the procuring of love as the way to "earn our salvation" and convince ourselves we are worthy persons. That often creates what is called "codependency"—a form of self-salvation through needing people or needing people to need you (that is, saving yourself by saving others). On the other hand, much relativism reduces love to a negotiated partnership for mutual benefit. You relate only as long as it is not costing you anything. So the choice without the gospel is to selfishly use others or to selfishly let yourself be used by others. But the gospel leads us to do neither. We

do sacrifice and commit ourselves, but not out of a need to convince ourselves or others that we are acceptable. We can love the person enough to confront when that's needed, yet stay with the person even when it does not benefit us.

4. Approach to suffering. Moralism takes the "Job's friends" approach, laying guilt on yourself. You simply assume, "I must be bad to be suffering." Under the guilt, though, there is always anger toward God. Why? Because moralists believe that God owes them. The whole point of moralism is to put God in your debt. Because you have been so moral, you feel you don't really deserve suffering. Moralism tears you up, for at one level you think, "What did I do to deserve this?" but on another level you think, "I probably did everything to deserve this!" When the moralist suffers, then, he or she must either feel mad at God (because I have been performing well) or mad at self (because I have not been performing well) or both. On the other hand, the relativist/pragmatist feels justified in avoiding suffering at all costs—lying, cheating, and broken promises are okay. But when suffering does come, the pragmatist lays the fault at God's doorstep, claiming that he must be either unjust or impotent. The cross shows us, however, that God redeemed us through suffering. God suffered not that we might not suffer but that in our suffering we could become like him. Since both the moralist and the pragmatist ignore the cross, they will both be confused and devastated by suffering.

5. Approach to sexuality. The relativist sees sex as merely biological and physical appetite. The moralist tends to see sex as dirty or at least a dangerous impulse that leads constantly to sin. But the gospel shows us that sexuality is to reflect the self-giving of Christ. He gave himself completely without conditions, so we are not to seek intimacy while holding on to control of our life. If we give ourselves sexually, we are to give ourselves legally, socially, personally—utterly. Sex is to happen only within a totally committed, permanent relationship of marriage.

6. Approach to one's family. Moralism can make you a slave to parental expectations, while relativism sees no need for family loyalty or the keeping of promises and covenants if they do not "meet my needs." The gospel frees you from making parental approval an absolute or psychological salvation, for it points to how God becomes the ultimate Father. Then you will neither be too dependent on nor too hostile toward your parents.

7. Approach to self-control. Moralists tell us to control our passions for fear of punishment. This is a volition-based approach. Relativism tells us to express ourselves and find out what is right for us. This is an emotion-based approach. The gospel tells us that the free, unconditional grace of God "teaches" us to "say no" to our passions (Titus 2:12) if we listen to it. This is a whole-person approach, starting with the truth descending into the heart.

8. Approach to witness. The pragmatist would deny the legitimacy of

evangelism altogether. The moralist person does believe in proselytizing, because "we are right and they are wrong." Such proselytizing is almost always offensive. But the gospel produces a different constellation of traits in us: First, we are compelled to share the gospel out of generosity and love, not guilt. Second, we are freed from fear of being ridiculed or hurt by others, since we already have God's favor by grace. Third, we learn humility in our dealings with others, because we know we are saved by grace alone, not because of our superior insight or character. Fourth, we are hopeful about everyone, even the "hard cases," because we ourselves were saved only because of grace, not because we were likely people to be Christians. Fifth, we are courteous and careful with people. We don't have to push or coerce them, for it is only God's grace that opens hearts, not our eloquence or persistence or even their openness. All these traits create not only a winsome evangelist but an excellent neighbor in a multicultural society.

9. Approach to human authority. Moralists will tend to obey human authorities (family, tribe, government, cultural customs) too much, since they rely so heavily on their self-image of being moral and decent. Relativists will obey human authority either too much (since they have no higher authority by which they can judge their culture) or else too little (they may obey only when they know they won't get caught). That means either authoritarianism or anarchy. But the gospel gives you both a standard by which to oppose human authority—if it contradicts the gospel—and an incentive to obey the civil authorities from the heart, even when you could get away with disobedience.

10. Approach to human dignity. Moralists often have a pretty low view of human nature—they mainly see human sin and depravity. Relativists, on the other hand, have no good basis for treating people with dignity. Usually they have no religious beliefs about what human beings are. (If people are just chance products of evolution, how do we know they are more valuable than a rock?) But the gospel shows us that every human being is infinitely fallen (lost in sin) and infinitely exalted (in the image of God). So we treat every human being as precious, yet dangerous!

11. Approach to guilt. When you say, "I can't forgive myself," it means there is some standard or condition or person that is more central to your identity than the grace of God. If you cannot forgive yourself, it is because you have failed your real god, your real righteousness, and it is holding you captive. The moralist's false god is usually a god of their imagination that is holy and demanding but not gracious. The relativist's false god is usually some achievement or relationship. God is the only God who forgives—no other "god" will.

12. Approach to self-image. Without the gospel, your self-image is based

upon living up to some standards—whether yours or someone else's imposed upon you. If you live up to those standards, you will be confident but not humble. If you don't live up to them, you will be humble but not confident. Only in the gospel can you be both enormously bold and utterly sensitive and humble. For you are both perfect and a sinner!

13. Approach to joy and humor. Moralism eats away at joy and humor—because the system of legalism forces you to take yourself (your image, your appearance, your reputation) very seriously. Relativism, on the other hand, will tend toward cynicism as life goes on. This cynicism grows from a lack of hope for the world: in the end evil will triumph—there is no judgment or divine justice. But if we are saved by grace alone, then the very fact of being Christian is a constant source of amazed delight for us. There is nothing matter-of-fact about our lives, no "of course" to our lives. It is a miracle that we are Christians, and we have hope. So the gospel that creates bold humility should give us a deep sense of humor. We don't have to take ourselves seriously, and we are full of hope for the world.

14. Approach to "right living." Jonathan Edwards points out that "true virtue" is possible only for those who have experienced the grace of the gospel. Any person who is trying to earn their salvation does "the right thing" in order to get into heaven, or in order to better their self-esteem, or for another essentially self-interested reason. But persons who know they are totally accepted already do the right thing out of sheer delight in righteousness for its own sake. Only in the gospel do you obey God for God's sake and not for what God will give you. Only in the gospel do you love people for their sake (not yours), do good for its own sake (not yours), and obey God for his sake (not yours). Only the gospel makes doing the right thing a joy and delight, not a burden or a means to an end.

B. THE GOSPEL AND THE CHURCH

1. Approach to ministry in the world. Moralism tends to place all the emphasis on the individual human soul. Moralistic religionists will insist on converting others to their faith and church but will ignore the social needs of the broader community. On the other hand, "liberalism" will tend to emphasize only amelioration of social conditions and minimize the need for repentance and conversion. The gospel leads to love, which in turn moves us to give our neighbor whatever is needed—conversion or a cup of cold water, evangelism and social concern.

2. Approach to worship. Moralism leads to a dour and somber kind of worship that may be long on dignity but is short on joy. A shallow understanding of "acceptance" without a sense of God's holiness, on the other hand, can lead to frothy or casual worship. (Meanwhile, a sense of neither God's love nor

his holiness leads to a worship service that feels like a committee meeting!) But the gospel leads us to see that God is both transcendent and immanent. His immanence makes his transcendence comforting, while his transcendence makes his immanence amazing. The gospel leads to both awe and intimacy in worship, for the Holy One is now our Father.

3. Approach to the poor. The pragmatist tends to scorn the faith of the poor and see them as helpless victims needing expertise. This is born out of a disbelief in God's common grace to all. Ironically, the secular mindset also dismisses the reality of sin, and thus anyone who is poor must be oppressed, a helpless victim. Moralists, on the other hand, tend to scorn the poor as failures and weaklings. They see them as somehow to blame for their situation. But the gospel leads us to be (a) humble, without moral superiority, knowing that we were spiritually bankrupt but have been saved by Christ's free generosity; (b) gracious, not worried too much about "deservingness," since we didn't deserve Christ's grace; and (c) respectful of believing poor Christians as brothers and sisters from whom we can learn. It is only the gospel that can bring people into a humble respect for and solidarity with the poor.

4. Approach to doctrinal distinctives. The "already" of the New Testament makes us bold in our proclamation. We can most definitely be sure of the central doctrines that support the gospel. But the "not yet" requires charity and humility in nonessential beliefs. That is, we must be moderate about what we teach except when it comes to the cross, grace, and sin. In our views, especially our opinions on issues that Christians cannot agree on, we must be less unbending and triumphalistic (believing we have arrived intellectually). It also means that our discernment of God's call and will for us and others must not be propagated with overweening assurance that our insight cannot be wrong. (Unlike pragmatists, we must be willing to die for our belief in the gospel; unlike moralists, we must keep in mind that not every one of our beliefs is worth fighting to the death for.)

5. Approach to holiness. The gospel's "already" means we should not tolerate sin. With the presence of the kingdom, we are made "partakers of the divine nature" (2 Peter 1:4). The gospel brings us the confidence that anyone can be changed, any enslaving habit can be overcome. But the gospel's "not yet" means that our sin remains in us and will never be eliminated until the fullness of the kingdom comes. So we must avoid pat answers, and we must not expect quick fixes. Unlike moralists, we must be patient with slow growth or lapses and be aware of the complexity of change and growth in grace. Unlike pragmatists and cynics, we must insist that miraculous change is possible.

6. Approach to miracles. The "already" of the kingdom means that power for miracles and healing is available. Jesus demonstrated the kingdom by healing the sick and raising the dead. But the gospel's "not yet" means that nature

(including us) is still subject to decay (Rom. 8:22–23) and thus sickness and death remain inevitable until the final consummation. We cannot expect miracles and freedom from suffering to be such normal parts of the Christian life that we will glide through our days with no pain. Unlike moralists, we know that God can heal and do miracles; unlike pragmatists, we do not aim to press God into eliminating suffering.

7. Approach to church health. The "already" of the kingdom means that the church is now the community of kingdom power. It is therefore capable of mightily transforming its community. Evangelism that adds "to their number daily those who [are] being saved" (Acts 2:47) is possible! Loving fellowship that destroys "the dividing wall of hostility" (Eph. 2:14) between different races and classes is possible! But the "not yet" of the kingdom means Jesus has not yet presented his bride, the church, "as a radiant church, without stain or wrinkle or any other blemish" (Eph. 5:27). We must not then be harshly critical of imperfect congregations nor jump impatiently from church to church over perceived blemishes. Error will never be completely eradicated from the church. The kingdom's "not yet" also means to avoid an overly severe imposition of church discipline and other means to seek to bring about a perfect church today.

8. Approach to social change. We must not forget that Christ is even now ruling in a sense over history (Eph. 1:22–23). The "already" of grace means that Christians can expect to use God's power to change social conditions and communities. But the "not yet" of sin means there will be "wars and rumors of wars." Selfishness, cruelty, terrorism, and oppression will continue. Christians harbor no illusions about politics nor expect utopian conditions. The "not yet" means that Christians will not trust any political or social agenda to bring about righteousness here on earth. So the gospel keeps us from the overpessimism of fundamentalism (moralism) about social change and also from the overoptimism of liberalism (pragmatism).

SUMMARY

All problems, personal or social, come from a failure to apply the gospel in a radical way, a failure to get "in line with the truth of the gospel" (Gal. 2:14). All pathologies in the church and all its ineffectiveness come from a failure to let the gospel be expressed in a radical way. If the gospel is expounded and applied in its fullness in any church, that church will begin to look very unique. People will find in it both moral conviction yet compassion and flexibility.

Source: Timothy Keller, "The Centrality of the Gospel" (© 2000 by Timothy Keller, 2000). This article appeared in adapted form in chapter 3 of *Center Church* (Grand Rapids, MI: Zondervan, 2012).

9

Increasing Racial, Ethnic, and Global Diversities in Church Leadership

JORGE LARA-BRAUD

"Hispanic-Americans and the Crisis in the Nation," 1969

Jorge Lara-Braud (1931–2008) was born in Mexico and came to the United States to attend high school at the Presbyterian Pan American School in Kingsville, Texas. He continued his studies in the United States at Austin College and Austin Presbyterian Theological Seminary. In 1966, Lara-Braud became the director of the Hispanic American Institute, a collaborative effort of The United Presbyterian Church in the United States of America (UPCUSA) and the Presbyterian Church U.S. (PCUS) to promote the educational and professional advancement of Hispanic Americans and support bicultural and bilingual ministries. The Institute was located at Austin Seminary, where Lara-Braud also offered courses in missiology. In his career, Lara-Braud also taught at San Francisco Theological Seminary and served in various leadership positions for the National Council of Churches and the Presbyterian Church (U.S.A.). During his tenure directing the Hispanic American Institute, Lara-Braud wrote insightful and incisive papers calling for more genuine partnerships between white Presbyterians and Hispanic Americans. In 1967, Lara-Braud presented to the Synod of Texas (PCUS) a paper on forming effective ecumenical relationships that warned against conflating solidarity with racial-ethnic or socioeconomic homogeneity. The paper was widely distributed among Presbyterians (and other Protestants) in the United States. Two years later, Lara-Braud presented this paper to the UPCUSA General Assembly, and it was recommended to local congregations for study.

I. A MINORITY NO LONGER INVISIBLE

Hispanic-Americans constitute the second largest ethnic minority in United States of America. There is reason to believe their number has by now gone beyond the figure to 10,000,000. Given their present rate of growth, by the end of this century their number will be around 22,000,000. Contrary to popular belief the vast majority, more than 80 percent, are urban dwellers, and even a larger percentage are United States citizens. These people are here to stay. Nevertheless, their significance is hardly understood by either church or nonchurch groups.

At present this is largely the result of the nation's overwhelming concentration on the convulsions within the black community. Read, for instance the daily newspapers and the church publications dealing with the "crisis in the nation." One looks in vain for a parallel concern with Hispanic-Americans. Here and there references to them are found, to be sure. Seldom, however, are we told the facts experienced by Hispanic-Americans themselves. Except for some recent Spanish-speaking immigrants from Latin America, notably Cubans, who have brought with them considerable professional, managerial, and technological skills, the rest of the Hispanic-American community is not faring much better than the black minority. . . . Nevertheless, for the nation and the churches Hispanic-Americans remain largely an invisible minority.

History sheds some light on the reason why Hispanic-Americans became a forgotten minority. The acquisition of Spanish-speaking citizens by the United States was largely the result of military conquest. The Texas War of Independence of 1836, the Mexican War of 1846–48, and the Spanish American War of 1898 left little or no choice to former Mexican and Spanish citizens but to accept the accomplished fact of United States citizenship. Conquered people have a way of gradually being reduced to humble hewers of wood and drawers of water. Eventually, a convenient stereotype builds around them: simple, child-like, indolent folk requiring no more than the bare essentials of life, a periodic fiesta or two, and the sporadic application of legal and economic force, lest cultural deviancy transcends the tolerance of a society bent on melting differences away.

The stereotype persists. Officially approved history school textbooks tend to portray the continued existence of the conquered Hispanic-American as a passive onlooker of the booming development of his former lands by the energetic conqueror from the North. Seldom are we told of the key role played by the back-breaking labor of the conquered peoples in building the railroad, mining, sheep, cattle, and agricultural empires of the newly acquired United States territories. Rarely, if ever, are we told of the strikes since the

1920[s] of historic import and major economic significance in the industries built with their sweat and blood. The omission on both counts, their toil and their protest, turns out to be a classical conspiracy of silence. For response to the first has been consistent exploitation. Response to the second has been brutal repression. . . . The combined legacy of military conquest, cheap foreign labor, and exile immigration, not surprisingly, has resulted in an image of a people in dire need of social and cultural rehabilitation if they are to qualify for full-fledged citizenship.

Hispanic-Americans, however, have repudiated the idea of rehabilitation as a condition for their share in the American Dream. In fact, it may be truthfully said that no other group has more generously amplified the principle on which that dream is based, unity in diversity ("e pluribus unum"). As an ethnic family it encompasses the whole gamut of the racial strains known to man, Indianhood being its most prominent component, and Spanish the language of its soul. What it pleads for is the same acceptance of its difference by the larger society, while it pledges its unconditional loyalty to a free, democratic, and pluralistic United States of America. Let the disproportionate record of heroism and casualties of the Spanish-speaking in the last three major United States wars stand as a perpetual memorial to their unwavering allegiance to the country. . . .

II. THE ROLE OF THE CHURCH

The church, committed as it is to an "inclusive fellowship," for a long time also treated Hispanic-Americans as objects of cultural rehabilitation, i.e., "Americanization." Apparently, in their case, the principle of inclusive fellowship would best be served by eventual absorption into typical United States social institutions, on the assumption that they themselves would favor an accelerated acquisition of the social, cultural and economic equipment that would enable them to perform in the mainstream of national life, no longer as strangers in the land. Provision of permanent facilities, ministries, and liturgies designed to retain their language, values and traditions was considered unwise long-range strategy. Halfway houses should be adequate. Other "language" minorities had been able to blend themselves within two or three generations almost imperceptibly within the so-called American melting pot, why not they? Is it any wonder that today most of our Hispanic-American congregations beat all the marks of marginality?

What seems to have escaped the strategists was simply that the parallel between Hispanic-Americans and other "language" minorities turns out to be no parallel at all. In the first place, the living organism of Hispanic-American culture was already deeply rooted in this American soil a good many years before the arrival of Pilgrims or Puritans. Hispanic-Americans may validly reverse Robert Frost's famous line, "The land was ours before we were the land's." Despite the traumas of military conquest, of dispossession of lands by legal chicanery, of prejudicial treatment of cheap laborers, and condescending acceptance of bewildered exiles, the very blood stream of the Hispanic-American organism has never ceased to be replenished. Meanwhile Latin America has been rediscovered south and north of the Rio Grande following the tremors of the Cuban revolution. Being a Spanish-English bilingual is no longer quaint or un-American. Practically all major institutions of higher learning have initiated programs of Hispanic-American studies. And in the new climate of hemispheric interaction, it is not surprising for 62,000,000 border crossings to be made by Mexicans in 1967, for 57,000,000 to be made by United States citizens, and for 386 weekly flights from Latin America to land in Miami, exclusive of the "freedom" flights which bring nearly 1,000 Cubans every week for relocation throughout the nation. The strategists were wrong. Hispanic-Americans are here to stay, to increase, and to become United States citizens with a difference: as a bilingual and bicultural community.

Society is not likely to take serious ecclesiastical pronouncements calling for fair dealings with Hispanic-Americans, when the church itself allows for little or no participation by them in its process of decision-making. By and large, the church continues to view them as objects of mission. Provisions for them are still largely in terms of benefaction, through such institutions as mission churches, houses of neighborly service, schools, clinics, and mission outposts. These institutions were legitimate at one time. Their unmodified perpetuation calls in question the maturity of Hispanic-Americans to be themselves agents of mission. It also raises serious doubts about the stewardship of the church's resources.

Hispanic-Americans genuinely rejoice in the church's overdue attention to the plight of black Americans. In fact, they consider the black struggle vicarious. Without it, the clamor of other neglected minorities would meet everywhere with the rankling syndrome of delayed redress. Much promise is seen as churches allocate "crisis" monies to the black community for programs of self-determination. But the lesson is lost on no one, really. Unless a minority mounts a vigorous campaign of open resistance against legal, institutionalized violence, it will continue to endure the nightmare of the wretched. Like black Americans and other exploited minorities, then, Hispanic-Americans demand nothing less than restitutional justice: the freedom and resources to determine their lives in consonance with their rich cultural traditions, and with the pluralistic ideal of American society.

III. CULTURAL GENOCIDE OR PLURALISM

Hispanic-American traditions constitute a humanistic treasure house without which the life of this nation and its churches would be sadly impoverished. As children of Cuauhtemoc and Atah[u]alpa, el Cid and Don Quixote, Hidalgo and Bolivar, Juarez and Marti, Nervo and Dario, the black saint, Martin de Porres, the Indian Virgin of Guadalupe, the blond European Madonnas and the Mestizo Christ, they are constitutionally disinclined to racial prejudice. Their own mestizaje (whether physical or psychological) has richly endowed them with antibodies against the virus of racism. Among them, honor is put before gain, human life is held sacred over "humane" causes, the wisdom of the old is the measuring rod for the dreams or fads of the young, the primacy of being is affirmed over the tyranny of doing, human existence is protected from the enslavement of the machine, freedom is valued more than life in times of threat to one's native or adopted country, and by race ("raza") is meant that ideal of universal solidarity to which they pay tribute on October 12, not so much as Columbus Day, but as "El Dia de la Raza."

The tragedy is that these traditions have been more hindered than enhanced. In fact, Hispanic-Americans still contend with an institutionalized system of rewards and punishments based on the relative success or failure with which one can abandon his "foreign" ways and adopt those more typical of the homogenized mainstream. Even then, those who so "succeed" more often than not discover that despite the silent trauma of self-denial, they have not quite arrived. Their physical features, the remnants of an accent, their Spanish surname still identify them with that vast "unrehabilitated" mass of the blood kin they mistakenly thought they had divorced themselves from. The results are frequently pathological. Alienated success types are driven farther and farther apart from their ethnic family by promotional overexposure. But few can escape the inner sense of the outer denunciation of a sell-out. Under those conditions, self-hatred is inevitable, and self-justification indispensable. When this alienated success type is put in a position of authority over his own ethnic family, especially, law enforcement, an appalling miscarriage of justice often results. In the mirror of the name, face, speech, dwelling and ways of those unfit people his self-rejected image is magnified a thousand-fold. The mirror or his "success" must go. He cannot have it both ways. Much regret has been expressed about lack of leaders among Hispanic-Americans. If by leaders we mean those rewarded with positions of power for rejecting or suppressing their ethnic family, then we should all rejoice for their shortage or weep for their abundance.

Happily, genuine leadership has been coming to the fore since the return of the World War II Hispanic-American veterans to civilian life. No ethnic minority had received as large a proportion of Congressional Medals of Honor, and few had sustained as many casualties. If their lives were sacred enough to offer in times of war, they were sacred enough to respect in times of peace. The G.I. Bill provided the first basic opportunity for thousands to complete high school or college. Signs were still to be seen in many cities and towns. "No Mexicans allowed." "No Latins accepted." Bringing down the barriers of blatant discrimination in public facilities in and out of court provided many with the testing grounds for leadership development. The drive for self-assertion was greatly accelerated by the beneficent radiation fall-out of the black struggle for human rights. Today, it is both heartening and frustrating for Hispanic-Americans to count on an impressive crop of leaders of every variety, while "La Causea" ("the cause," i.e., the advancement of the Spanish-speaking family) inches its way through modest victories and galling set-backs. . . .

What is likely to confuse even their well-disposed monolingual and monocultural fellow Americans is the marked compensatory emphasis they will have to place on truths and features essential to the survival of the Hispanic-American legacy that this society has been bent for decades on phasing out of the national scene.

This will call for:

1. A stern but loving rebuke to the Church, both Roman Catholic and Protestant, for failing to stand with them in their struggles for justice. Except for its impressive pronouncements on protective farm labor legislation and the courageous solidarity of some of its clergy and laity with the unionizing efforts of farm workers, it has consistently sided by silence or endorsement with the forces ranged against Hispanic-American self-determination. The worst indictment is its practice of consigning them to second-rate positions, salaries and facilities. It is terribly inconsistent for this derelict institution to exhort other institutions not to be derelict in the profoundly human issues of freedom, dignity, and equality. Indeed, its moral right to mission in Latin America is seriously compromised by its neglect of Spanish-speaking Christians in the United States of America. Yet as Christians, Hispanic-Americans stubbornly hold on to the hope of the Church's intrinsic potential for becoming once again the champion of the disinherited.

2. A vigorous demand for bilingual and bicultural education of their children beginning at the pre-school level, which entails a much greater use of Spanish in their communities.

3. A determined effort to correct the inequities of inferior education in schools and districts with a large number of Spanish-speaking students (among Mexican-Americans and Puerto Ricans 80 percent never finish high school).

4. A larger appropriation of symbols of redress taken from the history of liberation struggles in the Caribbean and south of the Rio Grande (heroes, slogans, and military imagery).

5. A vocal demand to equalize their representation on school and draft boards, grand and petit juries, higher employment echelons, and policy-making bodies—all of them spheres in which they are at present woefully underrepresented.

6. A strong protest against the distortion of their image perpetuated by history textbooks, public media advertisements, church mission publications, and public opinion bigotry.

7. A vigorous denunciation of the usually underreported but excessively frequent incidents of brutality suffered at the hands of law enforcement officers who often mistake their differentness for criminality (a few Americans endure a greater degree of overpolicing, and, as a result, a more inflated incidence of arrests and indictments).

8. An increased resistance to the present level of their young men drafted into the armed services. (Vietnam casualties among Mexican-Americans, for instance, are roughly double in comparison to their percentage of the population of the Southwest). As long as Hispanic-Americans have looked upon military conflicts as a legitimate defense of democratic freedoms, they have volunteered in disproportionate numbers. The Vietnam conflict, however, is increasingly being viewed by them as illustrative of the inequity of the draft system to the detriment of the poor. They are pained by the tragedy of being drafted to suppress a national liberation movement, not unlike the liberation longed for by the down-trodden Spanish-speaking of the United States of America. The act of volunteering must not necessarily be seen an endorsement of that type of conflict, but rather as one of the few outlets for the unemployed or the undereducated to obtain some basic training opportunity through the armed services.

9. A mounting pressure to bring about protective legislation for their numberless farm workers not covered yet by the National Labor Relations Act, and also for the thousands who manual skills have been mechanized out of existence, who plead in vain for retraining programs instead of the indignity of welfare. Demonstrations, boycotts and strikes will no doubt be the answer to lack of correctives.

10. A relentless exposure of discriminatory practices, many of them perpetuated by governmental and quasi-governmental agencies (school boards, armed services installations, public utilities, and firms under federal compliance contracts).

11. A concerted drive for the kind of self-determination that will make it

possible to shape their most basic social institutions: schools, churches, neighborhood councils, communications networks, recreational centers—in short, their right to a community expressive of their bicultural heritage.

No institution of society should be more sympathetic with those legitimate aspirations of Hispanic-Americans to be their true selves than the Church, whose mission is to provide conditions for authentic existence. Cesar Chavez speaks for the vast majority of them in answering the question, "What do we want the church to do?"

"We don't ask for more cathedrals[.] We don't ask for bigger churches or fine gifts. We ask for its presence with us, beside us, as Christ among us. We ask the church to sacrifice with the people for social change, for justice, and for love of brother. We don't ask for words. We ask for deeds. We don't ask for paternalism. We ask for servanthood."

Source: Jorge Lara-Braud, "Hispanic-Americans and the Crisis in the Nation," in Minutes of the General Assembly of The United Presbyterian Church in the United States of America, Part I: Journal, San Antonio, Texas, May 14–21, 1969 (Philadelphia: Office of the General Assembly, 1969), 662–67, 670–71.

GAYRAUD S. WILMORE

"Blackness as Sign and Assignment," 1977*

Gayraud S. Wilmore was born in Philadelphia, Pennsylvania, and graduated from Lincoln University, the first degree-granting historically black university in the United States. He was drafted into the U.S. Army during the Second World War and fought in an all-black regiment in Italy. During his military service, Wilmore received a call to pastoral ministry upon witnessing the anguish of war and the cruelty of humankind. He began his career as the pastor of Second Presbyterian Church in West Chester, Pennsylvania, and part of his ministry involved working toward desegregating the city's elementary schools. Wilmore's son was the first African American student to attend the integrated school. Wilmore continued his religiously motivated social activism as an executive in The United Presbyterian Church in the United States of America and professor at Pittsburgh Theological Seminary, Boston University School of Theology, Colgate Rochester Divinity School/Crozer Theological Seminary, New York Theological Seminary, Interdenominational Theological Center, and United Theological Seminary in Dayton, Ohio. Wilmore has produced several significant scholarly books on African American religious history, black theology, and Presbyterianism. This sermon was originally published in an anthology of black

*Scripture quotations are the author's own translation.

9.1   Jorge Lara-Braud, n.d. (Presbyterian Historical Society, Philadelphia, PA)

9.2   United Presbyterian Church of North America Map of Home Missions, 1953
(United Presbyterian Church of North America Women's General Missionary Society,
image from Presbyterian Historical Society, Philadelphia, PA)

Presbyterian preaching and provides an illuminating vista into Wilmore's theological analysis of the African American religious experience.

Son of man, you dwell in the midst of a rebellious house . . . Therefore, . . . prepare for yourself an exile's baggage . . . for I have made you a sign for the house of Israel. EZEKIEL 12:2–3, 6

Many people are confused about blackness. The term is used in many different ways today and the result is that most of us are thoroughly confused. Black Power, Black Pride, Black Studies, Black Theology—what are we to make of blackness? Is the word nothing more than a kind of arbitrary synonym for Negro, colored, or Afro-American—or is a there a more substantive meaning related to something eminently significant about us as a people? Let me put it another way: Is there a profound religious meaning in the idea of being a black people?

Let me put it squarely before you. I believe that black Christians—the black church in Africa and America—should articulate the theological meaning of blackness that arises from our religious experience as a people. I believe that we need to understand blackness as both a sign and an assignment from God.

I

Ezekiel is given a sign and an assignment from God. He had no choice in the matter. God didn't ask him if he would like to take on this assignment. He simply said: "Son of man, I have made you a watchman over the house of Israel. I am giving you a sign to take to these people. If you carry my sign and no one heeds it, they will be the worse for it, but you at least will be saved. If, on the other hand, you refuse to carry it and people do not get the message that I am sending to them, I am going to take out their punishment on you."

Ezekiel is asked to do a strange thing. He is to enact a kind of pantomime of the Babylonian exile. He is told by God to dress himself up like an exile, put an exile's baggage upon his shoulders, and go out through the city walls in the darkness of night, as one going sadly under great burden into captivity. In this way Ezekiel himself becomes a sign. He portrays a humiliated, captive people who have turned their backs upon their God and must suffer the consequence of being uprooted and driven out from the comfort and safety that God has given them. Ezekiel, with his exile's clothing and baggage, was God's message. He symbolized in his own being what God was saying to the people. He was not told to stand on the corner and preach this message. He was not asked to write and publish it. He had to leave his own home for a time, pack his belongings and put them on his back, dig through the city wall and go out into the blackness of night— "for I have made you," said God, "a sign for the house of Israel."

Let us substitute the color of blackness for the exile's clothing and for the baggage that Ezekiel carried by God's command. Certainly colors are used in all human societies as signs or symbols. From the most ancient and primitive people to our modern society, colors have been understood to convey powerful messages. The color symbolism of white Western societies has come, of course, to dominate most of the world. Wherever the white man has gone, his color symbolism—the assignment he has given to certain colors—has tended to become standard.

A simple example is the meaning of traffic signals. No matter where you are—in Hong Kong, Dar es Salaam, Santiago, or Atlanta—red means danger, yellow means caution, green means go. What about black and white? There is some ambiguity about these colors. But generally speaking, in Europe and America painting, literature, and cultural artifacts have conveyed the message that white symbolizes truth, beauty, purity, and goodness, while black symbolizes shame, impurity, ignorance, and evil.

Western symbolism—carried around the world by Western armies and missionaries—has made people believe that God himself decreed that "white is right, brown can stick around, but black must go back." More than that, according to this symbolism, God is white and Satan is black.

Did God authorize this symbolism? Of course not. Nor did black people authorize it. White men, by the sheer power of their culture—their money, guns, and Bibles—made this kind of white/black symbolism operative first in Europe and America, later in South Africa, and now all over the world. But just as the white man can make up his mind about the meaning of blackness and back it up by his interpretation of the will of God, we black people can change that meaning.

This is no idle matter. Colors convey powerful religious meanings, as the history of liturgics shows. And if a white preacher like the Rev. Buchner Payne can say that God chose whiteness because there is no darkness in him and that there can be no darkness in heaven, a black preacher can say that God chose blackness because God is mystery and cosmic fecundity, for there can be no white, lifeless sterility in heaven!

II

What I am really saying is that we black people have a right, even a responsibility, to interpret the Christian faith in such a way as to make blackness a profound expression of our religious experience. Even though black experience has usually been betrayal, suffering, and affliction, we can read the meaning of that experience in positive rather than negative terms, because of what we know about God and his relationship to those who trust in him.

One day men came and reported to Jesus about some Galileans who had fallen into Pilate's hands and had been killed. Luke does not tell us the questions they asked, but they probably had to do with whether Jesus thought this tragic event demonstrated the sinfulness of the victims. In other words, was this God's punishment for their sins? "No," said Jesus, "but the same thing could happen to you if you do not repent of yours!" On another occasion when the disciples passed by a man born blind they asked, "Rabbi, who sinned, this man or his parents, that he was born blind?" Jesus answered, "It was not that this man sinned, or his parents, but that the works of God might be made manifest in him."

The implication of both of these incidents is that God permits tragedy and hardships to come upon us for mysterious reasons of his own, not necessarily because we are offenders more than others. Indeed, he may even command some people to bear greater burdens than others in order that his will may be known. He summoned Ezekiel to bear the symbol of exile and captivity and sent him out into the darkness as a sign of what had been prepared for a rebellious people. While the false prophets lied about how much God was going to bless the people, Ezekiel dramatically portrayed the grim reality of their real situation.

Is there a lesson for us in Ezekiel's prophetic assignment? I believe so. In the face of man's false sense of security, in the face of his illusions about who he is and what he is able to accomplish by his own hands, in the face of his lies about truth and justice, blackness and the black experience of suffering and oppression stand as God's witness to reality, to the truth about life. Blackness is the way life really is. It is a sign of affliction and oppression, not of punishment and corruption. And there is a vast difference between the two that requires a complete revision of the color symbolism of Western culture. Blackness is indeed a symbol of what we have suffered, but we may bear it proudly not only because we have learned how to survive and sing the songs of Zion in a strange land, but because, like Ezekiel, God has called us in our blackness to bear a message to all people.

In *The Gift of Black Folk*, Du Bois speaks of the black presence in America as tragedy reflected in the sorrow songs or spirituals, but he saw in the black experience something that said a great deal about the vulnerability of all human existence, about the elemental nature of suffering and woe, about death as a natural and inevitable part of life. This is the message of blackness assigned by God himself. . . .

Blackness is a beautiful sensitivity to the hard, tragic dimension in life—a part of living that everyone must learn to negotiate, because, whether rich or poor, famous or infamous, black or white, we are all pitiable, vulnerable human beings and we have to go down into the pit together. Blackness is a message to the world that a man's arm is too short to box with God; that he is so high you can't get over him, so low you can't get under him, so wide you can't get around him—you must come in by the Door. And that Door is the door of trials and tribulation which is personified by Jesus. That Door is what makes a people both humble and strong. . . .

III

I have been talking about blackness as a symbol of perennial human condition. Blackness is also the message that man must struggle against every power that seeks to subdue and dehumanize him. Blackness symbolizes the truth that even though you may be down, you are not necessarily out. And by God's grace you will rise again.

Jesus Christ is crucial to black Christianity because darkness was his experience, and we know something about darkness. The Good Friday spiritual asks the question, "Were you there?" And the unspoken answer is, "Yes, we were all there when the Nigger of Galilee was lynched in Jerusalem." Is there any wonder that we can identify with him?

Black people, whether in America or in Africa, know Jesus as the Oppressed Man of God, who fraternized with harlots and sinners, who helped the poor and lowly, who struggled against the powers of evil in church and state, who was crucified in apparent defeat. We, of all the people of the world, can identify with that story because that is precisely what blackness has meant for us—lowliness, struggle, and defeat. Like Jesus on the cross, we too have cried out against the darkness in our flesh and in our environment, "My God, my God, why have you forsaken us?"

But as Jesus stood the test, we too stood the test, singing our blues and gospel, finger-popping all the while. As his strength was made perfect in weakness, so was ours. We never stopped struggling against the powers of oppression, poverty, and racism, and I believe we never will, because we have learned from Jesus that life itself is a struggle, and if you can't stand the heat, you will never be able to work in the kitchen. "In the world you have tribulation; but be of good cheer, I have overcome the world."

Blackness, therefore, is God's message through us to all people that to resist, to struggle, to wrestle, fight, and pray—and yet laugh and sing and "get happy"—is what it means to be a human being. Human beings know how to love and have compassion and get along with people in this world.

We do indeed have enemies and we have by no means conquered them within or without. But we continue to struggle with hope because we believe that even in death we shall be victorious through the Oppressed Son of God who conquered death, even death on the cross. That is why, as strange as it may sound in a world dominated by Western symbolism, we can speak of Jesus as our Black Messiah, because in so doing we chain ourselves not only to his cross but to his resurrection from defeat; we make blackness the sign and symbol not only of his struggle but also of his glorious victory which we will share.

Source: Robert T. Newbold Jr., ed., *Black Preaching: Select Sermons in the Presbyterian Tradition* (Philadelphia: The Geneva Press, 1977), 166–72.

CHOI, MOON YOUNG

"From the Kitchen to the Pulpit: A Korean Woman Pastor's Journey," 2006*

Choi, Moon Young was born in South Korea and came to the United States in 1987 to first support her spouse's study at Princeton Theological Seminary and then to pursue her own theological education. In 1995, she completed a master's thesis, "The Self and Korean Church Women: A Feminist Perspective," at the Graduate Theological Union in Berkeley, California. This essay was originally published in an edited volume celebrating the ordination stories of Presbyterian women in the United States. Choi was an associate pastor of Contra Costa Korean Presbyterian Church in California and member of the Presbytery of San Francisco when she wrote about her journey from South Korea to the United States. Korean Americans constituted the fastest growing racial-ethnic minority group within the Presbyterian Church (U.S.A.) in the last decade of the twentieth century. Choi's poignant reflections on gender, spirituality, and ecclesial authority in Korean and Korean American Presbyterianism reveal some of the complexities and ambiguities as both women and persons of color more fully entered into church leadership.

"Mom, you cannot be a pastor!"
"What . . . Why?"
"Because you are a woman!"
"Then, what about your dad?"
"He can be a pastor!"
"How come?"
"Because he is a man!"

*Scripture quotations in this article are from the New Revised Standard Version of the Bible and are copyright © 1989 by the Division of Christian Education of the National Council of the Churches of Christ in the U.S.A.

It sounds like a statement prohibiting women's ordination that has been heard repeatedly in Christian history. It was, however, a conversation between my daughter and me when she was only two years and nine months old. My husband and I were preparing for my ordination/installation service when my daughter suddenly jumped into our conversation and made this bombshell declaration. She had seen only male pastors in her life and could not envision her mother as a pastor. I was surprised to find that this little girl already had fixed ideas of gender roles in the ecclesial vocation. My husband and I laughed aloud, and I eagerly educated my daughter that women could also become pastors.

I heard a similar response from my mother, whose Presbyterian denomination in Korea does not yet ordain women. When I disclosed my intention to be an ordained pastor, my sixty-five-year-old faithful mother responded with worries and concerns: "Can't you believe in God just as you are? You can follow Jesus as Christian educator and pastor's wife like you are right now. Somehow, I find myself feeling unfamiliar and uncomfortable with a woman pastor."

Regardless of generation, I thought, the idea of a woman pastor appears new and strange in the Korean church context. These incidents are emblematic of my long struggle to be an ordained pastor.

FROM THE KITCHEN TO THE PULPIT

. . . Although it was certainly a challenge to start a M.Div. degree seven years after graduation from college, I was fascinated with the new life in the seminary. However, the field education requirement posed a challenge in my family relationship. Before I entered the seminary, I helped my husband's ministry, as was expected of the wives of Korean pastors. In most Korean churches, after the worship services Korean foods are served. Sharing food in ethnic churches is sharing cultural identity and nostalgia for the homeland. Pastors' wives usually play an important role in these meals.

My internship was in a different Korean church from the one my husband served. That posed a problem for both congregations and for me. When I arrived in the church for my internship, some people thought I was single. Finding that I was a married woman, especially a pastor's wife, they assumed we had some marriage problems. My husband's congregation seemed to perceive him to be a deficient pastor because his wife was not helping him.

As for myself, I felt a deep sense of guilt for going on my own journey. At times I tried to assuage my guilt by cooking and providing food for my husband's ministry in addition to working in my own church. Like many women in Korean churches, I had internalized the belief that only men, not women, were entitled to enter the pulpit. Thus I often felt inadequate and had difficulty owning my right to preach. After preaching, I would quickly rush to the kitchen as if that was where I belonged. It took a long time to develop self-confidence in the pulpit, free from this "kitchen-attachment syndrome."

INHERITING MY GRANDMOTHERS' GARDEN OF FAITH

. . . I have grown up with pride that I am a fourth-generation Christian, which is rare due to the relatively short history of Christianity in Korea. My paternal great-grandmother was first converted to Christianity, and her Christian faith was passed to my grandmother and my mother. I never met my great-grandmother because she died before I was born. But I remember how my grandmother was faithful and loved the words of God. My grandmother, born in 1900, like many women in her times, did not have public education and was illiterate. Yet because of her strong faith, my grandmother learned to read the Bible. In her later years, she had a stroke. I still remember how my grandmother made a great effort to copy the Bible on a faded notebook with her paralyzed left hand. . . .

Even though I grew up with women being active in church and attended a women's university where women were taught to be leaders, the idea of women's leadership at church had rarely occurred to me. It was because of the environment of my home church where women did not play leadership roles. . . . I had never seen an ordained woman pastor preaching or leading worship in Korea. I had never met ordained women elders participating in decision making, although about seventy percent of the congregation is women. Besides home visitations, most Presbyterian women's activities were focused on serving in the kitchen and preparing for a fellowship lunch or bazaar. Growing up in this church environment may have affected my self-identity as a churchwoman. At this moment, many women seminary students and M.Div. graduates of my home church are crying out for women's ordination with tears and prayer.

CHALLENGES IN MY ORDINATION JOURNEY

. . . I think there are four hurdles to ordination that my Korean colleagues and I have in common.

First there is a psychological hurdle. As mentioned above, I felt guilty and inadequate as a woman when I began my internship. In each step of the ordination process I wondered if I was headed in the right direction. Even after becoming a candidate, I deliberated for another six years before ordination. I felt I was not ready to be an ordained pastor. I found this sense of not feeling ready to be common among my female colleagues. It is quite a contrast to most male M.Div. graduates, who usually view ordination as a logical next step. . . .

The second hurdle is cultural. When I decided to attend a different church from that of my husband for my internship, I was considered "not the obedient pastor's wife." In the same way, I was considered "not a regular female *Jun-Do-Sa-Nim*"* when I followed the ordination process. It was not only my experience. When one of my Korean women colleagues asked the session to approve the inquiry phase during the ordination procedures, the Korean male senior pastor asked her, "Are you really going to be a pastor?" She was already an ordained elder and a M.Div. student. This question would never have been asked if she had been a male candidate.

The cultural ethos of the Korean church has been influenced by Confucianism. As in many Asian countries, Confucianism has been imbedded in Korean culture, affecting value systems and worldviews. Confucianism defines values and norms of behavior that involve a set of defined roles and mutual obligations.† It emphasizes hierarchical orders between king and vassal, men and women, husband and wife, and parent and child. Due to these orders, a notion of preferring a son to a daughter was popular in the traditional society. Although contemporary Korean society no longer rigidly follows these principles, the ideas persist either consciously or unconsciously even after immigration to Western society.

The third hurdle is biblical and theological interpretation regarding women's ordination. One Sunday I preached at the regular adult service as required for the internship. The senior male pastor happened to be out of town and had arranged for a woman elder to preside. He thought it would be better because the preacher was a woman. I also felt lucky to have the woman elder who was one of a few women elders in Korean churches in northern California. It was a very moving moment for me and for other women, because it was unheard of to have both a woman preacher and a woman elder leading worship on regular Sunday worship in a Korean church.

Later I learned that one male *Jun-Do-Sa-Nim* left our church because of that service. While working as an engineer, he had completed theological studies in a conservative seminary. He believed that it is "not biblical" for women to preach or lead worship and thus could not attend a church that did not follow the words of God. I felt deeply hurt by the comment. This incident threw me a big question about becoming an ordained pastor.

First Timothy 2:9–15, especially verses 11–12, is one of the Scripture passages most frequently quoted to oppose women's ordination: "Let a woman

---

*It literally means "evangelist." However, a student intern is usually called *Jun-Do-Sa-Nim* in Korean churches. While a male *Jun-Do-Sa-Nim* would become a pastor, a female *Jun-Do-Sa-Nim* is usually a permanent title for a nonordained woman minister.

†See Judith Bering's article "Confucianism," written for the Asia Society's *Focus on Asian Studies* 2, no.1 *Asian Religions*, (Fall 1982): 5–7.

learn in silence with full submission. I permit no woman to teach or to have authority over a man; she is to keep silent." Although I had learned the socio-cultural context of this text in my New Testament class and was well versed in the feminist theological perspective, I had no opportunity to respond to his seemingly unfair comments because he left.

Finally, there is a structural hurdle. I happened to get a call from the church where I did my internship. I became the second Korean woman ordained in the PC(USA) to receive a call to parish ministry in northern California. I feel so blessed and privileged. The number of female Korean seminary students has increased during the last decade. However, most Korean churches, not big enough to have associate pastors, prefer male pastors as their "solo pastor." So it is not easy for many female M.Div. graduates to have opportunities to receive a call. Outside Korean churches, they face barriers of race, language, and culture. One of my seminary colleagues came to the United States to become an ordained pastor because her denomination in Korea did not permit women's ordination at that time. Although she was looking for a call for several years after her graduation with a M.Div., she could not get a call despite all her efforts. Finally, she gave up and returned to Korea. I feel deeply sorry when I hear such stories. . . .

WHERE IS REV. CHOI, BY THE WAY?

My church has grown a lot in numbers since I was ordained, and we have three services on Sunday. Newcomers often do not know I am an ordained pastor. Furthermore, my name is gender neutral rather than feminine. When I am introduced to them as "Rev. Choi" by an usher, they often reply, "Are you Rev. Choi's wife?" Or sometimes they ask me, after first being told that I am Rev. Choi and even after talking to me for a while, "Where is Rev. Choi, by the way?" When I repeat that I am indeed the Rev. Choi, they usually respond with widened eyes, "I have never met a woman pastor in my life" or "I did not know a woman can also be a pastor." In these times, I realize there are not many spaces where women's leadership is visible and influential in the Korean church context even after ordination. I find my role and identity as a woman pastor often serves to educate these new members and the congregation to understand women's leadership in church. . . .

NEW PARADIGM: DREAMING OF SACK-DONG MINISTRY

Eight years ago, my daughter was born to us in our fourteenth year of marriage as God's gracious gift, after we had given up the hope of having a child. I pray that my daughter will grow up in faith with a sense of pride in her Korean identity. As a symbol of Korean heritage and her grandmothers' faith, I presented Sack-Dong clothes to her. Sack-Dong is Korean, traditional, rainbow-striped cloth. A Korean daughter would have worn Sack-Dong clothes once in her lifetime. With many bright colors equally beautifully shining, Sack-Dong clothes remind me of equality, harmony, diversity in unity, inclusiveness, and celebration.

Some Korean clergywomen make stoles out of Sack-Dong. I received one as my ordination present, and my Korean clergywomen colleagues wore the Sack-Dong stoles in my ordination/installation service. In these stoles I see a new paradigm of women's ministry in the Korean church context: Sack-Dong ministry. In contrast to the traditional hierarchical male-pastor-centered ministry in the Korean church context, Sack-Dong ministry is one that represents equality, harmony, diversity in unity, inclusiveness, and celebration. I dream of the ministry toward God's kingdom with these beautiful stripes: equality between women and men in partnership; harmony with both the ordained and laity; diversity of different cultures, races, generations, and perspectives in Christ; inclusiveness of the marginalized; and celebration of women's gift in ministry. In fact, Sack-Dong ministry as a new paradigm for women's ministry is nothing but the ministry of Jesus, welcoming children and women, accepting the sick and the poor, and embracing the sinners and the weak. I look forward to seeing these bright colors of Sack-Dong shining beautifully in my daughter's generation.

Source: Patricia Lloyd-Sidle, ed., *Celebrating Our Call: Ordination Stories of Presbyterian Women* (Louisville, KY: Geneva Press, 2006), 49–55, 57–59.

FAHED ABU-AKEL

"A Global Presbyterian Witness for a Global World Community," 2006

Fahed Abu-Akel was born in Kuffer-Yassif, a Palestinian village located between the Mediterranean Sea and the Sea of Galilee, and came to the United States to study in 1966. After graduating from Southeastern College in Lakeland, Florida, and Columbia Theological Seminary, he was ordained in 1978. He served as a pastor at First Presbyterian Church in Atlanta, founded the Atlanta Ministry with International Students, an organization that connects international students and scholars with local families and individuals, and taught world religions at Interdenominational Theological Center before his election as Moderator of the Presbyterian Church (U.S.A.) General Assembly in 2002. He became the first Arab American to hold the position and traveled across the United States and the world to represent the denomination and share his personal story. In this essay, which was originally published in an edited volume from 2006 seeking to assess the past, present, and future of the Presbyterian Church (U.S.A.), Abu-Akel reiterates the priorities he championed as Moderator and offers his perspective on Presbyterian engagement with peacemaking in the Middle East.

We Presbyterians can be "decent and in order" and at the same time influential and effective in bringing about constructive change! Now let me share with you my thoughts on these priority areas of our church life—spiritual renewal, local and global mission, unity in the midst of our diversity, and hospitality—and on peacemaking.

SPIRITUAL RENEWAL

Presbyterians in the twenty-first century must teach the basic tenets of the Christian faith based on our Reformed theology. In Austin, Texas, a 45-year-old man asked the associate pastor in the new membership class, "What is Easter and what is the resurrection?" Such questions point to several priority areas for our ministry and mission in what I would describe as a post-Christian America.

1. Christian education. We must teach the basic doctrines of our Reformed, Trinitarian faith about God, Jesus Christ, the Holy Spirit, sin, salvation, and how to grow spiritually in our personal and corporate faith. We need to move our people from an American "cultural Christianity" to a relevant New Testament expression of Christian discipleship. To accomplish this will require a vigorous emphasis on biblical literacy. Without a core of basic Bible knowledge, sermons and church school lessons will make little sense and spiritual growth will be limited.

2. Reading and studying the Book of Order. The Constitution of our church includes the Bible, the Book of Confessions, and the Book of Order. The Book of Order is not just for ministers of the Word and Sacrament, elders, and deacons, but should inform every member of our congregations. The first four chapters alone constitute a rich primer of our Presbyterian faith and heritage. Our people need familiarity with how and why we do what we do. Knowing the Constitution of the PC(USA) is a part of equipping the saints.

3. The priesthood of all believers and the importance of lay ministry. In the Reformed tradition, ministry and mission belong to all members of the body of Christ, not just those who are set apart by ordination for specific functions. The theology of the priesthood of all believers is very important to our branch of Protestantism. Engaging every person in the meaningful discovery of his or her gifts and Christian vocation assures an outgrowth of mission and ministry both within the walls of the church and into the community and world as we are commissioned to do. But there is another important aspect we must not miss. I can be your priest, and you can be mine; but I cannot be my own priest, nor

you yours. That demands a relationship that brings us into a healthy fellowship in need of each other. Spiritual renewal is realized when we go beyond just listening and learning, and put our faith into action where we live and work as well as where we go. Doing the work of the church is commendable, but true leadership involves enabling all to serve and enjoy participation in the gospel.

LOCAL AND GLOBAL MISSION

The invitation to each elder and member is to be involved in a local or global mission project that will help our people to be renewed spiritually. We need to challenge our members to experience the global church, to see how God is moving by the Spirit in Latin America, Africa, the Middle East, Europe, and Asia. Today, the Presbyterian Church is growing all over the world but not in the United States. Why? We Westerners in North America must learn from our mission partners in eighty nations why this growth is taking place and learn from them new ways our church grow. Living in the strongest military, economic, educational, and research nation does not guarantee spiritual renewal. We must humble ourselves and learn from our mission church partners new ways that God is working in Jesus Christ in these nations.

Our pastors and elders can help our members see that mission is done through effective partnership. The old colonial mission mentality is over. Change in global politics, commerce, and technology is happening faster than we have admitted as a church. The implications for our approach to the world in obedience to the Great Commission must be faced and prayerfully studied. Thank God for our missionaries and the Worldwide Ministries Division that help us recognize and respond to this fact. We can be thankful for the rich heritage of Presbyterian mission work in prior centuries, but we must also humbly and gratefully receive the reciprocal ministry and renewal these partner churches offer us in a new century and a changing world. We need the ministry and priesthood of our partnership churches, and they cannot do without the same from us. As a connectional church we must maintain these essential linkages given the body of Christ in the will and plan of God. Moreover, we need to communicate this phenomenon of worldwide church growth to all of our members. . . . Without mission, the church cannot survive. Mission is at the heartbeat of God. Throughout history God has spoken to his people through the prophets and through the written word of God, and finally God came to us in Jesus Christ two thousand years ago. In the incarnation, Jesus, Emmanuel, is God with us. God loved the human family so much that he came to us in Jesus Christ. The message of God to the world through the church must be to proclaim the birth, life, ministry, mission, death on the cross, resurrection from the dead, and the reality of the coming again of Jesus Christ.

UNITY IN THE MIDST OF OUR DIVERSITY

As Presbyterians, we talk a lot and like to discuss every issue that we face as individuals, families, and a denomination, in our congregations, communities, nation, and world. Our Reformed theology helps us to do that. Our differences must never outweigh what we hold in common. We should not become so wrapped up in single issues that we fail to see the whole picture. We must serve all to properly serve any, but in every generation we face new and sensitive issues that relate to our theology, our practice, and the biblical witness. The stress of these newly emerging issues can make us or break us. . . .

HOSPITALITY

. . . Hospitality opens hearts and doors, bonds strangers in friendship, and brings lifelong benefits to all. Hospitality is a Christian virtue and a practice urged upon the early church. Through the gift of friendship and hospitality Presbyterians have an opportunity to serve and to obey our Lord in a way that sows seeds of peace and understanding. . . .

We all know that the urban landscape of America has already changed. We live in a more pluralistic world than we have ever known. We have new immigrants in our midst from every nation under the sun. I challenge each congregation to see this new reality as an opportunity for mission, and not as a threat. Let us move in the Spirit of Christ and his gospel command and reach out to welcome these new immigrants and visitors to worship and to our homes. . . .

PEACEMAKING AND PRESBYTERIANS

At the beginning of this chapter I pointed out the signal role of Presbyterians in addressing the injustices that have reached the saturation point in the part of the world from which I come, that Christians, Jews, and Muslims everywhere identify as the Holy Land and Christians acknowledge as the birthplace of Jesus, our Lord. While we must never neglect those suffering from the heinous atrocities occurring in places like the Sudan and, earlier, in Rwanda and in other countries, I am convinced the ethnic cleansing and the linkages worldwide to the declared and hidden goals of the political powers in the Middle East, including the United States, are not only a physical and economic logjam but have held our world in spiritual captivity. We need to look for solutions rather than blame. I must reiterate the importance of our involvement and make a plea for us to renew our identity as peacemakers and reconcilers. . . .

The PC(USA) divestment policy is neither anti-Jewish nor anti-Israel nor anti-Semitic. Rather, our policy is "antioccupation." Our implementation of this step is studied, deliberate, and fair. Its provisions protect against using an unjust means to fight injustice.

The Presbyterian Church has been a friend of Israel from day one in 1948. Today more Jewish synagogues hold their Friday Sabbath worship services in Presbyterian sanctuaries than in sanctuaries of any other Protestant denomination in the United States. Jews and Presbyterians have long worked together to end racism in the United States and have worked for social justice and civil and human rights as leaders in our communities. American Jews and Presbyterians worked together effectively to oppose the apartheid system in South Africa. Today American Jews and Presbyterians must continue to work together for justice and peace for both Israeli Jews and Palestinian Arabs. We both know the basic facts on the ground in the West Bank—that occupation of the Palestinian people and Palestinian land is a key issue that must be resolved very soon. Peace can never be possible for either party if it is not possible for both parties.

America, the friend of Israel, helped make peace between Israel and Egypt. America helped Israel make peace with Jordan. I believe in coming days we can help Israel make peace with Syria, Lebanon, Iraq, Saudi Arabia, and every other Arab country. But if we fail to make peace between Israeli Jews and Palestinian Arabs, we will fail with our policy in the Middle East. The sooner we do justice to the Palestinians, to enable them to gain their freedom and to establish an independent Palestinian state in the West Bank, Gaza, and East Jerusalem, the sooner our nation will build credibility in the Middle East and around the world.

Beyond the foregoing matters, which seem self-evident, lies the plight of Israeli Arab citizens—Christians, Druzes, Muslims, and Bedouins who remained in the borders of the newly formed Israeli state in 1948. Theirs is a story that needs to be understood and addressed as well. All are affected. It is out of that particular Palestinian population that my own story emerged.

I grew up in a village twenty-five miles northwest of Nazareth in the Galilee of Palestine. I am grateful that my father and mother, five sisters, and two brothers helped me to be nurtured in the Christian faith. My native church was Eastern Orthodox, harking back to the original church established in the fourth century under Constantine. Worship was in the Greek Orthodox form. But it was my mother whose own beautiful tradition was to help us children to pray, to memorize and to recite the Psalms, the Gospels, the Lord's Prayer, and the Nicene Creed before we went to sleep.

As a four-year-old child, I still remember leaving home with my father, five sisters, and two brothers and leaving our mother at home alone. We went up to the mountains to a Druze Arab village called Yrka, and there we were put in a makeshift Palestinian refugee camp in tents. We stayed several months and then went back home to find my mother alive, but the new Israeli army had destroyed four nearby Palestinian Arab villages.

When Israel became a state on May 14, 1948, it was a day of celebration and independence to the Jewish people of Palestine, but a day of nakba or catastrophe and destruction to the indigenous Arab Palestinian population. On the land where Israel became a state, 418 Palestinian Arab Christian and Muslim villages and towns were destroyed, and more than 800,000 displaced Palestinian Arab Christians and Muslims were exiled and forced to move from their homes, lands, businesses, and places of worship. The issues of the right of Palestinians to return and the threat of transfer out of Israel to those holding citizenship must be brought before the world tribunal.

From this early beginning, through the grace of God and guidance of the Holy Spirit, I encountered two Scottish Presbyterian missionaries who came to live on the second floor of our home. How grateful to God I am for Dr. Doris Wilson and Ruth Lenox. Dr. Wilson helped me to give my life to Jesus Christ and became my spiritual mentor as I received my call to the ministry. With their encouragement I arrived in the United States on January 29, 1966, in Tampa, Florida, with one suitcase, one Arabic Bible, and an English-Arabic dictionary to pursue my education and to begin my new American journey. . . .

Where in all the world can a Palestinian Arab Christian who almost became a refugee—but was then nurtured by his Christian mother in the faith and witnessed to by two Scottish Presbyterian missionaries, who led him to come to the United States to study—thirty-six years later find himself elected to the highest position in his denomination? This could happen only in the church of Jesus Christ, and, in my case, only in our beloved Presbyterian Church (U.S.A.), and it could happen only in the United States.

My prayer for our beloved denomination and all believers is that we may together live and move and act obediently on the grace, mercy, and peace of our Lord and Savior Jesus Christ as we boldly embrace the future God has set before us.

Source: Robert H. Bullock Jr., ed., *Presbyterians Being Reformed: Reflections on What the Church Needs Today* (Louisville, KY: Geneva Press, 2006), 92–96, 98–100.

Index

CPSIA information can be obtained
at www.ICGtesting.com
Printed in the USA
LVHW03s1631111018
593278LV00014B/298/P